Published in the USA by:
BearManor Media
P. O. Box 71426
Albany, GA 31708
www.bearmanormedia.com

ISBN 978-1-59393-824-6

Printed in the United States of America.
Book design by Robbie Adkins, www.adkinsconsult.com
Cover and back cover design by Bunky Runser

TABLE OF CONTENTS

IV

Dedication

Dedicated to *Bride of the Gorilla's* "Assistant to Producer" Herman Cohen (1925-2002)—a wonderful guy, a wonderful friend. In this photo he poses, appropriately dressed, on the set of the Western *The Bushwhackers* (1952).

BRIDE OF THE GORILLA

(Realart, 1951)

Cast and Credits

Presented by Jack Broder Productions
65 minutes
Associate Producer: Edward Leven
Screenplay & Directed by Curt Siodmak
Photography: Charles Van Enger
Editorial Supervisor: Francis D. Lyon
Music: Raoul Kraushaar
Assistant to Producer: Herman Cohen
First Assistant Director: Richard Dixon
Art Director: Frank Sylos
Set Decorator: Edward Boyle
Men's Wardrobe: Elmer Ellsworth
Women's Wardrobe: Betty Zackin
Hairdresser: Ann Kirk
Makeup: Gus Norin
Sound: Bud Meyers
Special Effects: Lee Zavitz

From a *Variety* "Assignments" List (July 30, 1951):
Second Assistant Director: Ken Walters
Script Supervisor: Mary Gibson
Dialogue Director: Victor Stoloff
Props: John Orlando
Still Cameraman: Ed Jones

Barbara Payton (*Dina Van Gelder, later Dina Chavez*)
Lon Chaney (*Police Commissioner Taro*)
Raymond Burr (*Barney Chavez*)
Tom Conway (*Dr. Viet*)
Paul Cavanagh (*Klaas Van Gelder*)
Giselle Werbisek (*Al Long*)
Carol Varga (*Larina*)
Paul Maxey (*Mr. Van Heussen*)
Woody Strode (*Nado*)
Martin Garralaga (*Native Worker*)
Felippa Rock (*Stella Van Heussen*)
Moyna Macgill (*Mrs. Van Heussen*)
Uncredited:
Steve Calvert (*The Succarath*)

Acknowledgments

Many sincere thanks for favors great and small: John Antosiewicz, Michael F. Blake, Ted Bohus, Margaret Borst, Ron Borst, John Brunas, Michael Brunas, Lisa Burks, Bob Burns, Gerry Carpenter, Chris Casteel, Didier Chatelain, Herman Cohen, Joe Dante, Frank Dello Stritto, Rachael A. Dreyer, Richard Erdman, David Fuller, Scott Gallinghouse, Kerry Gammill, Beryl Hart, Walter Haussner, Richard Heft, Jia Jung, Igo Kantor, Dr. Robert J. Kiss, Madelynn Kopple, Craig Scott Lamb, John Landis, Dan Lewis, Donna Lucas, Boyd Magers, Scott MacQueen, Leonard Maltin, Greg Mank, Mark Martucci, Dave McDonnell, Ellen Meltzer-Zahn, Deborah Nadoolman, Tom Neal Jr., Ted Newsom, William Phipps, Felippa Rock, Alan K. Rode, Mary Runser, David Schecter, David J. Schow, Rich Scrivani, Curt Siodmak, Maria-Flora Smoller, Herbert L. Strock, William Swan, Don Taylor, Tony Timpone, Laura Wagner, Bill Williams and Wade Williams

JOHN LANDIS GOES BANANAS
Introduction by John Landis

"It's ironic to me that I'm now called a master of horror," says John Landis, "considering the vast majority of my films were comedies or musicals!"

The succarath—the monster haunting the South American jungle in writer-director Curt Siodmak's *Bride of the Gorilla*—takes its name from a creature found in folklore. Getting a succarath expert to write an introduction for this book seemed like the way to go, but it was hard to find one. Wellll, actually, I'm *assuming* that it *would* have been hard to find one, if I had tried.

So because *Bride's* succarath is played by a guy in a gorilla suit, we turn instead to Hollywood director John Landis, who has plenty to say about gorillas, gorilla suits, the movie guys who *wore* gorilla suits, the movies themselves—and even about Curt Siodmak. In a very informal chat transcribed for this book, he talks about gorillas both real and reel.

—Tom Weaver

I've *always* been a fan of monsters. But separate and apart from that, I've always been fascinated by apes, especially gorillas.

I really do like gorillas, in real life and the mythological gorilla, which I write about in my book *Monsters in the Movies* [2011]. In truth, gorillas are actually very mild creatures. Not like chimpanzees! Chimpanzees form groups that go to war with one another and they're cannibals, whereas the great apes, the gorillas, both the mountain and lowland gorillas, are really sweet and herbivores. But when they display their physical power, they can *look* ferocious. At the London Zoo for many, many years there was a gorilla called Guy, and I once saw him do something so amazing: In his enclosure was a gigantic truck tire, very, very thick, and I watched as he sauntered over to it and picked it up and *he flipped it inside out.* I'd never seen anything like that! It was such a casual display of strength. Also, in Rwanda, I went to visit the gorillas and it was incredible how strong they are, how they just snap giant eight-inch-thick bamboo stalks. But very sweet. My wife Deborah and I actually donated the funds to the L.A. Zoo to purchase a gorilla. We got to name him Jim after one of my attorneys, James Neal. He ended up in a zoo in Denver, Colorado, and he's had like four children since—Jim the gorilla, not Jim the attorney!

But despite how sweet gorillas really are, there is this whole myth about the gorilla as rapist, this great brute that shows up and drags off your women. That's a complete fantasy that was mostly propagated by a French-American named Paul Du Chaillu, who wrote *Stories of the Gorilla Country* and other books about his adventures in Africa in la Belle Époque. He created this mythology of gorillas attacking pygmy villages and carrying off the women, he just made it up. But once it was seized upon, then you had Edgar Allan Poe's story "The Murders in the Rue Morgue" which was an orangutan, but still a great ape, and in Western art you had all these images, in France especially, of the gorilla as rapist.

Nature in the Wrong: Far racier than *Bride of the Gorilla*, the Ed Wood-scripted *The Bride and the Beast* (1958) had a heroine (Charlotte Austin) who was a gorilla in a former life, and therefore not ill-disposed towards a hirsute suitor (Steve Calvert).

As for my love of monster movies and "gorilla suit" movies, that was a result of being born in 1950 and being part of "the television generation." I grew up in Los Angeles at a time when all the local TV stations around the country showed tons of old movies—everything from the Hal Roach "Little Rascals" and Laurel and Hardy to Godzilla movies. The RKO stations broadcast *Million Dollar Movie*, where the programming was kind of insane. For a week, *Million Dollar Movie* would show the *same* movie every night at 8 p.m. and then twice on Saturday and twice on Sunday. So if it was something like *Mighty Joe Young* [1949] or *The Ghost Breakers* [1940] or *Abbott and Costello Meet Frankenstein* [1948], a kid could literally memorize it! *King Kong* [1933] and *Mighty Joe Young* would be on television all the time, I saw them as a little boy and they were very emotional for

me. *The Son of Kong* [1933]—I must've been about seven when I saw it, and the ending just totally destroyed me. I was weeping—weeping and sobbing! Thank God *Mighty Joe Young* had a happy ending!

Then the famous "Shock Theater" package of Universal monster movies was sold to local stations around the country, and that led to the rise of the local horror hosts. I devoured that stuff. I would watch the Aztec Mummy pictures, I would watch *any*thing!

When I was older, I would go to Hollywood Boulevard to see movies. I started going in the late '60s when Hollywood Boulevard was really "down," like 42nd Street. But it was also fabulous because it had at least 25 used bookstores where a lot of movie material was sold. Those were the days when you could buy a one-sheet for a dollar, and stores would

Out-of-work circus men Laurel and Hardy—and their new traveling companion Ethel the Human Chimpanzee (Charles Gemora)—search for pet-friendly lodging in *The Chimp*.

have cardboard boxes filled with movie stills you could buy for a dime.

Hollywood Boulevard was also packed with movie theaters, a lot of grindhouses, most of which are gone now. Among my favorite memories of Hollywood Boulevard are two movies I came across by accident. One was George Romero's *Night of the Living Dead* [1968] which I saw as part of a double feature when I was a mail boy at Fox. I was totally unprepared for that film, and I thought it was fantastic. Another one I saw like that was *The Texas Chain Saw Massacre* [1974] at some triple feature. There used to be a place called the World Theater where you could see three features for a dollar. You'd go in there and they had a guy, a very large black guy, with a baseball bat, patrolling the aisles to keep order. It was a rowdy crowd! You could see remarkable stuff amidst all the dreck, but it was *all* entertaining. For many years I saw literally every movie that came out, foreign, domestic, art house, grindhouse,

whatever. Although it was seedy and kind of dangerous, I loved Hollywood Boulevard then.

Getting back to monster movies and "gorilla suit" movies: I'm fond of bad gorilla suit movies and good gorilla suit movies. Years ago, they used to use gorillas [actors playing gorillas] in movies as it was like a cheap McGuffin; for instance, it'd be a haunted house movie but actually there was just a gorilla running around. All you needed was a guy in a suit. There were all these people who had their own, like Emil Van Horn and "Crash" Corrigan, so producers would hire them *and* their suit. This is why, in a lot of B pictures, you see the same gorilla suits all the time. When I was in tenth grade, I staged a play and I actually had a gorilla guy, Janos Prohaska, in it. He was *the* gorilla guy for *The Outer Limits* and other shows, and he often showed up with his suits on Irwin Allen shows where he was supposed to be an alien monster so they'd like add a horn or something to his suit! He was amazing, that guy. Physically, it was extraordinary what he could do.

Charlie Gemora was probably the greatest of the gorilla performers. A movie I adore is *The Monster and the Girl* [1941]. I'm not joking, I believe it to be a terrific movie. It's a wonderfully sincere, beautifully made low-budget picture, shot on the lot. It looks great, it has a great cast and it is this amazing melange of genres: It's a mad-scientist-puts-a-human-brain-into-a-gorilla movie, but it's also a boy-and-his-dog movie and a white slavery movie and a courtroom drama and a film noir and a gangster movie. It's just delirious, I love that picture. And *sad*—it's a *sad* movie, the ending's so dark. It's got everything, and I really like that.

Charlie Gemora, who played the gorilla in that, is probably the best of all the gorilla suit guys. He was a little Filipino guy whose job, really, was in the art department, he was a sculptor. I really do think his

John Landis as Schlock.

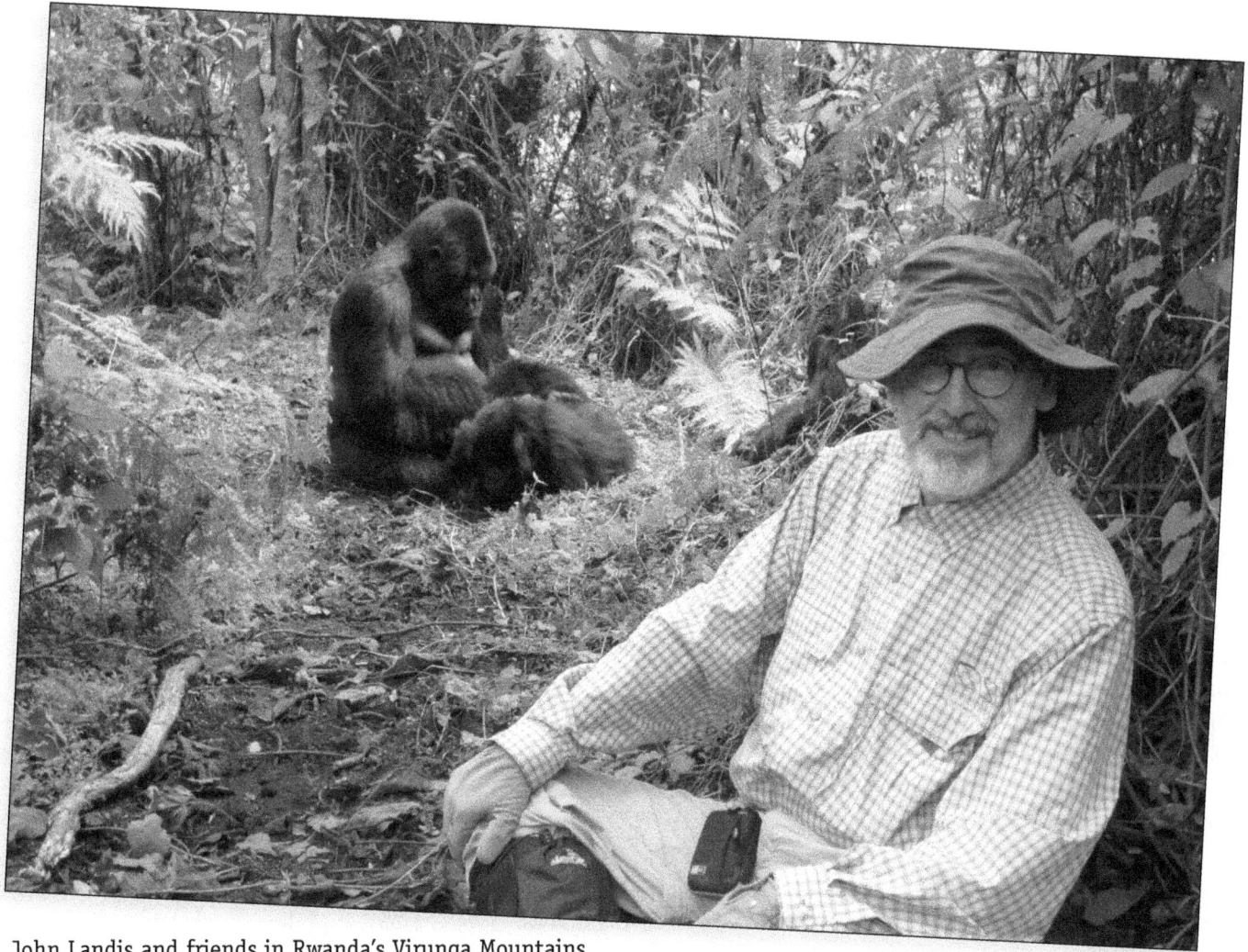

John Landis and friends in Rwanda's Virunga Mountains, June 19, 2013. (Photo courtesy John Landis and Deborah Nadoolman)

performance in *Monster and the Girl* is remarkable. He was very innovative with his various gorilla suits: He was the first guy to use water bags to give his belly and his breast weight and movement, he used arm extensions, and he was able to realize a remarkable range of expressions from essentially an immobile mask.

Have you seen the Laurel and Hardy short *The Chimp* [1932]? That's Charlie Gemora playing "Ethel the Human Chimpanzee," wearing an early ape suit of his—and a tutu! [*Quoting an Oliver Hardy line of dialogue from the movie:*] "Ethel, will you stop dancing and come to bed?!" Then in Laurel and Hardy's *Swiss Miss* [1938] there's one of the great moments of surrealism in cinema, it's positively Dada: For some reason Stan and Ollie have to carry an upright piano across a suspension bridge in the Alps, and a gorilla [Gemora] comes the other way. Wild!

I met Rick Baker when I was 21 and he was 20 and right away one of the things we bonded on was,

we shared this passion for gorillas and gorilla suits. Rick did the makeup for *Schlock* [shot in 1971, released in 1973, Landis' first movie, in which he plays an ape-like Missing Link]. My *intention,* when I wrote *Schlock,* was for it to have a bad gorilla suit. That was part of the joke. But then I met Rick Baker. I think his budget was $5000, and all the molds had to fit in his mom's oven. The film deserves its title, it's a terrible movie, but what's interesting about it is that Schlock himself became much more of a character because the makeup was so expressive. It was astonishing to me that Rick made a character that was both believable *and* schlocky. You accept him as a living being but he is also raggedy, rough around the edges, like a gorilla suit!

Schlock was shot in 12 days and for 11 of them I was in makeup. It was made in the summer, during a heat wave that's still listed as one of the hottest in California history. We were shooting in Agoura and, I'm not exaggerating, it averaged 108 degrees during shooting, and some days it was 110! So being out there in that makeup was ridiculous. And the sweat…! It was quite an experience. I am still astounded I survived, but I was 21, and you have a lot more stamina then!

Now, as to the subject of this book, *Bride of the Gorilla*. That was one of those pictures I first saw on TV. First of all, it's called *Bride of the Gorilla* so immediately it's about gorillas fucking women [*laughs*]—you know what I mean? It's sort of up-front about it, the same way as *The Bride and the Beast* [1958], the same way as a sexploitation picture from the '30s called *Forbidden Adventure*, which was basically black ladies dancing around topless and a guy in a gorilla suit. I have a wonderful poster from that movie.

Anyway, *Bride of the Gorilla*…this movie was written and directed by Curt Siodmak and he was quite a character. I met him at some Forry Ackerman function and out of nowhere he came out with this statement that took me aback. I've since heard that he said it often, but I was hearing it for the first time. Curt Siodmak said, "Hitler was the best thing that ever happened to me." He explained that without the Nazis, he never would have fled Germany and come to Los Angeles and had his career and his nice house. I think it was "just talk" but [*laughs*]—but it was still kind of a shocking thing to say!

Curt Siodmak was actually far more influential than people give him credit for, because a great deal of the "mythology" that he created while writing *The Wolf Man* [1941] and other Universal movies became accepted as true folklore. He had as much impact on this stuff as Bram Stoker. So many things we attribute to vampires and werewolves were inventions of Hollywood screenwriters. For example, we know that silver bullets can kill a werewolf, and that "fact" is mentioned in *The Wolf Man*. Well, Mr. Siodmak told

me that he heard *The Lone Ranger* on the radio and the Lone Ranger used silver bullets, and he thought, "Silver bullets! *That's* a good idea!" Years ago, when *The Wolf Man* came out on DVD, David Skal made for Universal Home Video a *Wolf Man* documentary [*Monster by Moonlight! The Immortal Saga of* The Wolf Man, 1999] and asked me to host it. All *I* did was stand there and read the narration, but David put that together and it's excellent. And in *that*, Siodmak talks about the process of writing *The Wolf Man* and makes a number of comments that are quite astute and interesting. Curt Siodmak left quite a legacy.

Curt was *insanely* jealous of his more successful brother Robert, a distinguished director of A-pictures. *Bride of the Gorilla* was Curt's first movie as director and it's not very good. I know that he wanted Lon Chaney to play the lead [the Barney Chavez role] but Chaney read it and said no [*laughs*], so he's miscast as the police commissioner. The movie's notoriety all surrounds the sensational Barbara Payton who had quite a scandal-ridden life. This was the first of her "downfall movies": She was under contract to Warner Brothers and Jack Warner was angry with her because of her bad behavior and punished her by saying, "Okay, I'm renting you out." But she actually gives a good performance in the film. And it was a big break for Raymond Burr [one of his first co-starring roles].

Bride of the Gorilla…it's not very good. It's a B picture and it was made on a very low budget and it uses a lot of stock footage. But it does have this kind of steamy, tawdry atmosphere around it. It's not an Ed Wood movie, it's not inept, it's just…nothing special. But it *does* have a gorilla suit!

THE MAKING OF BRIDE OF THE GORILLA
By Tom Weaver

Introduction

The Universal Monster Express made its first station stop on February 12, 1931, depositing *Dracula* at New York City's Roxy Theatre, and continued to roar through the U.S. (and much of the rest of the world) for 15 years. Other first-class passengers included the Frankenstein Monster, the Mummy, the Invisible Man and the Wolf Man.

The WereWolf of London, the Invisible Woman, the Ape Woman, the Mad Ghoul and others rode in coach. The Creeper shivered in an empty freight car.

Universal became known as the Studio of Horrors and the payoff was fairly handsome: From 1931 to 1944, the brood of screen monsters poured $10,000,000 in profits into Universal's coffers, about $750,000 net annually, "with some years showing considerable excess over that figure" (*Variety*).

But the train got to the end of the line in 1945. *House of Dracula*, the caboose, rolled into theaters in early December, its passengers a travel-weary, worse-for-wear Dracula, Wolf Man and Monster. That same month Universal made *She-Wolf of London*, monster-less despite the title, and the following month (January 1946) *The Cat Creeps*. The last day of *Cat Creeps* production marked the end of an era: The studio's horror cycle had come to a close.

Just as other studios had followed Universal's lead in the 1930s, producing their own chillers in the moneymaking wake of *Dracula*, they did the same in the mid-1940s, letting horror movies disappear from their production schedules the way Universal had. Occasionally there were indications that a public appetite still existed for monsters, the success of Film Classics' *Unknown Island* (1948) for instance; the year following the release of this dinosaur adventure, it was on track to gross 400 percent more than its negative cost. *Abbott and Costello Meet Frankenstein*, which provided a comeback for the Monster, Dracula and the Wolf Man, was Universal's second cheapest production of 1948 but also one of its top moneymakers.

Monster movie fans of the late '40s may have been deprived of their favorite characters' new adventures, but even in those pre-TV, pre-"Shock Theater" days, it was still possible to get an occasional fright film fix: In 1947, Realart Pictures contracted with Universal to begin reissuing their oldies, and Hollywood's greatest ghouls once again haunted American theaters.

Then in 1951, Realart's president decided to branch out into motion picture production. His company's third movie was its first horror flick and, perhaps understandably, it reeked of Universal influence: They hired screenwriter Curt Siodmak, one of the architects of Universal Horrors, as well as Universal's top terrornaut of the war years Lon Chaney, and teamed them on *Bride of the Gorilla*.

Bride of the Gorilla Synopsis

Barney Chavez…he's like a beast. An animal, with animal instincts…!

—Klaas Van Gelder

Klaas Van Gelder, owner of a rubber plantation in Spanish American jungle land, dislikes his plantation manager, the libidinous Barney Chavez. Klaas also feels neglected by his much-younger blonde wife Dina, a former dancer. *And* he probably notices that Barney, a brawny young buck, is a better match for Dina than a glum, pious bookworm like himself. With all this agita, you'd think Klaas would have high blood pressure, but his is so low that his physician, Dr. Viet, barely hears his heartbeat.

The heart is deceitful above all things, and desperately wicked: who can know it? I the Lord search the heart, I try the reins, even to give every man according to his ways, and according to the fruit of his doings.

Film Bulletin called the succarath "about as frightening as a baby monkey." From the looks of this photo, Lon Chaney would disagree!

Dinnertime at Van Gelder Manor: Klaas sits at the head of the table with a king-sized Bible and reads aloud those appetite-suppressing verses, then turns to Barney and accusingly asks, "You know about the complaint of that worker…*and his daughter*?" Apparently it's not just rubber trees getting tapped on this plantation. Barney tries to brush it off but a stressed-out Klaas fires him, then leaves the room. Dina, bored out of her gourd by her jungle existence, and obviously attracted to Barney, makes goo-goo eyes at him across the table and tells him in an urgent-sounding whisper, "Don't go away…don't leave…"

Now that he knows that Dina has feelings for him, Barney's course of action becomes clear. He catches Klaas alone in the garden and they have a man-to-man talk fated to be cut short by homicide. Barney says that he and Dina love each other; Klaas clouts him with a right; Barney notices a snake on the ground nearby and gives Klaas a forearm shot to the bread basket which puts the older man on his back next to the slithering reptile. One snake bite later, there's one more widow in the world.

Watching from the darkness behind bushes is Al Long, a wizened servant woman; she has it in for Love 'Em and Leave 'Em Barney because of his mistreatment of Dina's tawny native maid Larina. While Barney invades Dina's bedroom, urging her to go away with him, Al Long places a few leaves from a Pe de Guine plant over Klaas' eyes and chants, "Cursed shall be da murderer dese eyes have seen. Cursed shall be… Barney…Chavez! He shall be like uh animal… that hunt…in da jungle! Da jungle will haunt him…to his death!"

Police Commissioner Taro, conducting his inquest at Van Gelder Manor, thinks Barney killed Klaas, but he lacks the evidence needed to make a pinch. Al Long lies that she witnessed Klaas' death and that Barney wasn't involved— because she knows *her* vengeance will be swifter and crueler than the law's. That night she squeezes the juice of a Pe de Guine leaf into a glass while intoning, "Oh, Pe de Guine. Cloud his mind…change Barney Chavez into uh animal…in his eyes, he shall be uh animal!"

Barney and Dina are spliced at Van Gelder Manor. At the party that follows, Al Long prepares a drink for Barney that makes him woozy, and he sees—or perhaps he just *thinks* he sees—his right hand become black, swollen and cracked (a nice lap-dissolve transformation). Panicked, he dashes into an

When interviewed in his 80s and 90s, Curt Siodmak recalled that in every *Bride* scene shared by Raymond Burr and Chaney, "I watched their antagonism for each other penetrate their acting. Sparks of hatred flew from their eyes." One wonders if, in his old age, he was actually remembering the antipathy their two **characters** had for each other.

adjoining room. When Barney looks again, his hand is back to normal but, still shaken, he refuses to rejoin the party. That night, as Dina is preparing for bed and Barney is pouring champagne, jungle noises get his attention. Breathy and wide-eyed as he exits through exterior doors into the garden, he suddenly becomes the Roderick Usher of the rubber tree world, saying he can hear a bird that flies without making a noise; "I even hear the *snakes*!" Called out by the "voices" of the jungle, he rushes away on his wedding night. Looking swarthier and sweatier than usual, he prowls amidst the animals and snakes (stock footage that looks like it's from Thomas Edison days), and watches as his hands blacken. Subjective shots take us to the edge of a pool, and we see reflected on the surface of the water a succarath—a monster that looks like a guy in a gorilla suit. A *great deal* like a guy in a gorilla suit. Okay, *exactly* like a guy in a gorilla suit.

Dina later finds Barney unconscious in the garden. Feverish and delirious, he's treated by Dr. Viet. "The face in the water!" he babbles. Dina can tell that Dr. Viet is

in love with her, letting him down firmly with, "Barney's my husband, for better or for worse."

Turns out to be "worse": Word spreads that the jungle is again plagued by a succarath, which Taro defines to Dr. Viet as "a demon that tears living animals to shreds with its claws, and then feeds upon them. *Has* been known to attack humans, also." Summoned to the Van Heussen plantation, Taro examines the body of a slaughtered cow and talks to a native worker who describes the succarath as huge and red, with the head of a man and the teeth of an alligator. There's bogus suspense as Barney feverishly ambles around Van Gelder Manor and sees himself in a full-length mirror as a succarath. Amidst thunder and lightning, a subjective shot takes us into Dina's bedroom where hairy hands reach out for the sleeping girl, then withdraw.[1] Taro is certain that Barney is the succarath and that he will be brought to justice: "The jungle will see to that."

Dina, searching in daylight for her errant husband, finds him caught by the ankle in one of the steel animal traps set for the succarath. That night, Barney is himself again, even romantic and sincere-sounding as he and

Bride and gloom: Dina and Barney's passion for one another has prompted Barney to commit murder and will climactically lead to the lovers' death. What's *Duel in the Sun* (1947) got that *Bride of the Gorilla* ain't got??

Dina plan a trip to Paris and London. But Al Long doubles down on her spell-casting, and by the time Van Heussen arrives the next day to pay $100,000 for the Van Gelder plantation, Barney has again disappeared into the jungle. He returns home two days later, telling Dina in awestruck tones that in the jungle, he can see further, climb as if he had wings, smell 1000 smells—a speech culminating in an emphatic "The jungle's my *house*—it *belongs* to me!" Three of Barney's workers arrive to collect their pay so that they can move away from this succarath-haunted area, and notice that his hands are covered with dried blood.

Viet tells Dina that Barney may have been poisoned with a drug that causes hallucinations and schizophrenia; "These natives have many ways of driving a man out of his mind." Viet adds that he, like Taro, thinks that Barney killed Klaas so therefore his conscience may be the cause of his derangement. And if that's true, Dina may be on his hit list, since she reminds him of his crime.

The Van Gelder Manor servants have run away and the workers quit so it's now just Dina and Barney.

The latter knows he must choose between Dina and the jungle—and, to the dismay of his presumably still untouched bride, he again hurries out into the night. Dina plunges after him into his screeching jungle haunts, across the veldt of violence, past puma fang and boa coil. The camera (sometimes handheld, sometimes with hairy hands in front of it) stalks her. Eventually the camera catches up with Dina, who screams and flees. Soon we see her motionless in the arms of the succarath.

Taro and Viet come a-running, firing their guns up into a tree where *something* is hiding; there's a Barney-sounding cry as *something* drops to the jungle floor. We now see Barney and Dina on the ground near the base of the tree. As Viet hurries to Dina, Barney crawls to the edge of a dark pool and sees on its surface a succarath reflection (same shot as before). It then turns into a Barney reflection as, dying, he drops face-first into the water. Taro removes his hat and walks away as a distraught-looking Viet cradles the lifeless Dina. The jungle has punished Barney for his crime.

Bride of the Gorilla:
The Production History

Harris-Broder Pictures Corp., New York, has changed its name to Realart Pictures, Inc. Outfit is a film investing corporation, dealing primarily in reissues and foreign releases.

It recently acquired some 300 Universal reissues, on which it has made a deal with Film Classics for release of ten a year for five years.

The Realart saga began—in the pages of *Variety*, anyway—with this August 27, 1947, announcement of their deal with Universal. A much fuller account of the birth of Realart Pictures appeared in the show business bible several years later, January 25, 1956: *Variety* interviewee Matty Fox, who had joined Universal in the mid-40s as executive vice-president, revealed that the studio's big problem in mid-1947 was a looming $3,000,000 deficit for the fiscal year ending on August 31. Fox felt that the only way to turn things around in the two months remaining was to get a separate company to make a substantial down payment on the re-releasing rights to their backlog of films.

Fox canvassed the top reissue outfits who declared that the project was impossible. The *Variety* article continued, "He finally got some 'cloak-and-suitors'[2] to establish the company and arranged a loan, and Realart went into business as of July 31 with a ten-year pact with U-I. Terms of that pact were that Realart would get 35 percent of the gross, and would pay out $3,250,000 right on the barrelhead. Thus, Universal showed a $250,000 profit that year, and Realart came into being." (A 1950s article on Embassy Pictures founder Joseph E. Levine tangentially mentions that he, too, was among the organizers of the Realart deal.)

On September 10, 1947, *Variety* reported that Realart had already prepared its first two double-headers: a "Black" twin-bill of the Karloff-Lugosi *The Black Cat* (1934)[3] plus the same stars' *Black Friday* (1940), and a "Lady" combo of *The Lady from Cheyenne* (1941) and *Lady in a Jam* (1942). Other early twin bills, according to a December *Variety* blurb, were *Tight Shoes* (1941)-*Butch Minds the Baby* (1942) and *Green Hell* (1940)-*Pittsburgh* (1942). By September 1948, when Realart celebrated its first anniversary with a national convention and sales meeting in New York, they had already re-released 40 Universal features and eight Westerns. According to the Scott MacGillivray-Ted Okuda *Filmfax* article "Play It Again, Jack! Remembering Realart, the Re-Releasing

Company" (June-July 1993), some of Realart's first Universal reissues were advertised in such a way as to create the impression that the movies were new; "This practice was later modified in the interest of fair advertising, and promotions soon proclaimed the pictures 'A Realart Re-Release.'"[4]

Realart prexy Paul Broder also had other irons in the film-world fire: The enterprising head of an independent theater circuit in Detroit, Paul opened a theater in that city's Willow Run Airport in early 1948 and planned to establish a string of such theaters in air terminals across the country. The Willow Run theater was equipped with 16mm and 35mm projection equipment and showed newsreels and short entertainment programs. By June, however, the Airlines Terminal Theater had flopped, "folding after four months of operation because of lack of business" (*Billboard*, June 5).

Meanwhile, Realart kept spewing out dual bills exhumed from the Universal vaults, sometimes capitalizing on current events to generate a bit more business. Their 1948 re-release of W.C. Fields' *My Little Chickadee* (1940) and Olsen and Johnson's *Crazy House* (1943) was nothing special box office-wise. But in 1949 the late W.C. was suddenly very much back in the public eye as Robert Lewis Taylor wrote about the comedian in a series of eight *Saturday Evening Post* articles. Realart responded by pulling the *Chickadee-Crazy House* combo and replacing the latter with a second Fields film, *The Bank Dick* (1940). This new and improved double-header was a big hit. Realart prepared a second Fields twin bill, *You Can't Cheat an Honest Man* (1939) and *Never Give a Sucker an Even Break* (1941), for the fall of 1949, timed to appear when Taylor's articles were scheduled to be published together as a Doubleday book.

According to an announcement made by Realart sales-distribution veepee Budd Rogers at the company's second anniversary New York convention (late October 1949), the four Fields films did tremendous business (especially in the New England area) as a result of the Fields book. Reissues were gaining in popularity, Rogers proclaimed, giving Realart a greater number of exhibitor accounts. By this point, Realart was up to 165 features, 38 Westerns and four serials reissued nationally. But Paul Broder was no longer the head man: An October 8, 1949, *Billboard* article on his brother Al called Paul the "recently resigned" president of Realart Pictures. On November 10, 1949, *Variety's* page one items included a New York-datelined blurb revealing that Realart veepee Jack Broder had been elected prexy of the outfit.

The Spotlight

Hollywood's legion of independent producers, and even the major studios, have been forced to sit up and take note of an ambitious newcomer to the ranks of moviemakers, who, in one short year, has become the town's biggest volume producer of independent pictures. He is Jack Broder, a one-time successful exhibitor, and more recently the head of his own national distribution organization—Realart Pictures.

During his first year as an independent producer, Broder has turned out eight films, including "Basketball Fix," "Two-Dollar Bettor," "Bride of the Gorilla," "The Bushwackers," "Bela Lugosi Meets a Brooklyn Gorilla," "Kid Monk Baroni," "Breakdown," and "Battles of Chief Pontiac."

During the next 12 months, Broder expects to equal that output, and possibly even attain his eventual goal of ten personal productions per year. At the same time, he hopes to corral a half-dozen outside pictures.

More and more, Broder expects to enter into profit-sharing deals with "name" stars and directors, in order to give the product added lustre without involving prohibitive cash outlays. Moreover, he will continue to invest his own money in outside productions for Realart release, but only in cases where well-established stars head up the casts.

Broder tells FILM BULLETIN that nothing definite has been worked out on the rumored merger of his company with Lippert Productions. "Ever since the sale of the Lippert exchanges," he said, "Mr. Lippert has been using some of Realart's field representatives. However, any discussions of a merger are temporarily at a standstill."

The success of the Realart distribution company led Broder to dispose of most of his theatres, and when the re-issues began to slow down at the boxoffice in the early '50's, he embarked on his current program of producing new pictures. Jack Broder lets no grass grow under his feet.

JACK BRODER

Jack Broder, president of Realart Pictures.

Then of course there were the horror re-releases, Realart's biggest claim to fame according to decades of Monster Kid lit, and possibly some of the company's bigger moneymakers, although I've yet to find anything in contemporary sources to confirm that. In the Realart Pictures file at New York's Lincoln Center is an undated flyer Realart used to advertise the availability of *Dracula* and *Frankenstein* (1931). Emblazoned across the top is **SMASHING ALL RECORDS,** and below is a reproduction of a Western Union telegram sent from Marty Levine of Brandt Theatres to Jack Bellman of Realart's 630 Ninth Avenue, New York, office:

CONGRATULATIONS[.] TO BREAK RECORDS DURING HOLY WEEK IS A SENSATIONAL ACCOMPLISHMENT. YOUR COMBINATION OF *FRANKEN-STEIN* AND *DRACULA* IS SMASHING ALL RECORDS. IT GROSSED TWO WEEKS OF AVERAGE BUSINESS IN THREE DAYS. YOU AND AL BRODER DID A GREAT JOB. MANY THANKS.

Many Realart posters for Universal Horrors became collectors' items, says longtime items collector John Antosiewicz:

It was never a case where Realart used the original Universal poster design and simply replaced **Universal presents** or **A Universal Picture** with **Realart presents** or **A Realart Picture.** They created their own poster designs for each size—one-sheet, half-sheet, insert, three-sheet, lobby cards, pressbook. It was a mixed bag: Many are okay and a number are terrible, but some Realart pieces are very attractive and blow away the original Universal posters. The *Abbott and Costello Meet Frankenstein* half-sheet, for example. Some of the Realart posters for titles like *Dracula, Frankenstein* and *The Mummy* sell for a couple thousand each, if not more.

Reissues reached their peak in 1949, with the major studios, plus Eagle Lion, Film Classics and Realart, re-releasing a total of 136 old favorites. But, according to a *Variety* article, "Momentum gained by reissues in the past year is easing off with filmgoers showing more selectivity in their choice of oldies. Discriminative attitude is said to have been caused by an overdose of mediocre reissues during the past couple of years. However, top-quality oldies, according to exhibs, are holding up moderately well and in several cases are doing as good or better than some of current product." Because Realart had access to such a huge bloc of movies, they still had plenty of decent titles to work with, and even some hall of famers, like 1930's Best Picture Oscar winner *All Quiet on the Western Front*. Such was the prestige of *All Quiet* that on July 11, 1950, Realart kicked off that movie's comeback with a special screening and cocktail party at L.A.'s ritzy Ambassador Hotel.

Due to the public's current interest in war-themed films, *All Quiet* did good business in some situations, smash business in others. When Universal wound up its fiscal year on October 31, 1950, part of the studio's estimated $1,500,000 profit was income received under its reissue deal with Realart. The arrangement was "working out exceptionally well for U, giving it an income of better than $100,000 a month for the last few months of the fiscal year," *Variety* reported on December 6. "It is expected to increase still farther." The article continued,

> U made the deal with Realart in 1947, receiving $3,250,000 against a percentage. There was a recoupment arrangement by which the reissue outfit wasn't to begin paying the percentage until it had recovered its advance payment. The advance was completely recouped in the middle of this year and the percentages thereupon began to go to U.

Two years later, the *Variety* article "Realart Reaps Reissue Riches" (September 17, 1952) revealed that the outfit had so far re-released 300 Universal flicks. "Our reissues are averaging between 5000 and 8000 dates," said Jack Broder. "Some have reached such stature in the last five years that they have been re-booked at yearly intervals. Some, comparably, are doing far better in the re-release than they did the first time out." The most popular reissues to date, according to the article, were *Destry Rides Again* (1939) and…*Spoilers of the Sea*? There doesn't seem to be any such movie. There was a 1936 Universal B called *Sea Spoilers* with John Wayne and Nan Grey, but surely *that* wasn't one of Realart's two biggest attractions. Perhaps 1942's *The Spoilers* (1942), also with Wayne, is the movie in question.

Jack Broder Productions

After years of distributing movies, at last Jack Broder felt the urge to *make* some, and he started with a pair of pictures whose stories may have appealed to *him*.

Monster Kids know Herman Cohen as the producer of drive-in horror hits like *I Was a Teenage Werewolf* (1957), *I Was a Teenage Frankenstein* (1957), *Horrors of*

A family man's (John Litel) horse track betting leads to larceny in *Two Dollar Bettor*, the second movie from Broder's indie unit. Up until two days before the start of shooting, John Ireland was slated to star; he objected to script changes and asked for his release.

the Black Museum (1959) and more; in 1951 the 25-year-old Hollywood newcomer was working as an assistant to Broder. Cohen described Broder to me as someone who enjoyed playing cards for money and betting on the horses. Broder's first two movies, *The Basketball Fix* and *Two Dollar Bettor* (both 1951), both involved gambling—as did a third, *Kid Monk Baroni* (1952). *Bettor* and *Basketball* also featured crooks, and according to Cohen, Broder was "close friends" with a few of them too…

"Jack Broder owned theaters in Detroit so he knew members of the Purple Gang," Cohen told me. "Broder was close friends with them the way, say, Frank Sinatra was with Sam Giancana. The Purple Gang had spread to Las Vegas by this time, and once a month a guy from Vegas, from the Sands Hotel, would show up at Broder's office with a big briefcase—full of cash. They were investing in Broder. The Purple Gang invested in Jack Broder and the Realart reissues. I was meeting all kinds of straaaange people that would come to his office. It took me a while to figure it out." Cohen also recalled signing a number of documents for Broder without knowing what he was signing; a half-century later he laughed to me, "The FBI could have come in and wanted to interview *me*, in those days!"[5]

Cohen told me that Broder's first movie was *Two Dollar Bettor*, but according to 1951 trade paper production charts, *The Basketball Fix* was shot in March, *Two Dollar Bettor* in late April and early May. *Basketball* was a torn-from-the-headlines tale: At the beginning of 1951, two former Manhattan College basketball players admitted to police that, bribed by gamblers, they had "fixed" games during the 1949-50 season. Next three City College players were arrested on bribery charges, along with one of the masterminds of the scheme. In the coming weeks, in dribbles and drabs, dozens of players were snatched up by the long arm of the law and deposited in courts very different from the ones they were used to. The story escalated into college athletics' greatest scandal. Madison Square Garden was the epicenter but the crooked activities had been going on nationwide.

The Basketball Fix began production in mid-March, when the real-life scandal was still unfolding and police fingerprint ink still wet on the hands of some of the players and bookmakers involved. The most prominent player caught up in the mess was black college kid Sherman White, at that moment the sport's leading scorer; the equivalent character in the movie was played by Marshall Thompson, white as a mayonnaise jar and 25 years old and yet playing a high schooler. *The Basketball Fix* was completed in just eight days, with d.p. Stanley Cortez a main factor in the speed of production.

Broder's *Two Dollar Bettor* followed with a grim tale of a bank comptroller (John Litel) hooked on playing the ponies; he goes from bet to worse when he runs out of his own money and starts using the bank's. It was directed by Edward L. Cahn, "a talented man, he should have been making big pictures," Cohen told me. "But he only did B pictures, he never got a break 'cause he was too nice of a guy. And very talented. I learned a lot from him."

The movies Broder was preparing to make were *not* going to be released by Realart: Realart executive vice-president Budd Rogers announced in New York on April 30, 1951, that Broder's production company had no connection with Realart Pictures. "Realart's contract with Universal-International, for distribution of U-I's oldies, prevents reissue company from handling any other product," *Variety* stated in their coverage of this announcement. Around this time, a *Hollywood Reporter* item mentioned the possibility that *The Basketball Fix* would be purchased and released by RKO.

For their third movie, Jack Broder Productions turned to horror…

Enter Curt Siodmak

Directing adds life to the hermit existence of the writer. I wrote screenplays on speculation. Should I sell one, I could ask the company to let me direct it. Or was that wish a product of sibling rivalry, to show my brother Robert [Robert Siodmak, director of several '40s film noir classics] that I also knew where the camera should be placed on the set? My agent Lester Salkow sold my screenplay, *The Face in the Water*, to Realart Film Production, a company so stingy that before they spent a nickel, they raised the bull on that coin from a calf.

—Curt Siodmak, in his 1997 autobiography
Even a Man Who Is Pure in Heart

Back in the year 1951 BMKE (Before Monster Kid Era), the wide assortment of horror and sci-fi titles on German-born screenwriter Curt Siodmak's résumé gave no one nerdgasms, in Hollywood or anywhere else. Today, however, with some of his movies enshrined among the greats of the genre by generations of fans, his is among the revered names from that era (revered by Monster Kids, anyway). Between 1937 when *Kurt* Siodmak arrived in America, and 1951's *Bride of the Gorilla*, his name had been seen in the credits of more than two dozen films. More than half of them were in the horror or sci-fi vein, a few of them forgettable (*The Ape, The Invisible Woman, The Climax*), a few highly regarded (*The Wolf Man, I Walked with a Zombie*), most falling somewhere in between. Many of his movies feature characters whose yen for brain transplants (and/or related shenanigans) outpaced the logic behind them.

On the eve of the start of *Bride of the Gorilla* production, Hollywood columnist Edwin Schallert devoted some ink to Siodmak and an unusual deal that

Curt had made with his older brother Robert: "I came here in 1937 and Robert arrived here two years later," Curt told Schallert, continuing,

> I had managed to obtain a break as a writer but I also had the ambition to direct.
>
> However, it seemed easier to interest people in the directorial ability of Robert at the time.
>
> So we made an agreement. I would write and he would direct and neither of us would become identified with the other's activity. I thought it was a good arrangement at the time because it was to prevail only until he was established. But it turned into a Frankenstein.
>
> Every time there were negotiations for me to direct a picture the producer would say, "I thought this was Robert Siodmak. I want Robert Siodmak." And there I was out in the cold. This happened many times.
>
> Finally, now that he is in Europe [Robert was then making *The Crimson Pirate* with Burt Lancaster in Italy], I have been able to sneak in a couple of pictures.

According to Schallert, the "couple of pictures" to which Curt refers were *Bride of the Gorilla* and Summit Production's *A-Men*; I assume that the latter became *The Magnetic Monster* (1953).

Robert's reaction to Curt's decision to branch out into directing?: Again from Curt's autobiography: "Robert and Babs, his wife, were shocked when they learned that I wanted to become a director. They rushed to my house very upset, Robert green in the face, as he tried to talk me out of such a dangerous adventure.[6] What if I had a big success? That would cut into his glory as one of the top directors of Hollywood." (Without wishing to sound unkind, or to get ahead of the story, Robert had as much to worry about with Curt as Billy Wilder [*Double Indemnity*, *The Lost Weekend*, *Sunset Blvd.*, *The Big Carnival*, *Witness for the Prosecution*] did when *his* brother W. Lee Wilder turned director and started dotting the Hollywood landscape with his flicks

The Siodmak brothers, Curt (on left) and Robert, in a 1929 photo. Robert apparently wanted only one director in the family. And, according to a *Filmfax* interview with Curt, Robert also wanted only one *Siodmak* in the family: Robert asked Curt to change his name to Curt Patrick!

the way a cow dots a pasture.)

Siodmak, on the eve of turning 49, got an early birthday present: at last, an offer to direct a movie. On July 13 *Variety* published the news that Jack Broder Productions had signed him to direct *Bride of the Gorilla*.[7] According to this same blurb, "Cast is not set as yet," but ideas were floating around in *some*body's head: In the Xerox copy of the script which I own (reproduced in this book), the very first page is a list of the characters and a mini-description of each, and next to five of the descriptions, barely legible, are handwritten names, obviously the names of performers under consideration for each role:

Barbara Payton and Franchot Tone, the actor less remembered today for his acting roles than for being belted nearly into extinction by *another* Payton boy toy, Tom Neal. The month Barbara was born, November 1927, Tone was appearing in his first Broadway play (wait for it): *The Belt*! His libido kept calling him back to Payton the way Al Long's curse gave Barney Chavez uncontrollable urges to take to the jungle.

Alongside Klaas Van Gelder is **DON-ATH**, undoubtedly Ludwig Donath, the Austrian-born stage and movie actor who specialized in playing Nazis in Hollywood movies during World War II, and later played the father of Al Jolson in *The Jolson Story* (1946) and *Jolson Sings Again* (1949).

Alongside Dina Van Gelder is "**LUEZ, CHARLITA**." Luez has to be Laurette Luez, of *Prehistoric Women* (1950) infamy, and Charlita has to be (duh!) Charlita. She may have missed out on *Bride of the Gorilla* but she co-starred in Broder's next jungle jamboree, the way-out *Bela Lugosi Meets a Brooklyn Gorilla* (1952).

Next to Barney Chavez is **RANDALL**. *Randall?* A stumper for me. Stuart Randall, who did do a couple Broder movies? Perhaps a (misspelled) Ron Randell?

Underneath Al Long is **REY**. Maybe Rosa Rey, the Spanish movie actress who occasionally played maids and housekeepers? Most memorably for readers of this book, she played an Al Long-type character—a Haitian maid who makes a voodoo doll—in *The Face of Marble* (1946). Her husband Martin Garralaga *is* in *Bride of the Gorilla*, as the plantation worker who says he's seen the succarath.

And alongside Taro is **SOKOLOFF**, no doubt Russian-born Vladimir Sokoloff, an actor Monster Kids remember as the high school janitor in *I Was a Teenage Werewolf* (1957), the Supreme in *Beyond the Time Barrier* (1960), the old man buried with his winning lottery ticket in *Mr. Sardonicus* (1961) and more. Western fans think of him first as *The Magnificent Seven*'s (1960) village elder, exhorting the men of his bandit-plagued town to buy guns: "Go to the border. Guns are plentiful there!" Aficionados of Golden Age Hollywood Classics remember Sokoloff as painter Paul Cezanne in *The Life of Emile Zola* (1937) and the old Spanish guide in *For Whom the Bell Tolls* (1943). Probably *no one* remembers that in 1935, when he was a Max Reinhardt star working in Paris, Universal announced that they were prepared to sign him for the title role in their upcoming remake of *The Hunchback of Notre Dame* (eventually never made).

One day after the abovementioned "Cast is not set as yet" *Variety* blurb came a two-paragraph *Los Angeles Times* story "*Bride of Gorilla* Soon Will Star Barbara Payton," disclosing that the sexy blonde leading lady would top-line the coming Broder flick. "The Payton engagement, under a borrowing deal from William Cagney Productions, removes this star from the suspended list. She was put on suspension for refusal to play in *Close to My Heart* [1951] at Warners, according to report…" Payton was also the subject of the lede story in Louella Parsons' July 14 column (actually written on the date by Dorothy Manners): It amusingly began by noting that Payton, "who soon becomes the bride of [actor] Franchot Tone, stars in *Bride of the Gorilla* and no one is kidding her more about the title than the bridegroom-to-be."

Payton might have been a nymphomaniac, actor Mickey Knox told interviewer Patrick McGilligan in the book *Tender Comrades: A Backstory of the Hollywood Blacklist*. He continued:

> She really enjoyed sex. She kept me in bed once for three days and nights, even feeding me in bed. She wouldn't let me get out of bed. I had to crawl on my hands and knees.

Payton, a product of Cloquet, Minnesota, was a relative newcomer to Hollywood when she co-starred at age 22 with James Cagney in his producer-brother William's *Kiss Tomorrow Goodbye* (Warner Brothers, 1950), a violent gangster movie. But from this premature peak she toppled into a couple of supporting parts, fifth-billed in the Gary Cooper Western *Dallas* (Warners, 1950), as dull-witted renegade Steve Cochran's girlfriend, with waist-length blonde hair, and William Cagney Productions' Western *Only the Valiant* (Warners, 1951), as one point in a love triangle with Gregory Peck and Gig Young. Next came a loanout to the King Brothers for the Civil War yarn *Drums in the Deep South* (1951). Perhaps her career doldrums were partly caused by the steady drip-drip-drip of bad publicity her off-camera capers were receiving. How bad? According to Herman Cohen, bad enough that Jack L. Warner wanted her off his WB payroll pronto. Cohen recalled for me,

> [Jack Broder] played cards with Jack Warner at the Friars, at the Hollywood Athletic Club on Sunset Boulevard and what have you. They would play for money. Jack Warner mentioned that he had this cunt [Barbara Payton] under contract, doing nothing, sitting on her ass, and Jack Broder said, "Gee, I need a young, sexy girl for this film I'm gonna do." And Jack Warner

said, "*Take* her! You can *have* her." They didn't like her [at Warners]—she was fucking everybody on the lot. I think we paid hardly nothing to borrow her from Warners, Jack Warner said, "I gotta get rid of that cunt." So…it was a very cheap deal for Jack Broder to borrow her from Warners. …Oh, she gave *me* a great blow job when she first arrived. I was a young kid, I was scared stiff. She thought she was a cat, and she put whiskers over her eyebrows and on her lips. Drew them on. She thought she was a cat.

Lending credence to Cohen's claim of having had sexual relations with that woman…Miss Payton: In her lurid 1963 autobiography *I Am Not Ashamed*, Payton said that she and her boyfriend, actor Tom Neal, loved cats "and occasionally we'd make-up as cats and play games and eventually they'd end up in love-making."

Hollywood insiders had to know that Payton's downward spiral (going from a co-starring, attention-getting Warners role, to bad publicity, to small parts, to suspension, to *Bride of the Gorilla*) meant that she was bound for neverlasting stardom. Cohen is sure that Payton knew it too: "She was very unhappy about being loaned to do *Bride of the Gorilla*."

Lon Chaney

The *L.A. Times'* "*Bride of Gorilla* Soon Will Star Barbara Payton" item also mentioned the casting of Raymond Burr, and added, "There is a possibility that Lon Chaney will also join the production." Two days later, July 16, *Variety* announced, "Lon Chaney and Raymond Burr have the male leads." *Bride of the Gorilla* marked a return to monsters for Chaney who, outside of two stints as the Wolf Man (*House of Dracula* and *Abbott and Costello Meet Frankenstein*), hadn't been in a monster movie for seven years perhaps to the day: *The Mummy's Curse* began production on July 26, 1944, *Bride of the Gorilla* on July 26, 1951.

In the first half of the 1940s, when Universal was Monster Central, Chaney was its top terror star…but it appears that back then, he aspired to something more than yak hair, neck electrodes and mummy wrappings. He disliked the long makeup ordeals, venting to an interviewer on the set of *The Mummy's Ghost* (1944) that people were nuts to spend money to see Mummy movies. Universal director Reginald LeBorg told me that Chaney, in his horror heyday, expressed a desire to play "a gentleman" in a movie. Universal's Inner Sanctum mysteries gave him the chance to portray an assortment of gents, a neurologist, a college professor and a research chemist among them. The critical consensus on his performances made it plain that he'd have been better off sticking to his monsters.

By 1945 Universal had assigned him the roles of the Man Made Monster, Dracula, the Frankenstein Monster, Kharis (three times) and the Wolf Man (four)—not to mention the six Inner Sanctums, Western heroes and villains, comedic characters and more, permitting no grass to grow under his 12W shoes. But a few months after *House of Dracula* wrapped, Chaney refused to sign a new deal with Universal (the dispute was over money) and left to freelance. And then Universal morphed into Universal-International, their movies became a bit more (well, a *lot* more) sophisticated and, as one columnist put it, they "ordered Dracula and the Wolf Man to the showers."

In the interim between Chaney's split with Universal and his 1948 return to the studio to reprise the Wolf Man in *A&C Meet Frankenstein*, the actor had appeared in just four movies, one an indie, another a Monogram. Perhaps he began to miss the days of steadier work (and steadier paychecks), yak hair and all. With monster movies temporarily out of style, 'twould appear that *Chaney* was out of style also. He thought he could remedy this himself: During the making of *A&C Meet Frankenstein* he told columnist Bob Thomas that, with screenwriter Curt Siodmak, he was organizing his own production company to create new characters "more horrible than any yet seen on the screen." Thomas ended the story at this point with a sarcastic-sounding "I can hardly wait."

Two and a half years (and only a handful of additional movies) later, Chaney was back to talking about making his own monster flick, *The Lizard Man*. In the October 1950 article "Here's a Monster Film with a Message," he claimed that since 1948 he had received letters from all over the world asking what had become of the monsters. (In another article written at about the same time, he said that these letters were penned by "everybody from morons to doctors.") "The studios in the past made a serious mistake in their monster films," the actor claimed, continuing:

> They tried to make them too horrible, and eventually ran out of ways to do it. [In *The Lizard Man*,] the goon will be a very sweet goon who kills people only to protect a young girl. That was the secret of my father's monstrous success. You ended by feeling sorry for him. …It will be a monster film and a travelogue combined. And the lizard man's protection of the little girl will have a message.

Lon Chaney had an almost boyish look when playing the title characters in *Man Made Monster* and *The Wolf Man*. Just ten years and a lake's worth of liquor later, he looks middle-aged and careworn in *Bride of the Gorilla*. The script describes his character, Taro, as "a tall, handsome, brown-skinned man."

According to the article, Chaney was also spending time "perfecting makeup to puff out his jowls like a lizard." In another October 1950 article on Chaney, this one by Alice Mosby, he said most of the same things about the state of movie-monsterdom and *The Lizard Man* but added a few details, like the fact that kids followed him as if he were Hopalong Cassidy and imitated his Wolf Man howl. Regarding *The Lizard Man*, he said it will be "anti-adultery, which should satisfy the religious groups, and I hope to film it at a national park like the Grand Canyon so it will be educational. Like a travelogue." In a June 1951 column, Hedda Hopper wrote that, despite current rumors, Chaney would not be remaking any of his father's old pictures. She quoted Jr. as saying, "Both Claude Rains and Charles Laughton tried, and neither was very successful. No matter how good you were, the public would still think you didn't come up to the old films. It's like remembering the pies your mother used to make." Hopper wrapped by saying, "Lon, bearded up for *Flame of Araby* [1951], just wants to be a good character actor."

In the run-up to the production of *Bride of the Gorilla*, Edwin Schallert made a monkey of himself when he included a funny slip-up in his July 21, 1951, *Los Angeles Times* column: "Curtis Bernhardt, the writer, [is] undertaking his first directorial assignment in Hollywood [on *Bride of the Gorilla*]." Oops. Curt *Siodmak*, not Bernhardt, Edwin! German-born Bernhardt began directing in his native Germany in silent days, and made his Hollywood directing debut at Warners in 1940 with the romantic *My Love Came Back*, a surprise sleeper. Since then he'd directed many more WB pictures with stars including Bogart, Davis, Crawford, Stanwyck and Ida Lupino. One hopes that Bernhardt skipped reading the *Los Angeles Times* that day.[8]

Lights! Camera! Inaction!

This is jungle. Lush. Green. Alive with incredible growth. As young as day; as old as time. I, Taro, police commissioner of Itman [phonetic spelling] County which borders the Amazonas [phonetic] River, know it as well as any man will *ever* know it. Isn't it beautiful? But I have also learned that beauty can be venomous. Deadly! Something terrifying, something of prehistoric ages when monstrous superstitions ruled the minds of men. Something that has haunted the world for millions of years rose out of that verdant labyrinth. Let me tell you

how the jungle itself took the law into its own hands…

　　　　—Police Commissioner Taro (Lon
　　　　Chaney) narrating the opening of
　　　　Bride of the Gorilla

Bride of the Gorilla began shooting on Thursday, July 26, at Sam Goldwyn Studios, formerly the historic United Artists Studios.[9] Its interiors *and* jungle exteriors were shot on sets. Herman Cohen had a memory of finishing the picture in ten days, but according to contemporary sources and also to director Siodmak, it took only seven. Seven days is surprising because, Siodmak admits, on the *first* day the movie didn't really *have* a director!:

> There is a difference in writing a scene or standing behind a camera, to visualizing that scene and to giving it life. At the first minutes of shooting I was in a catatonic state, but the crew and the actors, sensing my mental coma, came to my rescue. I saw Barbara walking through the jungle, the camera moved on its track, the actors spoke their lines. The experienced crew guided me through the first hours of production. I was not told that Jack Broder, who had watched me, wanted to replace me, but the actors and crew threatened to walk out. The next day I already felt like an old-timer.

Cohen didn't mention Siodmak's catatonia, but did recall an equally vexing problem posed by having a heavily accented German in the director's chair: "I was the only one who could understand Curt Siodmak's English, so they all came to *me*: 'What did he say? What did Curt say?'"

Fortunately for newbie director Siodmak, he had written an action-lite script, one that a detractor might call a *no*-action script: The two-punch fight between Barney and Klaas is *it* for the 65-minute movie. But *Bride* has compensations for easy-to-please Monster Kids, for example, plot ties to Siodmak's calling card to screenwriting respectability, *The Wolf Man*:

With the names Lon Chaney and Siodmak in the credits, and Larry Talbot- and Maleva-like characters in top roles (Barney and Al Long, respectively), it's hard to watch *Bride of the Gorilla* without visions of *The Wolf Man* dancing in your head. But the dance doesn't end there, especially with the Pe de Guine plant an integral part of the plot, as wolfbane was in *The Wolf Man*. Then, too, there's Commissioner Taro, minion of the law, who's the equivalent of the Universal movie's Capt. Montford; and Dr. Viet, who's part physician, part psychiatrist, and tags along with Taro on the succarath hunt, like *The*

Presumably what's happening in this behind-the-scenes photo is that a camera operator has donned the gorilla suit (with camera attached to his shoulder) to get Gorilla P.O.V. shots that include his hands.

Wolf Man's Dr. Lloyd. In *The Wolf Man*, as well as in *WereWolf of London* (1935) before it, the werewolf seeks to kill the one he loves best (Gwen in *The Wolf Man*, Lisa in *WereWolf of London*); in *Bride*, Succarath Barney is driven to try to kill the one who reminds him of his crime (Dina).

"[Curt Siodmak] had written *The Wolf Man* ten years before," Michael Weldon observed in his *Psychotronic* magazine review of *Bride of the Gorilla*, "but the logic of this Realart release (a gorilla in South America?) is closer to a *Jungle Jim* or *Bomba* movie."

Then there's the Maleva counterpart Al Long, played by Gisela Werbisek. She *puts* the curse on Barney to make him suffer, whereas Maleva tries to *ease* Larry's suffering, so the two characters couldn't be more different. But Al Long, a tiny, heavily accented, witch-like old woman hanging around the edges of this man-into-monster story, nevertheless gives off unmistakable Maleva vibes.

In *Even a Man Who Is Pure in Heart*, Siodmak wrote that Gisela was a famous comedienne

with a face so lined and homely that it crossed the borderline of ugliness and made her fascinating to watch. She also had a morbid wit. A Jewish refugee in Hollywood, she said she never would be able to understand America "where the Jews are gangsters and the Goyim are bankers." She also complained that in Austria she was called Gisella, in Berlin Gisela, but her name in America was pronounced "Scheissele," "Little Shit" in German. She was married to Franz Piffl, whose brother was the archbishop of Salzburg. Piffl, on account of his enormous [girth] and giant body, was in constant demand as an extra in pictures, while Gisella got only one single job, the native witch in my film.[10] In Vienna where she had been rich and famous,

According to a Phantom of the Movies review, *Bride*'s Gisela Werbisek (left) is "clearly channeling Maria Ouspenskaya [from *The Wolf Man*, right], minus the latter's wizened charm." One Internet wag describes Gisela as looking "like the elderly Buster Keaton in drag"! (*Bride* photo courtesy Ronald V. Borst/Hollywood Movie Posters)

she had kept Piffl in Sacher tart and cream. When she was in Hollywood, he had to make her breakfast and serve it to her in bed before he left for the studio.

Interestingly, if any of this stuff is interesting, Siodmak's original idea for *The Wolf Man* was that viewers would never be certain if the man bitten by a wolf actually goes on to transform into a wolf himself, or if it's all in his head. Universal wanted an on-screen monster so that approach was ditched; we frequently see Larry as the hairy, fanged monster. Siodmak salvaged the "Does he or doesn't he become a monster?" notion for *Bride*, which he initially called *The Face in the Water* because in his original script, his intention was that viewers would only see the monstrous version of Barney through Barney's eyes, in reflections. (Notice too that Al Long, when putting her curse on Barney, specifies, "In his eyes, he shall be uh animal!")

But footage of the succarath—*not* seen through Barney's eyes—is seen here and there throughout the movie, so unless viewers have also been hexed by Al Long, then Barney *does* undergo a transformation. The first boo-boo comes in the wedding scene, where we get a subjective shot of Barney's hand becoming black and monstrous; in

the subsequent group shot his hand is normal in the split-second that we see it before he jams it into his coat and flees from the room. Later we get an unaccountable two-shot of Barney looking into the mirror with the succarath reflected in the glass.

Dina's daytime search for Barney includes a shot of the succarath, seen from the back as he pushes his way through some brush, and then a second shot in which he is dimly and distantly sorta-seen. The finale puts the final nails in the coffin of "Does Barney really transform?" with a shot of succarath hands reaching into a shot from the right side of the screen, and then an extended money shot of the monster carrying Dina.

Even when the succarath *is* the reflected Face in the Water, Siodmak blows it. When you see your reflection in water, you're right side up; in *Bride*'s shots of the water's surface, the succarath is upside down, which means that we viewers, with *our* eyes, are looking at the succarath's reflection from the opposite side of the pool from the succarath.

Also, one can't help but wonder if a human Barney— even a Barney who *thinks* he's a succarath—is capable of bare-handedly breaking the necks of cows and tearing their hides to shreds. The fact that natives claim to have

If Barney only imagines that he transforms into the succarath, then **Bride** viewers should see the succarath in the mirror through *Barney's* eyes, in a Barney point of view shot, and not the way it's seen in the movie (identical to this photo).

seen the succarath adds to the overwhelming "Barney *does* transform" body of evidence. Another vote is cast in the "He turns"/"He *doesn't* turn" controversy by the musical score: One cue is titled "He Turns"! (In the world of the supernatural, all things are possible, so we won't ask what happens to Barney's *clothes* as he shape-shifts into the phone booth-sized succarath and back again.)

When I interviewed Siodmak, I pointed out that *Bride's* premise (the succarath is just in Barney's imagination) is spoiled by shots of the beast, and Siodmak grumpily maintained, "They forced me to do that—sometimes you can't fight 'em."[11] In the script, Siodmak did indeed stress that shots of the succarath should be subjective: At the bottom of page 53 of the script in this book, it says:

The CAMERA is the gorilla. Care should be taken that Barney sees him[self] as an animal,

but nobody else. Barney would look at himself in any mirror, believing he is the ape. Anything and any part of his body within his vision is part of the GORILLA. But when other people look at him, the picture would change into that of Barney.

That said, at the bottom of script page 96, when Dina is cornered by the monster, Siodmak calls for a shot of "[t]he gorilla, walking toward her, rearing on his hind legs."

"[Siodmak] was from Europe—a very serious man— and when he did *Bride of the Gorilla*, he thought he was doing *Gone with the Wind*!" Cohen told me. "He was very serious about everything. …I genuinely think he thought he was doing a big, *big* picture. …Of course, to him I was 'the kid': 'Hey, kid,' 'Listen, kid…' But he did do a good job on the picture, for what it was—we made it with spit."

Raymond Burr brings a raw, dangerously elemental edge [to Barney]. Yet when he speaks of the jungle and his newfound senses…, his tone becomes almost poetic, and one can see the genuine longing in his eyes.

   —Bryan Senn in his book *A Year of Fear*

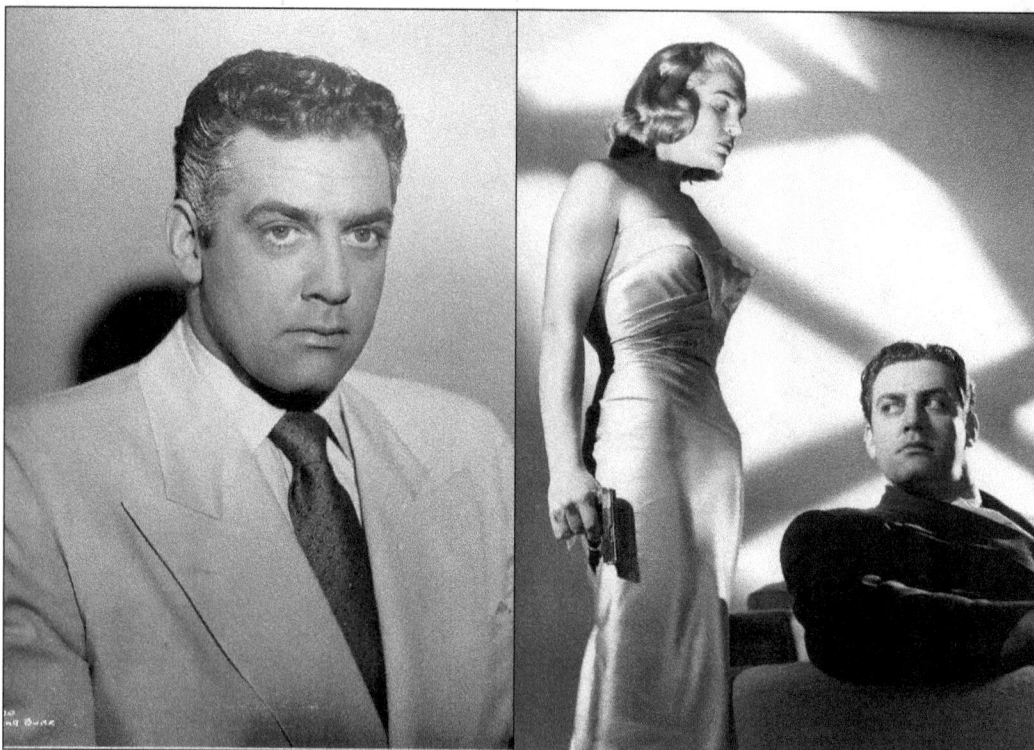

According to one movie historian, the pre-*Perry Mason* Raymond Burr "filled the fat heavy niche for most of the period between the death of Laird Cregar and the appearance of Victor Buono." In a '60s interview, Burr talked about his long run of scoundrel roles and admitted, "I began to run out of ways of being bad."

The only *Bride* actor that a 21st-century Joe Average *might* know is Raymond Burr, ubiquitous on TV for decades as Perry Mason in the 1957-66 TV series, decades of reruns and latter-day TV movies. It's always a pleasure to see Burr in *anything*, no matter which side of the law he's on—but in 1951 when the 34-year-old actor was third-billed in *Bride*, there weren't a lot of movies in which he'd played anything *but* blue-ribbon bad men. Whether in drama (*Desperate, Raw Deal, Pitfall*, more) or comedy (*Love Happy*), modern setting or Old West (*Code of the West, Station West*) or older (*Bride of Vengeance, The Magic Carpet*), the movie's stars had to watch their backs once Ray got the notion to hasten their arrival in the Hereafter. *Bride* is fortunate in the services of Burr, who cuts a rather trim (for Raymond Burr), ruggedly handsome figure and gives the best performance in the movie.

After Burr shot to TV stardom as Perry Mason, word got out that the actor was as good a human being as his movie characters were bad—and his movie characters were very, *very* bad. Burr was proxy parent to orphans throughout the world, gave to charities and, perhaps most impressively, made many trips to South Vietnam on his own dime to entertain American servicemen in front line positions. By 1965, he'd spent more time in that war zone than any other American actor, hopping from one post to another by helicopter.[12] Herman Cohen told me that once Burr took the role of Perry Mason, "it was wonderful, because Raymond became a millionaire. Not too many people knew it [in the '50s and '60s], but Raymond Burr was gay, and he sent…one, two, three…he sent about *four* young guys [boyfriends] to medical school, paid for them to go. He kept it very quiet, but I knew what was going on."

Curt Siodmak wrote in *Even a Man Who Is Pure in Heart*, "Ray, a homosexual, disliked Lon, and vice versa. Whenever they had a scene together I watched their antagonism for each other penetrate their acting. Sparks of hatred flew from their eyes. No director could have coaxed more convincing scenes from any actor."

And *Chaney* occasionally wore a green carnation (if you know what I mean)—according to Siodmak, anyway. In many interviews Siodmak called him a homosexual or a latent homosexual, sometimes off the record (as with me), sometimes on. When pressed as to how he *knew* that, however, he'd say that he was basing the comment mostly on a vibe that he picked up when the two actors were together on the set.

When I told Herman Cohen about Siodmak's claim that Chaney and Burr didn't get along, he had no memory of that situation, and in fact scoffed, "We didn't have the *time* for them not to get along with each other.

Movie-wise *Bride of the Gorilla* was a stretch for Raymond Burr, then typecast as a baddie, with few on-screen opportunities for romance (or for obsessing over being a succarath!).

By the 1950s Tom Conway was doing less work for the top studios, but the majors' loss was Monster Kids' gain as he lent his talents to *Bride of the Gorilla* (pictured) plus *12 to the Moon* (1960) and producer Alex Gordon's *The She-Creature* (1956), *Voodoo Woman* (1957) and *The Atomic Submarine* (1959). (Photo courtesy Ronald V. Borst/Hollywood Movie Posters)

We made the whole picture in ten days [actually seven days] and we came in under budget. So there was no time to fight, not at all. But, on this picture, there were no friends among the actors."

"I quickly found out that the art of directing is based 80 percent on public relations, to make the actors believe in the importance of their job, and 20 percent on technique," Siodmak wrote in his autobio, continuing:

> The actor Tom Convey [*sic*] was contracted for one shooting day. I felt he was only interested in collecting his thousand dollar salary and then go fishing.

I humbly asked him: "Tom, thank you for accepting that very small part. But your scene is the pivot of that film. I depend on your skill as an actor or I'll have no picture." That plea touched his actor's ego. "My lines should sound like cynical jokes," he said, relishing my accolade, "that will make the public dislike me and feel sorry for poor Barbara."

Aside from getting Conway's name wrong, he also wrongly remembered that Conway had only a small part and that he played an unsympathetic character rather than the clement chap he actually plays. (It's obvious that Siodmak's copy of *Bride of the Gorilla*…if he *had* one…got very few plays at Casa Siodmak: He described the movie as set on a farm on a Pacific island!) His claim that Conway worked just one day on *Bride* also sounds fishy, as Conway appears in just about every other scene in the movie. If all of Conway's scenes were shot in one day, then it should have been possible to shoot the whole movie in two!

Late in Siodmak's life, when he was asked by interviewers if he liked directing, he usually went for a laugh by adamantly growling, "No!" To *Starlog*'s Lee Server, he said he loved it—but dig the reason why:

> As a writer, you get up and you don't feel good in the morning, how can you work? You cannot. But the director can come in like that and everyone says, "Good morning, sir. How did you sleep?" And the filmmaking machinery is all there. The actors can do their lines, the cameraman, the camera. The director can lie down and wait till he feels better. The movie takes care of itself. Directing is highly overrated. …*Anybody* can direct.

Well, if they don't mind having the reputation that Curt Siodmak had as a director (*Bride of the Gorilla*,

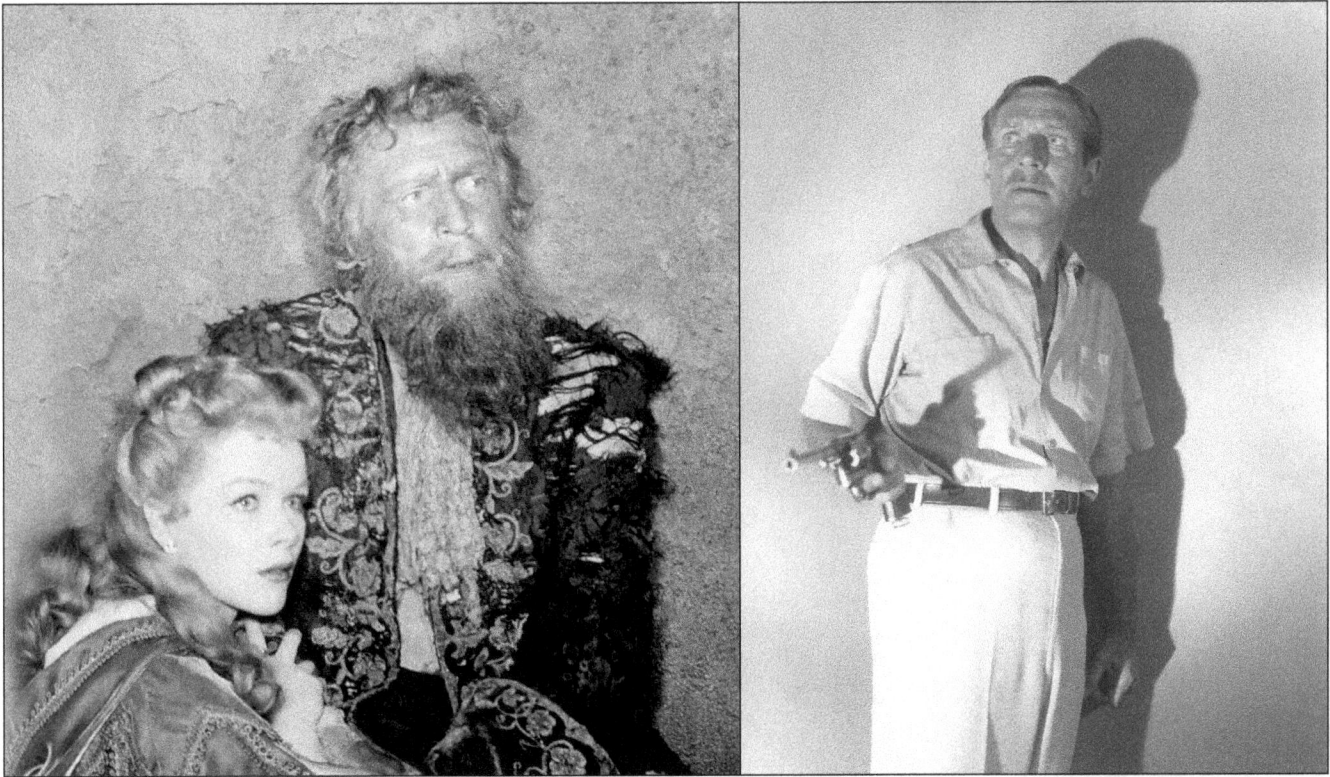

Paul Cavanagh was in the first three horror movies of the 1950s, all released around the same time in 1951: *Bride of the Gorilla* (pictured above right); *The Son of Dr. Jekyll*, as a police inspector on the trail of Mr. Hyde; and *The Strange Door* (pictured above left, with Sally Forrest), as a dungeon prisoner. (*Bride* photo courtesy Ronald V. Borst/Hollywood Movie Posters)

Curucu, Beast of the Amazon, Love Slaves of the Amazons, etc.), then yes, *anybody* can direct!

For hardcore movie fans, there are welcome faces in the small roles in *Bride*: Paul Cavanagh, the star of many minor and now-forgotten films of the 1930s, wears a fixed, troubled look as Dina's grump of a husband; we never do quite understand why she ever married him. Paul Maxey, seen in *Bride* as the Van Gelders' closest neighbor (40 miles away) Van Heussen, probably had his most memorable movie role as the mysterious fat man on the train in the top-notch film noir *The Narrow Margin* (1952). Baby Boomer TV fans might remember him as Mayor Peoples in scores of episodes of the comedy series *The People's Choice*.

"There also was a tall, handsome black, who played a native policeman, and who had half a dozen lines to speak," Siodmak wrote in *Even a Man…* "He was the former top football player Woody Strode. Frightened to have to act and stiff like a wooden Indian, I gave him confidence by rehearsing his lines with him so often that I dreamt of them. A natural talent, he quickly caught on to his new profession as an actor. For many years he became a motion picture star, playing in *Spartacus*, *The Professionals*, and other important pictures."

Seen in the wedding scene as Mrs. Van Heussen is Moyna Macgill, a Belfast-born stage-movie-TV actress and mother of a much *more* prominent stage-movie-TV actress, Angela Lansbury. Felippa Rock, playing Mrs. Van Heussen's daughter Stella in that scene, coincidentally came to America years earlier on the same boat as Macgill and Angela. Rock told me she had two encounters with Raymond Burr, on *Bride of the Gorilla* and, earlier, when the Pasadena Playhouse was preparing a semi-professional production of *Anne of the Thousand Days* with Burr as Henry VIII. "I auditioned for him, for the role of Anne Boleyn. I was far too young for the role, but he was very, very pleased with my audition and gave me a lot of encouragement. He was always very professional, he was charming, he was a gentleman."

> Don't, whatever you do, be fooled by the ape who chases scantily clad Barbara Payton in *Bride of the Gorilla*. It's really Steve Calvert, aptly-named head bartender at Ciro's…
>
> —Mike Connolly, "Just for *Variety*," August 3, 1951

Steve Calvert began finding work in movies in 1937 but over the years remained near the bottom of

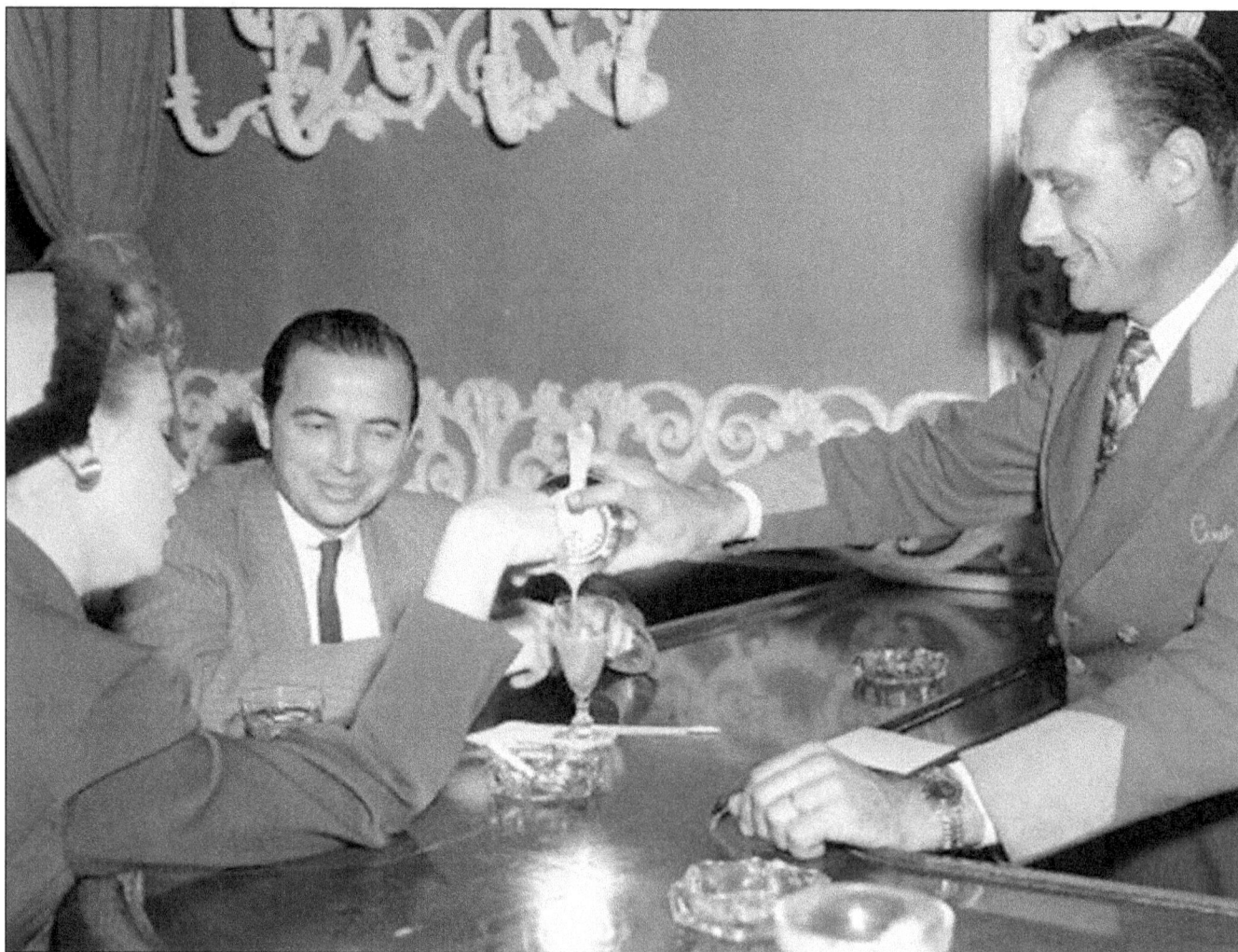

Served by a Succarath: Barflies at Ciro's, the famous Sunset Boulevard nightclub, get service with a smile from Steve Calvert, who moonlighted as a gorilla in several '50s films.

the Hollywood food chain (a photo double for Robert Lowery, an extra, etc.). He got a break in 1948 when B Western star Ray "Crash" Corrigan, apparently tiring of his sideline stint of playing gorillas, sold Calvert two of his outfits. Corrigan also tossed in a lesson in how to play a simian. "Calvert must have been a good student, because he picked up a lot of Corrigan's best moves," Bob Burns, king of the Monster Kids, told me. "Calvert was good enough to fool you: If you saw a Corrigan gorilla costume in a '50s movie and didn't know about Steve Calvert taking over, you'd still think it was Corrigan, because Calvert did an excellent job of 'capturing' him. The Three Stooges' 3-D short *Spooks!* [1953] is a good example, with Calvert doing a number of the things that Corrigan used to do, including the hands-over-the-face bit."

"You have to reverse your human instincts and thought patterns," Calvert told *Filmfax* interview Ted Newsom. "You don't walk around, you lumber through. You act ferocious—not because you're antagonistic, but

to scare the humans away so they won't give you any unwanted trouble." Right after giving an $1800 down payment to Corrigan, Calvert got a job playing a gorilla in a *Jungle Jim* movie (nine days, $200 a day…a total of $1800!). In addition to *Bride of the Gorilla*, he was seen as gorillas in *Road to Bali* (1952), *The Bowery Boys Meet the Monsters* (1954), *The Bride and the Beast* (1958), the serial *Panther Girl of the Congo* (1955) and several TV comedy programs, plus when he made public appearances. He was a Brooklyn-based beast in *Bela Lugosi Meets a Brooklyn Gorilla* (1952), another Jack Broder production. Calvert dropped out of "the business" in the 1970s and died of heart problems in an L.A. hospital in 1991. It's strange that Siodmak's characters' descriptions of the succarath are so outré (like a big cat, like a puma, like a demon, huge and red, with a head like a man and teeth like an alligator) when Siodmak knew that the creature would be played by a guy in a gorilla suit; his script's stage directions call it a gorilla and an ape. (When

Bela Lugosi (in vampire mufti) and his Brooklyn Gorilla (Steve Calvert) arrive at the *House of Wax* premiere in April 1953. The onlookers on the left are Richard Denning and his wife Evelyn Ankers.

talking or writing about this movie, it's hard to remember to call the succarath anything *but* a gorilla, especially with *Gorilla* in the movie's title.)

Despite its low budget, there were also good people behind the scenes, most notably editorial supervisor Francis D. Lyon[13], an Oscar winner for 1947's *Body and Soul*, and veteran d.p. Charles Van Enger, who did some expert work on the Universal Horrors *Night Monster* (1942) and *Abbott and Costello Meet Frankenstein*. Van Enger was behind the camera on a half-dozen Broder productions, from *Two Dollar Bettor* to *Combat Squad* (1953). In *A Year of Fear*, Bryan Senn commended Van Enger on his "evocative" *Bride* photography, "complete with deep-focus, mobile point-of-view shots, and shadowy images [that make] the potted plant jungle seem almost authentic." In one jungle scene, the moving camera "becomes" the succarath, pushing through foliage as it follows Dina. (It's reminiscent of a similar shot in an infinitely better movie: the camera trailing Betsy and zombie Jessica through the sugar cane to the *houmfort* in *I Walked with*

a Zombie.) Another striking moment, this one early in *Bride*: The movie goes from present-day to flashbacks via a dissolve from a shot of a fallen ceiling fan on the rubble-strewn floor of Van Gelder Manor, to a shot of a clean checkerboard floor, the shadow of the off-camera fan's spinning blades cast upon it, as we get our first look at Dina (Payton), dancing to south-of-the-border-style music in her strapless, sarong-like outfit.[14]

Dancing in the dark: A moody shot of the bewitching Dina (Barbara Payton) as we first see her in the movie. (Photo courtesy Ronald V. Borst/Hollywood Movie Posters)

The uninhibited (read: raunchy) 23-year-old Payton was a constant storm center and drama magnet, even during the few days it took to shoot *Bride of the Gorilla*. According to the 1951 rumor mill, she'd briefly became the scrumptious side dish of a few of the married stars with whom she'd appeared in her most recent movies. For the past several months she'd been the girlfriend of mid-level movie star Franchot Tone, whose claims to fame included an Oscar nomination for *Mutiny on the Bounty* (1935's Best Picture Oscar winner) and a late-1930s stint as Mr. Joan Crawford, star of seven movies in which Tone also appeared. A few of the other highlights of his rather, pardon the pun, high-Tone movie career: He appeared in four Jean Harlow vehicles, co-starred in another 1935 Best Picture nominee *The Lives of a Bengal Lancer*, and shared the screen with Bette Davis as she gave *her* first Oscar-winning performance in *Dangerous* (1935).

Over 20 years Payton's senior, Tone first saw her when he judged a Charleston dance contest in which she participated. It was love at first leer for Tone, who apparently got his kink on with bad girls. He began taking Payton out and soon announced that they were engaged. But for Barbara it was always sex o'clock and according to some accounts, being Tone's fiancée didn't keep the actress (who won that dance contest, by the way) from doing the horizontal hustle with other men.

And then, along came *the* other man. At a pool party, Payton met B movie actor Tom Neal: more "age appropriate" and quite a fine young animal. ("The minute I saw him in bathing trunks, I just flipped," Payton told pals.) A college boxer, he'd had a 44-3 record, 41 of his wins by knockout. In 1937, on a Florida beach, Neal and his muscles had caught the eye of a Sam Goldwyn talent scout and he was placed under contract to Goldwyn (and that same year supposedly came close to landing the lead in Goldwyn's *The Hurricane*). A short stint as a Metro contractee ensued, but afterwards Neal spent most of his time working for the smaller Hollywood outfits. At PRC he had his finest hour (and nine minutes) as the can't-catch-a-break chump in Edgar G. Ulmer's zero-budgeted noir *Detour* (1945).

Apparently Payton and Neal started going at it like a couple of bunnies. The July 12, 1951, "Just for *Variety*" column by Mike Connolly reported that Franchot Tone was on the eve of leaving for the east and wouldn't return until September, but Herman Cohen recalled for me that Neal *and* Tone were visitors to the *Bride of the Gorilla* set in late July and/or early August. Cohen knew enough about Barbara's sexploits to see the necessity of keeping the two actors apart: "We told the captain at the Goldwyn gate that, if Tom Neal was coming, call the

stage immediately, and *especially* if Franchot was there—Barbara had to get rid of him!"

Franchot told me that he lost his potency when he married Joan Crawford. She made him impotent. Then, later on, he fell wildly in love with [Payton]. He fell madly in love with her because she brought him back to life sexually.

—Mickey Knox, to interviewer Patrick McGilligan

Tone was a drinker. He'd *have* to be, to tell Knox that story and forget that, in the interim between Crawford and Payton, he and actress Jean Wallace had a couple of kids!

Post-Production

In the weeks before the start of production on *Bride of the Gorilla*, Joseph I. Breen of the Production Code Administration, Hollywood censor and "czar of all the rushes," closely read script drafts and showed his determination to keep a tight rein on the filmmakers; any movie where a gorilla took a "bride" was risqué business in that era. (See the **Notes on the Script** section starting on page 42.) Breen continued to keep tabs on Bride even after it was in the can: On September 14 he wired Margaret Ann Young of the Motion Picture Administration's Title Registration Bureau in New York:

BRIDE OF THE GORILLA APPROVED AUGUST 17 stop STORY DEALS WITH WHITE MAN IN AFRICA [sic] WHO COMES UNDER A CURSE AND BELIEVES HE IS TURNING INTO A GORILLA stop WE FEAR POSSIBILITY OF ALMOST INEVITABLE BAD EXPLOITATION stop STILLS ALREADY SUBMITTED HERE SHOW GORILLA CARRYING WOMAN IN ARMS TO EXPLOIT SUGGESTION OF BESTIALITY

If Jack Broder was worried that Breen might rain on his parade, even lightly, at least there was compensating good news for the rookie producer. In the summer of 1951, as the release dates of his first movies loomed, the gods smiled down upon Broder and *The Basketball Fix*: A new collegiate scandal broke as past cage stars for Bradley University in Peoria, Illinois, were placed in technical custody for taking gamblers' money to throw basketball games. A few weeks later the scandal was in the news yet again when a man described by a D.A. as "one of the worst of the Kansas City mob of

DAILY NEWS 5¢

3 CCNY STARS JAILED IN FIX

LIU, NYU Men, Big Bettor Also Held in Cage Bribery

Warner's Production.

Taking the idea for their first movie from current headlines, Broder's company also attempted to corner the market on monikers for such a movie, filing a slew of titles with the Motion Picture Association of America registry bureau: *Basketball Bribe, The Big Fix, The Black Fix, The Black Scandal, Cage Bribe, Cage Fix, Cage Scandal* and *Basketball Fix*. Ultimately *The Basketball Fix* was chosen.

killers and narcotics peddlers" became the object of a 48-state manhunt for having tried to "buy" the entire Bradley team in the 1948-49 season. Now, instead of *The Basketball Fix* being released months after the New York basketballers' 15 minutes of infamy, it would premiere in the midst of breaking news.

The next bit of good news for Jack Broder Productions: It was announced that Realart, which was allowed to distribute no product other than Universal oldies, *was* now being permitted to handle Jack's own movies. In early August, Realart closed a deal to release ten Jack Broder Productions a year, starting with *The Basketball Fix, Two Dollar Bettor* and *Bride of the Gorilla*.

Then came the incident which, if Hollywood was a fight arena, would be described as the Main Event.

Hollywood's most notorious mattress back, Barbara Payton, was forever flitting between Franchot Tone and Tom Neal. During *Bride* production she broke

things off with fiancé Tone and announced that she and Neal would be marrying; the very next day, Mike Connolly ("Just for *Variety*") revealed that Jack Broder had chartered a plane to fly her and Neal to Ensenada on August 8 for their wedding. Then she went back to Tone again, and then Tom again. Thursday, September 13, was a "Tone again" day, quite a full one in fact, even though she and Neal were supposed to be married in San Francisco upon the morrow(!). The last of Barbara and Tone's stepping-out stops during that long Thursday of renewed togetherness: Ciro's, where it's fun to think that they might have interacted with bartender Steve Calvert, *Bride*'s simian succarath!

A presumably drunk Tone and the presumably equally bombed bombshell at last called it a night and betook themselves to her apartment in the wee hours. Neal was there, drunkenly hosting a hastily arranged party, and he was madder than *two* wet hens. Words were exchanged, the mayhem in the a.m. reaching critical mass when Tone made the rather poorly thought-out decision to offer Neal a suggestion:

"Let's settle this thing outside."

The battle of the aesthete vs. the athlete began out on the lawn with Neal hitting Tone hard. How hard? Hard enough that he flew through the air and landed on the front page of the next day's newspaper. *Every* newspaper.

"It was one of the bloodiest fights I've ever seen," a neighbor said in one press account of the fracas. The overmatched Tone hadn't gotten in a single lick in this one-sided battle to the finish (Tone's finish), succeeding only in blocking every one of Neal's powerhouse punches with his face. Papers provided their readers with the "tale of the tape": Neal was 37 years old, Tone was 45. Neal was 180 pounds, Tone 155. Once an MGM pretty-boy actor, but now looking more like a jigsaw puzzle with a couple of pieces gone, Tone's carcass was carted off to a hospital where it was determined that he had sustained a concussion, a shattered nose and fractured cheekbone. For hours following Hollywood's most lopsided fight on- or off-screen, he was unconscious, his condition listed as serious.[15]

In Neal's version of events, it was Tone who was on the warpath and threw the first punch: "I wanted to settle this like grownups. But he insisted on fighting." Probably nobody bought it coming from him, especially with Payton in Tone's corner: "The first blow knocked Tone down and he was completely out. Then Tom beat him unmercifully," announced Payton, who'd seen it with her own eyes—one of them now black because she got in the way of a flying fist (Neal's).[16] A doctor operating on Tone's smashed-in face said he was praying that the

In *this* corner: Franchot Tone, born with a silver spoon in his mouth and raised in a society atmosphere. In movies, he specialized in "fancy dress" characters, often bland and with perhaps an unintended touch of the dork. He was battling out of his class when he went up against…

…hard-muscled he-man Tom Neal. His punches packed with dynamite, Neal rang Tone's bell (and re-arranged his features) in the first few seconds of Round One of their fight. "It *wasn't* a fight!" Tone's actor-friend William Phipps corrected me. "It was no more a fight than a man stepping on a bug is a 'fight.'"

actor would recover, "but only the Lord knows that for sure." The totality of the damage to Neal: swollen hands and knuckles on the day that he was supposed to be sliding a wedding ring onto one of his fingers. "We both wanted to marry Barbara," he told the press. "She was engaged to Tone when I met her two months ago. But she told me she wanted me because he was too dull. She said I was exciting."

The newspapers stayed on top of the story the way Neal allegedly sat on top of Tone administering his haymakers. And Payton became unstoppable in what appeared to be a campaign to provide them with a stream of sordid new developments to report. She scaled the hospital fire escape to see Tone, who on her second such visit proposed to her through the gauze with which his once patrician head was cocooned. And she accepted. That's *one* version of how it went down. Then there's the one Mickey Knox told McGilligan: "Barbara saved

Neal's ass. Neal was going to be sued by Franchot and also put in jail. So Barbara went to see Franchot in the hospital and said, 'Let's forget Tom Neal. You and I will get married. I love you. Let's put him out of our lives.' That was the thing he wanted to hear. He said okay, and he married her."

Tone had lost the battle, but won the whore.

Payton, Tone and Neal all went on to pay a price for their bad behavior; Barbara made her first payment a few days later, when it was announced that the femme lead in the upcoming feature *Lady in the Iron Mask*— promised to her—would now be going to Patricia Medina.[17] Payton probably hoped people would believe what they read in *The Hollywood Reporter*, that her doctor advised her that she was "too emotionally upset to undertake the role," but (per the September 19, 1951, *Los Angeles Daily News*) the real reason was the notoriety of her relationships with Tone and Neal.

Barbara Payton has withdrawn from *Lady in the Iron Mask*, but things might have been different if Franchot had worn one during the Battle of the Front Lawn.

—George E. Phair, "Retakes," *Variety*, September 20, 1951

Neal also became persona non grata in LaLaLand, and Tone of course had his looks halfway-spoiled for life. One bit of good news for embattled Barbara: According to Sheilah Graham's syndicated column (September 28), "Barbara's latest picture, *Bride of the Gorilla*, is being rushed out to 'benefit' from the publicity; and the personal appearance offers pour in!" September 28 was also the day that Payton and Tone married in the living room of Barbara's girlhood hometown of Cloquet, Minnesota. The union would have more ups and downs than a cocktail shaker, with Tom Neal continuing to make dramatic reappearances in her life.[18]

It was in this atmosphere that the Payton-starring *Bride of the Gorilla* was being prepared for release.

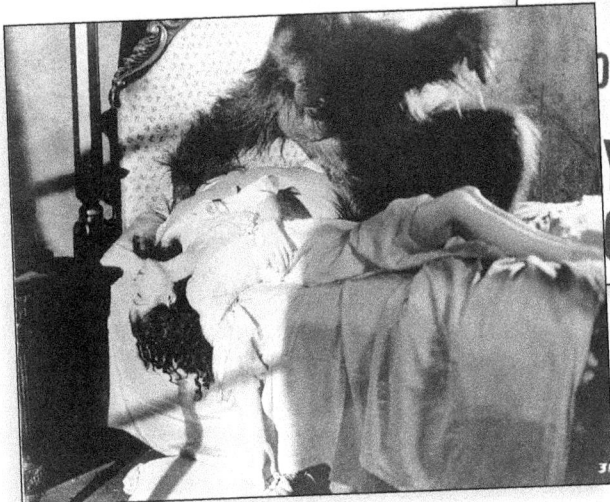

PRIMITIVE! PASSIONATE!
Nothing like it ever before!

JACK BRODER Productions presents

Bride of the Gorilla

Starring BARBARA PAYTON
[LO]N CHANEY
[RA]YMOND BURR
[T]OM CONWAY

Written and Directed by CURT SIODMAK

Yes, in the 1950s Realart was king of the hill in the reissue world...but that didn't make it okay for them to "reissue" a *Murders in the Rue Morgue* (1932) photo of Erik the Ape and Camille at the bottom of their *Bride of the Gorilla* posters!

HERE COMES THE BRIDE
Bride of the Gorilla Release History
By Dr. Robert J. Kiss

Theatrical first-run

Bride of the Gorilla made a low-key theatrical opening at a number of movie theaters across Southern California during the second week of October 1951, playing as second-feature on a bill with Paramount's feline frolic *Rhubarb* starring Ray Milland. The actual premiere, although not billed as such, took place on the evening of October 8 at the Baseline Drive-In in Highland, California, flagship venue of the Pacific Theaters chain in the area. The Baseline Drive-In was sufficiently sophisticated to broadcast the soundtrack over patrons' car radios rather than using speakers.

Although *Bride of the Gorilla* gradually opened in an ever-greater number of locations around the nation during the period from mid-October to late November 1951, newspaper publicity for the movie remained understated, even negligible. In numerous instances the picture effectively piggybacked on the success of whichever major studio release it was double-billed with. For example, at the Fox West Coast Theatre in Long Beach, California, from November 22, it played second fiddle to Paramount's *When Worlds Collide* for two hugely successful weeks of continuous shows beginning at ten a.m. daily, with the entire image-heavy newspaper campaign focussed on *When Worlds Collide* and only a single line of text (devoid of any taglines, credits or graphics) referring to the presence on the bill of "new thrill co-hit" or "2nd thrill feature" *Bride of the Gorilla*. The consistency with which *Bride* played to almost no fanfare opposite major new releases during these two months points toward a deliberate distribution strategy by Realart, with well-chosen placement of the movie allowing it to swiftly generate significant income against minimal outlay for publicity at this time.

A mink-clad Payton mugs for the camera in the arms of a "gorilla" in front of Minsky's Rialto, 336 South State Street, Chicago, during the run of the double-bill *Bride of the Gorilla* and *The Daltons Ride Again* (see partly visible posters for both behind them).

Syndicated columnists Sheilah Graham and Harrison Carroll had quipped in their respective September 29 and October 1 columns that producer Broder "has a laboratory working day and night readying prints" so that *Bride of the Gorilla* could be "rushed out to 'benefit' from" tabloid coverage of Barbara Payton's love triangle with Franchot Tone and Tom Neal. There was little sign of any truth to such suggestions during the movie's initial October and November playdates, but that all changed with the Chicago premiere (which, unlike any of the earlier screenings, was specifically billed *as a premiere*) at the Minsky's Rialto burlesque theater on December 6.

Bride of the Gorilla was pre-booked to appear at Minsky's Rialto for three weeks, with the venue's usual live stage shows withdrawn for the duration, and a five-minute personal appearance by Payton preceding screenings instead. Payton also posed for a camera outside Minsky's Rialto in the arms of a man in a gorilla suit, with the resulting publicity shot making its way into literally hundreds of newspapers and magazines the length and breadth of the nation. Furthermore, *Bride* was now accompanied by a salacious, exploitation-style promotional campaign asserting that the movie was "Adult Entertainment," "Banned Until Now" and being shown in an "Uncut Version." In the days immediately following the premiere, there was a sudden stream of United Press news articles alleging that Payton had reconnected with Tom Neal while in the Windy City for her Minsky's Rialto appearances, reigniting "Hollywood's most interesting triangle of the year." With repeated mentions of the movie's title and the venue where it could be seen, lengthy direct quotes from Payton and not-entirely-strenuous denials by Al Broder that anything untoward was going on, it is all but impossible to construe these articles as anything other than well-crafted publicity.

Ad from *The Capital Times* (Madison, Wisconsin). According to Joe Dante (in the "Trailers from Hell" installment devoted to the movie), *Bride of the Gorilla* is "only slightly better than its title suggests."

The Chicago release marked a decided shift in the way that *Bride of the Gorilla* was marketed. The "Banned Until Now! Uncut Version!" tagline was adopted for first-run screenings in numerous towns and cities. The picture's success in Chicago itself became a familiar reference point, with ads for the February 10, 1952, opening at the Orpheum in Atchison, Kansas, for example, proclaiming in headline-sized lettering, "4 Weeks in Chicago to Standing Room Only[19] and Now You Will Have a Chance to See the First Midwest Showing of This Most Different Adult Movie in History." And the widely seen Minsky's Rialto publicity shot of Payton in the arms of a man in a gorilla suit was republished, with an identifying caption, almost everywhere that the movie now played.

Having been given a staggered domestic release, *Bride* cannot be considered to have finished its first run until roughly the end of August 1952, by which time it had effectively reached communities of all sizes in all states. However, the film's theatrical potential hadn't quite been exhausted by this lengthy first run, throughout which almost no use had been made of it as a midnight horror show attraction. For Halloween 1952, however, the movie was made widely available as a special attraction, most frequently on a double-bill with one of the Broders' Realart reissues of lesser-known 1940s Universal horrors, in particular *Night Monster* or *Phantom of Paris* (a retitled *Mystery of Marie Roget*). Even though *Bride of the Gorilla* made its television debut in July 1953, a few months later it again received wide theatrical play as a special Halloween attraction, this time billed most commonly with Realart reissues of *The Mummy's Tomb* or *The Mummy's Curse*. Again, the degree of consistency in the picture's initially being held back from such use, and of its subsequent widescale deployment at Halloween 1952 and 1953, points toward a calculated distribution tactic by Realart.

As a standalone feature

Within the sample of around 900 movie theaters across the U.S. during the period from October 1951 to August 1952, 20 percent of all *Bride of the Gorilla* screenings took the form of a standalone presentation supported only by selected cartoons, novelties and other shorts. This form of presentation was far more common following the movie's December 1951 Chicago premiere, after which point the publicity campaign was better suited to showcasing the feature on its own merits. Standalone presentations were equally common in large cities, average-sized towns and rural communities. In some instances this was simply because single-bills were already the established norm in those locations. However, in many instances, local theater owners who usually screened double-bills evidently

Ai chihuahua! Scary fun at the Charro Drive-In in Brownsville, Texas, today one of America's most dangerous border towns.

trusted sufficiently in the drawing potential of *Bride* and its associated publicity—*or else were offered a sufficiently good deal by the Broders*—to break with regular practice and present this particular movie as a standalone feature.

With live stage show accompaniment

The early 1950s represented something of a peak period for variety and burlesque routines involving a scantily clad young woman and a man in a gorilla suit. When *Bride of the Gorilla* opened at the Fox in Oakland, California, in December 1951, graphic ads for burlesque duo Bartlett and King in their routines "The Gorilla and the Maiden" and "The Monster and the Maiden" (the latter involving a Frankenstein's Monster costume rather than a gorilla suit) at the city's El Rey burlesque house appeared alongside adverts for *Bride* throughout the Bay Area daily press, implying an association.

This association became real following *Bride*'s Chicago premiere, when Emil Van Horn and Carol Borgia—apparently on their own initiative, rather than on the basis of any deal with the Broders—offered their act "The Virgin and the Beast" to local theater owners, as a thematically linked live stage show accompaniment on the same bill as the movie. Right through to the conclusion of *Bride*'s first run, Van Horn and Borgia continued to appear alongside the film, performing at the Palace Theatre in Brownwood, Texas, as late as August 1952. Van Horn's provision of such

Variety predicted that *Bride* would provide a field day for exhibitors who delight in putting up "flash exploitation fronts." According to the Phantom of the Movies, "*Bride* knucklewalks in as an enjoyable B-movie throwback to the days when men were apes, women blondes, and budgets nearly non-existent."

live stage accompaniments for motion picture screenings predated his own stint before the cameras as a Hollywood gorilla performer in the 1940s, with his routine "Beast vs. Beauty" (an earlier incarnation of "The Virgin and the Beast") having been performed throughout the second half of the 1930s in support of such exploitation titles as *Jaws of the Jungle*, *Dark Rapture* and *Love Life of a Gorilla*.

Not all live stage entertainments co-billed with *Bride of the Gorilla* featured a man in a gorilla suit. At the Paramount Downtown Theater in Los Angeles from November 15, 1951, the movie played in support of top-billed "King of the Mambo" Pérez Prado and his orchestra and dancers, who at the time were at the height of their popularity in the U.S. This particular example is analogous to other *Bride* showings during October and November 1951, with the picture again essentially piggybacking on the success of a larger attraction on the bill.

Presentations with live stage show accompaniment account for barely one percent of screenings within the sample of around 900 movie theaters across the U.S. during the period from October 1951 to August 1952. However, since almost all such screenings were at larger urban theaters with heavy footfall, the (surely memorable!) experience may not have been quite so rare as it initially sounds.

Double-bills and tandem deals

Within the sample of around 900 movie theaters across the U.S., 78 percent of all screenings of *Bride of the Gorilla* took the form of a double-bill, making this by far the most common way to have originally experienced the movie during its first run. However, the vast array of co-features attested below covers almost all studios, budget ranges and genres, meaning that *Bride* had neither a "regular co-feature" nor even a regular *type* of co-feature. Even the most frequently attested co-presentation, Warner Bros' *Come Fill the Cup* starring James Cagney, accounts for just five percent of double-bill screenings in total, and was found exclusively as a title on which *Bride* piggybacked at theaters within a four-state area on the East Coast.

The extremely wide variety of different pictures with which *Bride* was co-billed should not be interpreted as signifying that the Broders were haphazardly supplying the feature as a one-off item, or that they lacked a distribution strategy to ensure greater placement of their product in theaters. A first hint of what was actually going on may be gleaned from the statistic that 18 percent of all *Bride* screenings on multiple-bills comprised a *second* Broder-controlled picture, either in the form of a new Jack Broder Productions feature or a Realart reissue. However, the Broders do not seem to have been focussed specifically on double-bills, but rather on "tandem deals"—that is to say, supplying a venue with a second Broder-controlled feature to appear on a bill either immediately prior to or immediately after *Bride of the Gorilla* playing there.

Fully 72 percent of all screenings of *Bride* within the sample, on single and multiple bills alike, were immediately preceded or followed by a bill at the same theater that also contained a Broder-controlled feature. A comparable pattern can be established with regard to the distribution of each of the Jack Broder Productions features manufactured·between 1951 and 1953, leaving little doubt that tandem deals were key to the Broders' approach to theatrical distribution.

Of course, contemporary moviegoers would hardly have been aware of such deals, and would have experienced and responded to *Bride* within the context of whatever else played on the same bill. One thing that some might have picked up on, though, was the presence of Lon Chaney in *both* movies on the bill, which was the case in some ten percent of all multiple-bill screenings from coast to coast! In this sense, it might be for the best (or at least, all the more understandable) that *Bride* was promoted primarily on the basis of the column-inches-grabbing Barbara Payton's name, in particular following the Chicago premiere; Chaney may have been almost too ubiquitous on new and reissue horror, Western and adventure bills at the time to really be showcased as a "unique selling point" for the movie. Indeed, a rather half-hearted promotional press piece featuring a photograph of Chaney, referring to him as "one of the foremost 'bogey-men' in Hollywood," and maintaining that he had prepared food for castmates throughout the shooting of *Bride*, was picked up by barely a handful of newspapers nationwide. Whereas no editor in the land appears to have been able to resist publishing the shot of Payton outside Minsky's Rialto.

All of the double-bill co-features attested within the sample are arranged alphabetically below. The month mentioned in each case is the earliest in which the pairing was encountered.

(*) signifies a slightly more substantial number of playdates

(**) signifies a regular affiliation of the titles (at between three and five percent of theaters)

<u>underscored titles</u> are Broder-Realart releases

January 1952	*An American in Paris* (Gene Kelly)
December 1951	*Anne of the Indies* (Jean Peters)
January 1952	*Assassin for Hire* (Ronald Howard)
July 1952	*The Atomic City* (Gene Barry)
December 1951 (*)	<u>*The Basketball Fix*</u> (Marshall Thompson)
December 1951	*Behave Yourself!* (Farley Granger)
March 1952	*The Belle of New York* (Fred Astaire)
April 1952	*The Big Trees* (Kirk Douglas)
May 1952	*Bonanza Town* (Charles Starrett)
January 1952 (**)	<u>*The Bushwhackers*</u> (John Ireland)
December 1951	*Callaway Went Thataway* (Fred MacMurray)
March 1952	*Captain from Castile* (Tyrone Power)
December 1951	*Cattle Queen* (Maria Hart)
June 1952	*Cavalry Scout* (Rod Cameron)
July 1952	*Champagne for Caesar* (Ronald Colman)
November 1951	*Close to My Heart* (Ray Milland)
January 1952	*Colorado Ranger* (Russ Hayden)
December 1951 (**)	*Come Fill the Cup* (James Cagney)
October 1951	<u>*Condemned to Hang*</u> (Franchot Tone; Realart reissue)
February 1952	*Crosswinds* (John Payne)
July 1952	*Cry Danger* (Dick Powell)
January 1952	*Dakota* (John Wayne; Republic reissue)
November 1951 (**)	<u>*The Daltons Ride Again*</u> (Lon Chaney; Realart reissue)
December 1951 (**)	<u>*The Daltons' Women*</u> (Lash LaRue; Realart reissue)
July 1952	*Decision Before Dawn* (Richard Basehart)
December 1951	*Detective Story* (Kirk Douglas)
May 1952	*The Eagle and the Hawk* (John Payne)
December 1951	*Elephant Stampede* (Johnny Sheffield)
February 1952	*Fixed Bayonets!* (Richard Basehart)
March 1952	*Flame of Stamboul* (Richard Denning)
January 1952	*Fort Defiance* (Dane Clark)
March 1952	<u>*Frontier Badmen*</u> (Robert Paige; Realart reissue)
November 1951	*The Gas House Kids in Hollywood* (Gas House Kids)
February 1952	*A Girl in Every Port* (Groucho Marx)
February 1952	*The Girl on the Bridge* (Beverly Michaels)
March 1952	*Gunslingers* (Whip Wilson)
May 1952	*He Ran All the Way* (John Garfield)
December 1951	*Highly Dangerous* (Margaret Lockwood)
May 1952	*Hoodlum Empire* (Brian Donlevy)
January 1952	*Hotel Sahara* (Yvonne De Carlo)
April 1952	*Hurricane Island* (Jon Hall)
February 1952	*I Was an American Spy* (Gene Evans)
February 1952	*I'll See You in My Dreams* (Doris Day)

December 1951	*International Burlesque* (exploitation)		November 1951	*The Red Badge of Courage* (Audie Murphy)
April 1952	*It Ain't Hay* (Abbott & Costello; Realart reissue)		June 1952	*Red Skies of Montana* (Richard Widmark)
March 1952	*It's a Big Country* (Ethel Barrymore)		April 1952	*Red Stallion in the Rockies* (Arthur Franz)
July 1952	*Jack and the Beanstalk* (Abbott & Costello)		February 1952	*Retreat, Hell!* (Frank Lovejoy)
April 1952	*Jeepers Creepers* (Weaver Brothers; Republic reissue)		April 1952	*Return of the Texan* (Dale Robertson)
February 1952	*Jesse James* (Tyrone Power; 20th Century-Fox reissue)		December 1951	*Reunion in Reno* (Mark Stevens)
May 1952	*Jungle Jim in the Forbidden Land* (Johnny Weissmuller)		October 1951 (*)	*Rhubarb* (Ray Milland)
			March 1952	*Rogue River* (Rory Calhoun)
December 1951	*The Kid from Kansas* (Dick Foran; Realart reissue)		January 1952	*Savage Splendor* (Denis-Cotlow Expedition)
February 1952	*The Lady from Texas* (Mona Freeman)		March 1952	*Scandal Sheet* (Broderick Crawford)
			August 1952	*Scaramouche* (Stewart Granger)
July 1952	*Lady in the Iron Mask* (Patricia Medina)		March 1952	*The Sea Hornet* (Rod Cameron)
February 1952	*Lady Possessed* (James Mason)		August 1952	*Shadow of a Doubt* (Joseph Cotten; Realart reissue)
January 1952	*Legion of the Lawless* (George O'Brien; RKO reissue)		June 1952	*She-Wolf of London* (June Lockhart; Realart reissue)
April 1952	*Lilli Marlene* (Lisa Daniely)		March 1952	*Short Grass* (Rod Cameron)
January 1952	*The Longhorn* (Wild Bill Elliott)		January 1952	*Silver City* (Edmond O'Brien)
April 1952	*The Lost Jungle* (Clyde Beatty; Republic reissue)		December 1951	*Sin Town* (Constance Bennett; Realart reissue)
February 1952	*M* (David Wayne)		February 1952	*Slaughter Trail* (Brian Donlevy)
April 1952	*Man Bait* (George Brent)		March 1952	*Smoky Canyon* (Charles Starrett)
December 1951	*Man in the Saddle* (Randolph Scott)		January 1952	*Smuggler's Gold* (Cameron Mitchell)
January 1952	*Mark of the Gorilla* (Johnny Weissmuller)		December 1951 (*)	*The Son of Dr. Jekyll* (Louis Hayward)
January 1952	*Mob Town* (Little Tough Guys; Realart reissue)		January 1952	*Starlift* (Doris Day)
			July 1952	*Station West* (Dick Powell)
June 1952	*Models, Inc.* (Howard Duff)		May 1952	*A Streetcar Named Desire* (Marlon Brando)
June 1952	*Montana* (Errol Flynn)		December 1951	*Submarine Command* (William Holden)
May 1952	*Oklahoma Annie* (Judy Canova)			
January 1952	*On Dangerous Ground* (Ida Lupino)		February 1951	*Swamp Fire* (Johnny Weissmuller; Specialty reissue)
February 1952	*On the Loose* (Joan Evans)		June 1952	*Tarzan's Peril* (Lex Barker)
December 1951	*Pancho Villa Returns* (Leo Carrillo)		February 1952	*Tembo* (Howard Hill Expedition)
			February 1952	*Ten Tall Men* (Burt Lancaster)
January 1952	*Partners in Time* (Lum & Abner)		March 1952	*Thunder in God's Country* (Rex Allen)
November 1951	*People Will Talk* (Cary Grant)		June 1952	*Thunder in the Pines* (George Reeves)
February 1952	*Pickup* (Beverly Michaels)			
August 1952	*Prairie Schooners* (Bill Elliott; Astor reissue)		April 1952	*Thunder Trail* (Charles Bickford; Favorite reissue)
February 1952	*Quicksand* (Mickey Rooney)		January 1952	*Thunderhead, Son of Flicka* (Roddy McDowall; 20th Century-Fox reissue)
December 1951	*The Racket* (Robert Mitchum)			

What was promised: "Her Clothes Torn Away Screaming in Terror! Her Marriage Vows Were More Than Fulfilled!" What was delivered: A morose jungle melodrama in which monster and girl don't meet until two minutes from the end—and the first thing he does is kill her!

May 1952	_Two-Dollar Bettor_ (Steve Brodie)	March 1952	_Warpath_ (Edmond O'Brien)
January 1952	_Two Tickets to Broadway_ (Tony Martin)	June 1952	_West of the Pecos_ (Robert Mitchum; RKO reissue)
January 1952 (*)	_The Unknown Man_ (Walter Pidgeon)	February 1952	_Westward the Women_ (Robert Taylor)
April 1952	_Wagon Wheels_ (Randolph Scott; Favorite reissue)	November 1951 (*)	_When Worlds Collide_ (Richard Derr)
		April 1952	_Yellow Fin_ (Wayne Morris)

Triple-bills

A small number of examples were located of *Bride of the Gorilla* playing on triple-bills during its first run. These particular multiple bills were attested exclusively at smaller drive-ins and collectively account for just one percent of the total for first-run screenings, making this an uncommon way to have first experienced the movie. It is surely no coincidence that the Broders supplied two of the three pictures on the first two triple-bills identified below.

July 1952	*House of Dracula* (Realart reissue) + *Red Mountain* (Alan Ladd)
March 1952	*The Mummy's Tomb* (Realart reissue) + *The Strange Door* (Boris Karloff)
March 1952	*Raton Pass* (Patricia Neal) + *Virginia City* (Errol Flynn; Warner Bros. reissue)

The Reviewers Roar

The Hollywood Reporter: The script itself is stereotyped chiller fare, but Siodmak's direction fills it with pace and sufficient quantities of action to make the brief running time fairly interesting.

Boxoffice: [T]he showmen who date and play it need not be more than ordinarily alert to realize that there is obvious and made-to-order merchandising fodder in the fact that Barbara Payton is the cast topliner.

Harrison's Reports: This is a mild program horror picture with some sex, made for those who enjoy melodramas of this type with a little "spice" in them. ... The action is mostly slow and "gabby"... None of the principal characters is sympathetic, with the exception, perhaps, of Lon Chaney, but he is negative. ...Strictly adult fare.

Motion Picture Exhibitor (whose reviewers never realized how annoying the word "okeh" is): Okeh exploitation film has the angles. ...Burr is okeh as the tormented victim of the curse. The theme lends itself to plenty of exploitation, and action houses should find this an okeh box office attraction.

Variety (whose reviewer saw *Bride* at the Goldwyn Studios where it was shot—on Halloween!): Picture is able to sustain a moderate amount of suspense in its unfolding, although the first half is over-dialogued and moves at a rather slow tempo. ...Cast is adequately set up, although it looked like the members raced through their assignments due to restricted shooting schedule.

The Harvard Crimson, Harvard University's daily student newspaper: If you like jungle movies in general, you'll like this one, especially since it has the additional charm of one Barbara Payton strutting her hour upon the screen in primitive-type dresses which point up her figure considerably.

Film Bulletin: *Bride of the Gorilla* offers front page personality Barbara Payton in the title role. Beyond this, [it] holds little entertainment value. The story is an off-the-cuff horror yarn, done better too often before to rate any special attention. ...[D]irector Curt Siodmak, working from his own script, seems incapable of filling the piece with the movement and action that might distract attention from the inept writing. The Payton publicity and horror aspects give this programmer some exploitation value, but otherwise it's just ordinary dual bill fodder.

Barbara Payton performs her romantic antics in the grand manner of a burlesque star on tour in legit. ... Raymond Burr is too accomplished an actor to dissipate his talents on nonsense like this.

The Cedar Rapids Gazette: [It's] a better-than-average "B" picture with a fine cast. ...Lon Chaney looks as if he feels a bit out of place in all this, and he can act better than he does in this one.

Oakland Tribune: Robert Mitchum and Barbara Payton, both of whom have been in the off-side Hollywood news on occasion, are sharing the screen of the Fox-Oakland this week in a pair of pictures called, respectively, *The Racket* and, so help me, *Bride of the Gorilla*.

Oddly enough the two "stars" have something in common beside a propensity for crashing the front pages; they are master and mistress of the deadpan or expressionless school of cinematic art, a gift that is not especially rewarding for the on-looker.

...If *The Racket* is no great shakes as a picture, it is positively an epic in contrast to *Bride of the Gorilla* whose presence in a first-run theater may be ascribed solely to the fact that one of its players is Mrs. Franchot Tone.

Mrs. Tone is beyond reason of a doubt the poorest excuse for the rating of "star" that has been offered in many a year. She has one expression—a blank one—that never changes; she reads "I love you" and "I'm afraid of him" in the same monotone, and she knows as little about acting as a first year junior high school student.

Her sole claim to fame is that Nature has equipped her rather generously in a certain section of her anatomy...

There's no point in mentioning the supporting players—they looked unhappy enough about it as it was. Like other folks, actors like to eat.[20]

NOTES ON THE SCRIPT
By Tom Weaver

This is a by-no-means-complete list of some of the interesting (or funny, or bizarre) ways in which the script and the finished film differ.

🍌 The undated script reproduced in this book is an early draft, probably the first draft. It seems safe to assume it's the draft critiqued by the Production Code's Joseph I. Breen in a letter he wrote to Jack Broder on June 27, 1951, two days after he (Breen) had a conference with Curt Siodmak. According to Breen's letter, Siodmak had agreed to all the asked-for changes *in* that letter.

🍌 Notice on the script's page of character descriptions that Barney Chavez and Klaas Van Gelder are the same age, "about 40." Taro and Al Long are called lapinos, "a mixture of Spanish and Indian." When Taro makes his first appearance in this script (page 17), lapino is now defined as "a mixture of Spaniard and Juiloto Indian." According to ad lines on *Bride*'s posters, a lupino is the mistress and the bride of a gorilla. Have you got all this?

🍌 Page 1 of the script specifies that there should be no music under the titles, just the sound of jungle animals, most noticeably the sound of a gorilla. Whereas the finished film's narration is spoken by Lon Chaney as Taro, this script calls for the narrator to be Klaas Van Gelder, who begins by mentioning that he's been killed(!). If Klaas *had* narrated the beginning and end of this movie, we could have added *Bride of the Gorilla* to the short list of "Narrated by a Corpse" movies (*Scared to Death*, 1947, and *Sunset Blvd.*, 1950).

Not found in the script included in this book: The Van Heussen plantation scene where Taro (Chaney) examines the dead cow and questions the native worker (Martin Garralaga, next to Chaney) who saw the succarath.

🍌 In the movie, Dina dances for a few seconds when we first see her, stopping when Barney makes his entrance. In the script (pages 2 and 3) she's dancing *and* singing, and continues dancing after Barney appears. Dina is apparently no fan of Al Long: When the servant approaches with drinks, Dina says sarcastically, "There is Al Long—seeing all…hearing all…never talks…"

🍌 Klaas fires Barney and walks out of the room. Dina asks Barney why Klaas is behaving this way. Barney: "You know as much as I do…to think of it—[*he grins*]—you know exactly half and I the other half!" Breen insisted on the elimination of that line "to remove any suggestion that there is an adulterous relationship between Barney and Dina."

Bride viewers get the impression that the Barney-Dina bedroom scene takes place on their wedding night; it immediately follows the wedding scene, and they have champagne in an ice bucket. But in the script, Dina has a line to Barney in this scene ("Something is bothering you—since the day we married...") that makes it clear that it's some time later.

🍌 Also on Breen's "Eliminate" list: The underlined part of Klaas' line to Dr. Viet, "What do you want me to do? Smile and keep my eyes shut while that big gorilla <u>is making love to Dina</u>?" The minder of moviemakers' manners also nixed this exchange between the two men:

VIET: Dina wasn't exactly a blank piece of paper when you married her… She had—lived before. She was a dancer in a night club…in Rio.
KLAAS: All right—I knew that. It gives her no excuse to cheat on me.

🍌 Not until Klaas and Barney are in the garden does Klaas mention "the complaint of that worker—and his daughter." Breen disallowed Barney's response: "I didn't take anything that wasn't given to me."

🍌 In the movie, Dina conveys to Barney that she loves him by whispering across the dinner table, "Don't go away…don't leave…" while looking at him with bedroom eyes; he responds, "That's all I need to know." In this script, he asks her flat out, "You do love me, [don't] you?" and she nods earnestly. In the trailer, we get to hear Barney speak that not-in-the-movie line. The trailer also gives us an over-Barney's-shoulder shot of Klaas punching Barney, different from the shot we see in the movie.

🍌 In the script, after Barney kills Klaas and enters Dina's bedroom, he takes her face in his hands and kisses her, and Dina "melts for a moment" (page 14). It was more like a melt*down* for Breen when he read that scene: "It is suggested that there be no physical contact between Barney and Dina in this sequence. His action of kissing her immediately after he has participated in the death of her husband is in eminent bad taste."

In the movie, Barney has no clue that Al Long put a curse on him. In this script, he and Dina watch from Dina's bedroom as Al Long performs her ritual over Klaas' body. In this script's inquest scene, Barney hears Viet and Taro talk about the fact that Al Long put a spell on Klaas' killer.

During the movie's inquest scene, Taro mentions the Pe de Guine plant and translates its name into English: "the plant of evil." In this script (page 20), Pe de Guine translates into "the foot of the god."

It isn't every movie melodrama where a man who's suspected of murder (in this case Barney Chavez), with the motive being the murdered man's wife, takes the widow in his arms at the day-later inquest and announces to everyone present (including a policeman), "We're going to get married as soon as possible. …You are invited to our marriage…all of you!" But that's what Barney does, in this script (page 23) if not in the movie.

Other in-the-script-but-not-the-movie touches are found in the wedding scene: Upon request, Dina dances to a record called "The Dance of the Candles"; and we see Barney Chavez's signature on the marriage papers and learn that his middle name is Albert. Other things we learn about Barney in this script: He hails from New Mexico (page 65) and was brought up on moonshine (page 34). On page 67 we get a bit of backstory on Klaas Van Gelder.

Party pooper Breen reminded the moviemakers that in the post-wedding bedroom scene (beginning on page 34), Dina's "thin, transparent, silk dressing gown" must conform with the Code requirements regarding women's costuming.

After Barney comes home from his first feverish jungle jaunt, Dr. Viet gives him a hypodermic injection. In the script (page 43) the doctor mentions that it was barbituric acid—but Breen ordered that omitted.

Pages 46 and 47: Gotta love the way Taro deals with the possible arrival of two "illegal aliens." Take a look.

During one of Barney's jungle forays, we were to have seen (from his distorted p.o.v.) an insect photographically made to appear gigantic, a similarly oversized-looking tadpole and a toad, and other "tiny animals blown up to giant size, revealing their frightening shape." Breen got frightened just reading about it, insisting that care be exercised in these sequences lest they become "unduly horrific." In 1954, *Killers from Space* somehow got away with a three-minute-plus-long scene of Peter Graves being menaced by photographically enlarged spiders, lizards, etc., a scene far more "intense" than the one proposed for *Bride of the Gorilla*.

We're told that, to catch the succarath, the natives set animal traps and staked a goat by each—and when we see Barney caught in a trap, there *is* a goat nearby, leashed to a tiny tree with a piece of rope. In the script (page 61), at the end of that scene, the young goat, "frightened, bleats in fear and tries to free itself. … While the animal strains miserably, Dina and Barney walk OUT OF SHOT." But in the movie, an injured, barely-able-to-stand Barney uncharacteristically takes the time to set the goat loose. *Very* characteristically, Breen warned that blood oozing through Barney's broken boot should not be excessively gruesome.

Barney caught in a trap, by the way, is another scene repeated from *The Wolf Man*. And several minutes later, there's a shot of Barney in a fogged-up section of the jungle set, reminiscent of the low-lying fog in *The Wolf Man's* forest scenes.

Actually, *Bride of the Gorilla* is more like an early *Wolf Man* script draft than it is to the finished film *The Wolf Man*. In that early draft, the protagonist is not Larry Talbot but Larry Gill, a visitor to Wales who gets wolf-chomped. No werewolf rears up in the script's remaining pages, just a four-legged wolf that roams the woods until one hunter's silver bullet finds its mark. Badly wounded, the wolf runs away; next we see (from behind) a badly wounded Gill collapsing near the edge of a pool of water, and seeing a monstrous wolf face reflecting back at him from the water's surface. After he dies, hunters arrive on the scene, roll the body over—and it's Larry Gill (not a wolf man)

As Klaas lies dead in the garden, Al Long puts Pe de Guine leaves on his face. This too comes from the Larry Gill *Wolf Man* script mentioned above: In its version of the scene where the body of Bela the gypsy lies in a crypt, his eyes are open, his grin is malevolent and the mark of the pentagram is on his forehead. His mother Maleva touches Bela's mouth with some wolfbane and the grin disappears; touches his eyes with wolfbane and they close; touches his forehead with wolfbane and the pentagram fades away. Now Bela has a happy smile.

For Universalholics, *Bride*'s plot similarities to *The Wolf Man* help it (make it more interesting) rather than hurt it; a certain amount of familiarity is no drawback in a genre piece, just as the same recurring faces in classic horror flicks create that agreeable "old home week" vibe.

After the death of Larry, this *Wolf Man* script calls for a subjective shot from the dead man's point of view; Maleva gives Gwen wolfbane and tells the crying girl to touch his heart with it, his cheeks, his lips and finally his eyes. Through her tears, Gwen happily says, "Look!... He's smiling...!"

In the movie, va-va-va-voom Dina (in her bedroom, packing to leave with Barney) gives some of her clothes to the va-va-va-va-voom Larina. But with no Larina in this script, Dina tries to give them to—Al Long (page 70)! *She* doesn't want them, so perhaps Dina should offer a few items to Dr. Viet: In this script, when Dina momentarily leaves the bedroom, Viet picks a dress up from her bed, "caresses it for a moment then throws it back on the bed" (page 74). Handle this scene with care, Joseph Breen stressed, "lest it be excessively sex-suggestive."

Nothing in the movie makes you think that the widowed Dina had any beef with her bookish husband Klaas other than his being distant, but in this script, she has unloving memories. Talking with Barney about selling the plantation (page 65), she looks around his bedroom and says, "This was Klaas' bedroom...this furniture...he sat on this chair...everything reminds me of him...I hate him more now since he is dead...I don't think he has left us!"

In this script's version of a subsequent scene in Dr. Viet's office, this dangerous dame lays all her cards on the table (page 87):

DINA: I know [Barney] killed Klaas...we never talked about it, but he knew I was on his side when I protected him that night...I lied to Taro. Barney had not been to my room—before Klaas had died. ...You might think I have no morals, because I don't feel badly about Klaas' death—I wanted him to die. If Barney had not done it, I might—one day—I hated him, since the day Barney came to us.

VIET: Klaas was kind to you!

DINA: I hated even his kindness!

Meee-owch! Curt Siodmak safaris into Robert Siodmak territory with a lady as loathsome as this script's Dina, and she pays the ultimate price *à la* the femmes fatale in Robert's films noir *Criss Cross* (1949) and *The File on Thelma Jordon* (1950).

Some readers of this book may be hoping to finally learn exactly what happens at the end of the movie. File that hope under "Life's Disappointments," because I don't know either. Shortly after we see the succarath carrying the unmoving Dina through the

Al Long (Gisela Werbisek) with her Pe de Guine plant, preparing to place leaves on the face of the dead Klaas (Paul Cavanagh). (Photo courtesy Ronald V. Borst/ Hollywood Movie Posters)

underbrush, Taro and Dr. Viet fire their guns into a tree whose upper branches are moving. There's an outcry and the sound of an impact on the ground; next we see Barney lying atop Dina's legs, then rolling away from her. Did he (in gorilla form) carry her up into the tree, and they were both shot and killed? Or killed in the fall? Or did Succarath Barney leave her on the ground at the foot of the tree, then climb the tree and fall out of it *onto* her, killing her? Or was she a goner (intentionally crushed to death by the succarath) before she even *got* to the tree? What we see on-screen would support all of these scenarios, and probably even a few more.

This script makes it appear that Barney *wants* Dina dead: On page 88 Barney, certain that she's going to want to accompany him on his next jungle jog, secretly takes the powder out of her rifle bullets, then replaces it in the rifle rack. Sure enough, Dina does insist upon tagging along, and does bring the rifle. Later, when the succarath stalks her, the gun doesn't fire. Then, on page 98, "The claws of the monster's right hand [close] around her throat. [In another part of the jungle,] Taro and Viet listen to a terrifying shriek, and the gorilla's triumphant cry." It seems clear that this script's Barney carefully plotted her murder and then committed it. Perhaps the reason Dina isn't choked by the succarath

in the movie was Breen's edict that that action "should be indicated out of frame, as much as possible."

A revised script was received by Breen on July 17 and he reacted to it two days later in a letter that called for many of the same changes as in his first letter; apparently Siodmak, after his June 25 promise to Breen to make these changes, either forgot or (in air quotes) "forgot." This second script, which I've never seen, had two endings, one in which Dina dies and another in which she survives. For Breen, the "Dina lives" version presented problems:

In the original script, both Chavez and Dina die as a result of their sins. The Code acceptability of this original ending is discussed fully in our letter to you of June 27th, 1951. In this letter, as you will recall, we told you that your story, which is an unusual combination of drama and melodrama, was not a proper vehicle for telling a true story of adultery. We therefore requested that Chavez and Dina not be engaged in a physically adulterous relationship. For the sake of the story, and inasmuch as Dina met her death at the conclusion, we did allow what might be termed a mental unfaithfulness on the part of Dina toward her husband, Klaas. This, in order to portray her as an evil woman who is punished for her sin.

On the other hand, in the present version (received July 17th) you have an upbeat ending in which Dina walks away in the arms of Dr. Viet. In order to render this type of ending acceptable under the Production Code, it will be necessary to remove from the body of the story, certain lines of dialogue and certain actions on the part of Dina which characterize her as an unfaithful wife.

There was new Dina dialogue that caught Breen's disapproving eye, including this comment to (I assume) Dr. Viet:

I knew how you felt about me ever since I've come to the jungle. You never had the courage to do anything about it. Barney did.

Breen said the last two sentences needed to be changed or eliminated. In a later scene, he found her line

"If ever you're unfaithful, I'll kill you," presumably spoken to Barney, "unacceptable, coming from the heroine of our piece."

What ended up on the screen, when *Bride of the Gorilla* was released in October 1951, strikes me as the weirdest of all possible worlds: Movie Dina is sufficiently "innocent" to deserve to be allowed to live, and to walk off into the jungle sunset with Dr. Viet—but she dies! With Movie Dina's only on-screen sin the telling of a lie at the inquest, her on-screen fate seems harsh.

For those wishing to know what the moviemakers intended at the end, the pressbook synopsis is no help: "Barney's transformation overpowers him, and he seeks out Dina and tries to strangle her. The Doctor and Taro, who have followed them into the jungle, shoot him dead, and he crashes to the ground." So in Pressbookville, but not in the finished film, Dina is *about* to be strangled when Taro and Dr. Viet ride to her rescue. The pressbook synopsis also misinforms us that Dina's native maid Larina "is really Klaas' half-caste daughter"; at least one of the trade reviews also made them mother and daughter.[21]

Embarrassing admission: I saw the movie many times before realizing Dina *was* dead at the end; I'd always given Barney all my attention in the closing seconds.

Taro (Chaney) never visits Al Long's (Gisela Werbisek) room in the movie; could this photo be from a scene shot but not included in the final cut? Notice Al Long's Pe de Guine plant in the foreground.

On page 9 of the revised script (which I have not seen), Barney strikes Al Long. It must have been quite a smackdown because Breen called it "unacceptably brutal" and recommended that, instead of Barney doing whatever's described on that page, he instead "merely slap her once with the back of his hand."

BRIDE OF THE GORILLA SCRIPT

By Curt Siodmak

BRIDE OF THE GORILLA

Original Screen Play

by

Curt Siodmak

UNTITLED SCRIPT
by
CURT SIODMAK.

Cast of Characters:

Klaas Van Gelder..............plantation owner, about 40 years
old, sutdious looking, a puritan.

Dina, his wife...............about 26, very handsome, charming,
a former dancer.

Barney Chavez................manager of the plantation, powerfully built, same age as Klaas,
slow moving, slow speaking, but
attractive to women.

Dr. Viet.....................a physician, government employee,
a man of about 35, slightly dissi-
pated by the tropical sun.

Al Long......................an old servant woman in Klaas'
house. She is a native, a lapino -
a mixture of Spanish and Indian.

Taro.........................a native, also a lapino. He is
police commissioner of the district.

Van Heussen..................a plantation owner, Klaas' neighbor,
middle-aged, fat, jovial.

His wife.....................very stout, and matronly.

Stella.......................their daughter, an anemic looking
young girl of about 17.

Nado.........................a native policeman.

Ferreno......................foreman of the rubber tappers, a
native - or negro.

The gorilla

FADE IN:

1   UNDERNEATH THE CREDIT TITLE the expanse of a tremendous
JUNGLE is seen (STOCK) TITLE:

THE BRIDE OF THE GORILLA

There is no music, but an uproar of many animal voices -
from the tiger's roar to the monkey's chatter - the shrill
voices of jungle birds, and the eerie barking of peccaries.
Above it, penetratingly, the unearthly noise of the gorilla
is HEARD. The CREDITS FADE AWAY, and the picture of the
JUNGLE CONTINUES IN DIFFERENT SHOTS. The voice of KLAAS
VAN GELDER IS HEARD.

                KLAAS'S VOICE
         I, Klaas van Gelder, plantation
         owner, was killed at the border of
         this jungle which stretches thousands
         of miles - an unclaimed wilderness,
         that has always known such crude
         and primitive things - as murder!
         No justice was done to my death by
         human beings. But something else -
         something not human - rose terrify-
         ingly from this verdant wilderness...
         something out of prehistoric ages -
         when monstrous superstitions oppressed
         the minds of men - something that
         might have haunted the world a million
         years ago: the jungle itself arose to
         avenge my death!

While the VOICE is talking, CAMERA PULLS BACK and in
different DISSOLVES shows STOCK SHOTS of jungle animals
fighting, of mountainous hills of termites, of snakes
2   slithering through grass, of age-old trees, reaching
THRU toward the clouds, and then CAMERA again travels over
10   the endless stretches of jungle to

                                 DISSOLVE TO:

11   EXT. PLANTATION HOUSE - DAY

A sturdy white building, surrounded by a garden which
borders on the jungle.

                KLAAS'S VOICE
         Van Gelder Manor... here I used
         to live...in this house built to
         withstand the onslaught of tropical
         rains, the searing sun...a house...

                                 DISSOLVE TO:

12   INT. PLANTATION HOUSE LIVING ROOM - DAY

CAMERA TRAVELS through the room, from MED. FULL to FULL.
The large room with its broken windows. Plants wind
their long-fingered creepers through the room. The walls
are cracked by the inclemencies of the weather, the arms
of giant lianas like petrified snakes, spout out of the
broken floor, strangulating the decaying furniture...a
large refectory table, heavy Dutch chairs, a gun rack,
settees, a coffee table in the middle of the room. The
curtains have dropped from their hangers above the windows.
The bamboo shutters are broken.

                    KLAAS'S VOICE (Cont'd.)
               ...built to shelter generations
               of Van Gelders, of which I was the
               last...

CAMERA STATIONARY THEN -

                                        SLOW DISSOLVE:

13   INT. PLANTATION LIVING ROOM - LATE AFTERNOON - DOLLY SHOT

The same room, but this scene plays years before the decay
of the house. It is late afternoon. The room seems to be
cool despite the humid heat outside. The refectory table
is laid with silver, candles in silver holders, mirroring
in the highly polished surface of the table. A native
servant attends. In a corner stands AL LONG, an old woman.
Silently she directs the servants. Al Long, a native, is
of indefinable age.

MUSIC IS HEARD, coming from an expensive phonograph. CAMERA
in a BOOM SHOT, focusses on DINA VAN GELDER. She is a
beautiful exotic looking girl. Dina is singing and dancing to the tune of the music. It is obvious that she was a
professional - her movements are that of a well-trained
performer. The music is Columbian (public domain). As
she dances the above-mentioned room can be seen. CAMERA
HOLDS HER as she looks up toward the door.

14   MED. CLOSE - BARNEY CHAVEZ

Barney is handsome in a brutal way; powerfully built, he
is about forty years old. He is dressed in tropical white,
the shirt is crumpled by the humidity. He stops, looking
at Dina, and smiles tiredly.

15   MED. CLOSE - BOOM ON DINA

Her face lights up, seeing Barney, and without interrupting
her dance, she smiles at him, dancing closer.

                                        (CONTINUED)

15   CONTINUED:

                          DINA
                 Hello Barney Chavez!

Now Barney is in the SHOT with her, but she dances out of
SHOT while CAMERA stays on him.

                          BARNEY
                 Good afternoon, Mrs. Van Gelder.
                 Have you got a bottle around?
                 It was an unpleasant day!

Dina enters the SHOT again, dancing.

                          DINA
                 Unpleasant? That's what you're
                 paid for by my husband!

Barney looks after her, amused, as she dances out of the
SHOT. Suddenly the phonograph needle jumps the track,
and as CAMERA PANS QUICKLY, Dina runs over to the machine
and turns it off. Barney walks toward her, until CAMERA
stays in MED. CLOSE. Dina pushes back her hair, and looks
at him.

                          BARNEY
                 Rubber's going up in price every
                 day...and I can't get hold of
                 enough workmen. And when I do they
                 run away to go into business for
                 themselves... The times when people
                 were allowed to have slaves!

Dina looks at him coquettishly.

                          DINA
                 Slaves! Aren't we all slaves...
                 somehow...

16   MED. CLOSE PAN SHOT

Al Long approaches with tray with drinks.

                          DINA
                      (sarcastically; in a
                       low voice)
                 There is Al Long - seeing all...
                 hearing all... never talks...

Barney turns to Al Long, he takes a glass from the tray
she is holding. But as he picks up one to pass to Dina
she shakes her head. Al Long leaves the SHOT.

                                        (CONTINUED)

16   CONTINUED:

                         BARNEY
               Have one...

                          DINA
               Thank you, no...I don't like the
               taste of it. After a while all of
               you will be soaked like the wick of
               a lamp...only able to glow as long
               as the vessel is filled with alcohol...
                    (she sighs)
               I'm bored, Barney...bored to death.

      CAMERA PANS as she walks over to a vase that stands on the
      phonograph. She picks up a bright flower, and puts it
      into her hair. She watches Barney as though to imprint
      his face into her memory.

                         BARNEY
               This is no place for a beautiful
               woman like you to bury yourself.
               A woman like you ought to have some
               fun. Life runs away pretty fast
               if you don't hold onto it with
               both hands!

                          DINA
                    (amused)
               Will you help me hold it, Barney?

      She looks up as the door o.s. opens.

17   MED. CLOSE - THE DOOR

      The door leads into the garden - there is another one
      leading to the servants' quarters and a third one leading
      to the living quarters. KLAAS VAN GELDER and DR. VIET
      enter. KLAAS is small, studious looking; he wears glasses.
      But his strong puritan face, his cold calculating eyes
      betray a will of iron, but also a lack of humor. With
      him is Dr. Viet, a man in his late thirties, attractive,
      but somehow dissipated by the tropical climate and drink.
      Klaas, stopping in the doorway, looks sharply at Barney
      and Dina, while Viet walks on.

                         DINA (o.s.)
               Hello Klaas, hello Doctor...

                          VIET
               Nice to see you, Dina...

18   REVERSE SHOT

      as Klaas walks up to Dina and Barney.

                                                    (CONTINUED)

18   CONTINUED:

>   KLAAS
>   I was looking for you, Barney.
>   You should've been at the warehouse...

>   BARNEY
>   The heat got me down, Mr. Van Gelder.

Al Long enters the SHOT with the tray, and offers one to
the doctor, who picks it up eagerly.

>   KLAAS
>   There was an accident, Barney, a
>   man got hurt.

>   BARNEY
>   They always get hurt. That's the
>   chance they take.

>   KLAAS
>   This one died. He wouldn't have
>   died if you had been on the job!

>   BARNEY
>   (crossly)
>   I got only two feet and two hands,
>   and two eyes. I can't be on two
>   places at the same time.

Dina enters the SHOT.

>   DINA
>   We're going to eat in a minute...
>   don't fight before dinner!
>   Now get ready, both of you!

>   BARNEY
>   I'd rather eat in my room, Mrs.
>   van Gelder...

He leaves the room, while Klaas looks after him, suppress-
ing a reply. Then he turns sharply and walks off in the
opposite direction. Klaas turns to Barney.

>   KLAAS
>   Chavez - you can pick up your
>   pay and leave.

>   BARNEY
>   That's all right with me, Mr. Van
>   Gelder, quite all right!

Dina looks shocked and surprised.

                                        (CONTINUED)

18   CONTINUED (1)

                          DINA
               What is all this? What have you
               got against Barney?

                          KLAAS
               I don't want him here any longer!

                          BARNEY
               Do you want me to leave straight
               away?

Klaas does not answer. He turns sharply and leaves the
room. Dina wants to follow, but Viet stops her.

                          VIET
               Stay here!

                          DINA
               But what has gotten into him?

                          VIET
               Stay here - let me find out!

He gets up and follows Klaas.

19   MED. FULL

as Al Long gives a sign to the servants to leave the room.
She too walks out of SHOT. CAMERA MOVES CLOSER on Dina
and Barney. Dina suddenly looks scared, and desperate.

                          DINA
               Barney...

Barney looks at her, finishing his drink and putting down
the glass.

                          BARNEY
               Did he spoil your appetite?

                          DINA
               Why is he acting that way?

                          BARNEY
               You know as much as I do...to
               think of it --
                    (he grins)
               -- you know exactly half and I
               the other half!

                          DINA
               But why...

                                        (CONTINUED)

19   CONTINUED:

>   BARNEY
> He has his spies -- that old
> woman... I bet she gives him
> a report every day...what's
> going on in this house - how
> many dogs have barked, and how
> many cats mewed! She's peeping
> through keyholes, I bet!

>   DINA
> Did you quarrel today with Klaas?

>   BARNEY
> I'm old enough not to be pushed
> around by anyone. I'm doing a
> job, and that's what I'm paid for.

He looks at Dina, angrily, gloweringly.

>   DINA
> It's that heat...

>   BARNEY
> I don't care what it is. I want
> to be treated right. That's all.
> Because he has the money doesn't
> mean he owns me. I don't need to
> stand for it!

>   DINA
> Don't go away - don't leave me!

She stretches out her hand. Barney melts a little. He
takes her hand, his voice is softer.

>   BARNEY
> If anybody has to go, it's him,
> not us!

>   DINA
> Let's go away together - I can make
> money - I can sing - and dance...

>   BARNEY
>   (evasively)
> You heard what the doctor said --
> Klaas is a sick man - he won't
> live long...not long enough to
> stand in our way!

He gets up and as CAMERA MOVES CLOSER he asks in a low
voice:

                                        (CONTINUED)

19   CONTINUED (1)

                    BARNEY
          You do love me, do you?

Dina looks into his eyes, unwaveringly, then she nods,
earnestly.

                    BARNEY
          That's all I need to know!

He walks out of the SHOT. Dina looks after him, and as
CAMERA MOVES INTO CLOSE, she covers her face with her
hands.

20   MED. SHOT

          other part of the large room where Al Long stands, quietly,
          blending with the shadow of the corner. She has watched
          the preceding scene and now, noiselessly, withdraws.

                                        DISSOLVE:

21   INT. KLAAS'S BEDROOM - NIGHT - CLOSE SHOT

          on an indicator to measure blood pressure. The mercury
          is sliding down as CAMERA PULLS BACK into MED. CLOSE.
          Klaas, the machine fastened to his arm, is sitting on
          the bed. Viet watches the pressure gauge. Then he takes
          the machine off Klaas's arm.

                    VIET
          You shouldn't excite yourself.

                    KLAAS
          What do you want me to do?
          Smile and keep my eyes shut
          while that big gorilla is making
          love to Dina?

Viet tries to humor Klaas.

                    VIET
          You know there are no gorillas
          in our part of the jungle!

Klaas, tired, hides his face for a moment, then he controls
himself.

                    KLAAS
          Barney Chavez...he is like a beast -
          he is an animal - with animal
          instincts. I should never have
          given him the job - but I never
          thought Dina would fall for him!

                                        (CONTINUED)

21   CONTINUED:

Viet takes out his pipe and starts cleaning it.

                        VIET
              It's the jungle. The jungle is to
              blame!

Klaas looks up surprised.

                        KLAAS
              Are you trying to defend Dina?

22   MED. CLOSE - ANOTHER ANGLE

                        VIET
              Dina wasn't exactly a blank piece
              of paper when you married her...
              She had - lived before. She was a
              dancer in a night club...in Rio.

                        KLAAS
              All right - I knew that. It gives
              her no excuse to cheat on me.

                        VIET
              You do love her, don't you?

                        KLAAS
                   (moved)
              I haven't got much without her!

Viet nods as he steps over to Klaas and for a moment puts
his hand on Klaas's shoulder.

                        VIET
              You got rid of Barney Chavez. That's
              your right. But still, I would take
              her away from here. A woman buried
              in this place for years...you got to
              make some allowances, if she gets a
              bit mixed up.

                        KLAAS
              You too got a crush on her, haven't
              you?

Viet looks startled, then he smiles.

                        VIET
              Sure I have...She looks good to
              any man...and that's a compliment
              to you!

He looks at his watch.

                                        (CONTINUED)

22   CONTINUED:

                         VIET (Cont'd.)
             Well, who am I to be giving advice!
             My private life isn't perfect either.
             - But as I live alone, nobody cares.
             That's the whole difference!

He walks to the door.

                         VIET (Cont'd.)
             I better go to bed...and you
             should too. I don't like seeing
             you take so little care of yourself.

                         KLAAS
             Good night, Viet.

                         VIET
             Good night.

23   MED. CLOSE - OTHER ANGLE

      as Viet leaves. The door closes o.s. Klaas is alone.
      He opens the large door leading into the garden. A multi-
      tude of animal noises are HEARD coming from the nearby
      jungle. The screen door separating the room from the
      garden is still closed. Klaas opens the collar of his
      shirt wider, as if he had difficulties breathing. Then
      he pushes open the screen door and walks outside.

24   EXT. GARDEN AND JUNGLE - NIGHT - FULL (STOCK)

      MED. CLOSE on a night animal - a lemur or any kind of
      half monkey, looking into CAMERA and disappearing, scream-
      ing in protest.

25   MED. CLOSE (STOCK)

      On a large animal - a lizard of tremendous size - scurrying
      away from CAMERA.

26   FULLER SHOT

      On part of garden and jungle (the set is a clearing bordered
      by strange trees and creeping plants). Klaas enters the
      SHOT. He stands in the moonlit garden, then walks on as
      CAMERA PANS.

27   MED. CLOSE

A tall, silent figure stands under a tree, now steps forward
as Klaas enters from the opposite side. It is Barney
waiting for Klaas.

                    KLAAS
          What are you doing here?

                    BARNEY
          I saw you leave your room. I
          want to talk to you!

                    KLAAS
          Tonight?

                    BARNEY
          Why not? I'd rather get it off
          my chest now.

                    KLAAS
          I don't want to listen. You can't
          tell me anything I haven't told you
          before!

28   MED. CLOSE - OTHER ANGLE

as Barney steps closer to Klaas. Klaas takes a flashlight
out of his pocket, and lets the light fall sharply on
Barney.

                    BARNEY
          I did a lot of good work for
          you. I didn't fall down on my
          job.

                    KLAAS
          Anything else?

                    BARNEY
          Okay, glad you agree with me.
          That's the only thing you've
          got the right to criticise: the
          work you pay me for.

                    KLAAS
          You know about the complaint of
          that worker - and his daughter.

                    BARNEY
          I didn't take anything that wasn't
          given to me. So what is it to you?

                                      (CONTINUED)

28   CONTINUED:

                              KLAAS
                    You are living in my house. I
                    demand that you conduct yourself
                    accordingly.

       He lowers the light and both men are in semi-dark, their
       shadows falling black on the moonlit ground.

                              BARNEY
                    In life a man sometimes gets into
                    a spot where he has to make a
                    decision, a big decision, Van
                    Gelder.

                              KLAAS
                    My decision has been made and you
                    know it.

29   MED. CLOSE DOLLY SHOT

       Klaas walks forward to pass Barney but Barney steps into
       his way.

                              BARNEY
                    Mine too. You are standing in my
                    way - and Dina's!

       Klaas stares at him stunned.

                              KLAAS
                    Did she ask you to tell me that?

                              BARNEY
                    She loves me - and I love her.
                    What are you going to do about it?

       Klaas lunges forward and hits Barney. The flashlight drops
       to the ground.

30   CLOSE - BARNEY

       as he wipes off a small trickle of blood from his lips.
       He does not lift his arms. He looks at the flashlight
       on the ground. His face suddenly tightens.

31   CLOSE (STOCK)

       a large snake staring into the light.

                                             (CONTINUED)

31   CONTINUED:

                        BARNEY (o.s.)
                Watch out, Van Gelder... A snake --
                a poisonous one...

32   CLOSE ON KLAAS

       as he turns and sees the animal. His face freezes in fear.

33   MED. CLOSE - OTHER ANGLE

       as Barney suddenly lunges forward, and with a short powerful
       stroke knocks the unsuspecting Klaas down.

34   CLOSE TRICK SHOT

       as the snake shoots forward.

35   CLOSE

       on Barney's face, as he stares at the man on the ground.

                        KLAAS (o.s.)
                      (choked)
                Help - Barney - help...

36   CLOSE

       Behind a cluster of leaves and bushes stands Al Long,
       almost blending with the background. Her face is frozen
       in terror, as she watches the scene.

37   CLOSE ON BARNEY

       as he watches the scene before him, with a cruel smile.
       He now turns - hearing a noise nearby.

38   CLOSE

       Al Long has disappeared - only the leaves rustle.

39   CLOSE ON BARNEY

       as he listens irritated, and suspicious.

                                        DISSOLVE TO:

40   INT. DINA'S ROOM - SAME NIGHT - CLOSE ON DINA

She is lying on her bed, behind the mosquito netting.
The shutters are not closed and the white light of the
moon falls into the room. Dina stirs and sits up as a
knocking on the door is HEARD.

                    DINA
          Who is it?

                    BARNEY (o.s.)
          Open up!

CAMERA MOVES BACK as Dina slips out of bed, puts on her
slippers, and walks to the door. She opens the door.

                    DINA
                 (frightened)
          You can't come in here at this
          hour... are you insane!

                    BARNEY
          I must talk to you...

He forces his way into the room and closes the door behind
him.

                    DINA
          Turn on the light.

Barney switches on the light. Dina turns to him as CAMERA
MOVES into MED. CLOSE.

                    DINA
          What happened to you? You've
          hurt yourself!

She touches his mouth and cheek where Klaas hit him.

                    BARNEY
          It's nothing...

He wipes his mouth with the back of his hand.

                    BARNEY
          I'm leaving early in the morning
          and you're coming with me!

He bends down and taking her face between his large hands,
he kisses her. Dina melts for a moment, then she frees
herself.

                    DINA
          Why not tell Klaas? I'm not
          afraid to talk to him!

(CONTINUED)

40   CONTINUED:

                        BARNEY
          What's the good? You told me you
          love me - not him!

Dina embraces him and hides her head on his shoulder.

                        DINA
          What will happen if he does not
          let me go?

                        BARNEY
          How can he hold you? Marriage
          is only a contract. Every
          contract can be broken.

                        DINA
          Where are we going to go?

                        BARNEY
          Does it matter? I can find a job
          at any plantation.

                        DINA
          Nobody will give you work out here -
          they all know Klaas - and they'll
          stick together...you know them!

                        BARNEY
          The world is bigger than this jungle
          patch.

                        DINA
          Barney - I'm afraid...
               (she is holding onto
                Barney)
          Why am I afraid, Barney?

                        BARNEY
          You will be happy with me. I
          promise you, you will!

Suddenly he looks up, and switches off the light.

41   MED. CLOSE

                        DINA
               (in a whisper)
          What is it?

                        BARNEY
          A light - in the garden...

42   LONG SHOT - THE GARDEN

as seen through French doors. A light is moving in the
garden, a swinging lamp. Al Long carries it.

                    BARNEY'S VOICE
          Who is it?

                    DINA (o.s.)
          It's Al Long!

43   INT. DINA'S ROOM - MED. CLOSE

on Dina and Barney as they stare through the window.

44   EXT. GARDEN - NIGHT

DOLLY and BOOM SHOT on Al Long. The animal noises are
HEARD loudly, shrilly, the cry of the night birds, the
howlings of the monkeys, and the far cry of the giant cats.
In her arm Al Long carries a small potted plant, with fat
leaves: the Pe De Guine, the foot of the god Guine, a mystic
South American plant; in the other hand she has an oil lamp,
which throws a yellow glow on the ground. She walks on and
then stops close to Klaas's body. The flashlight is still
lying on the ground but dying out, illuminating the motionless body. The old woman kneels down (CAMERA INTO CLOSER
SHOT), puts down the lamp and the plant.

45   CLOSE SHOT - AL LONG

kneeling down, picks two leaves from the tree and puts them
on the dead man's open eyes.

                    AL LONG
          Cursed shall be the murderer
          these eyes have seen. Cursed
          shall be the mind of the wrong
          doer. He shall be like an
          animal that haunts the jungle...
          The jungle shall haunt him to
          his death.

                              SLOW FADE OUT:

FADE IN:

46   INT. LIVING ROOM PLANTATION - DAY - PAN SHOT - MED. FULL

Barney, Taro, Al Long, Dr. Viet, Dina, a colored stenographer, a native policeman. Taro, the native commissioner,

                              (CONTINUED)

46   CONTINUED:

walks from the door to the large refectory table. He is
dressed in a resplendent uniform. CAMERA MOVES CLOSER.
On the table lie the flashlight, a couple of dry leaves of
the Pe De Guine tree. Some medicine bottles and pill boxes
of cardboard - the way the pharmacist delivers its medicines.
The stenographer is working with a noiseless portable machine,
the only sound that is HEARD. Taro, the commissioner, is a
LAPINO, a mixture of Spaniard and Juiloto Indian, a tall,
handsome, brown-skinned man. The policeman and the stenographer are Cholos - white and Indian blood mixed. It is
ominously quiet in the room. Barney is slumped in a wicker
chair, smoking a cigar. The doctor is staring out of the
garden door window. He has a drink on a stool beside him.
Dina, dressed in white, is sitting motionless at the table,
her hands clamped around the arm rests of her chair. Al
Long is standing near the door leading to the servants'
quarters. She is dressed in white - the mourning color of
the natives.

47   DOLLY SHOT

into CLOSE SHOT as Taro takes off his glasses (he wears them
for distance, not for reading). He picks up a document which
the native stenographer is typing out on the small portable.
The stenographer, having finished her job, picks up her
shorthand book and a pencil.

                         TARO
              You insist, Mr. Chavez, that
              the last time you saw Mr. Van
              Gelder was in this room?

Taro puts on his glasses and looks toward Barney.

48   MED. CLOSE - ON BARNEY

he puffs on his cigar.

                       BARNEY
              I gave it to you in writing.

49   MED. CLOSE - ON TARO

He nods, and puts down the document. The stenographer takes
down the conversation.

                         TARO
              We found imprints of shoes of the
              size and shape you're wearing near
              the body. Are you sure you weren't
              in the garden that night?

                                        (CONTINUED)

49   CONTINUED:

Barney gets up and walks over to the table, where he sits
down opposite Taro. His big frame is almost too large
for the chair.

                    BARNEY
          They are old footprints...but since
          you don't believe me, why don't you
          come straight out with what you
          want to say, commissioner! Why
          don't you ask me: have you killed
          Klaas van Gelder? You know I had
          a quarrel with him. You've got
          witnesses for that, haven't you?

                    TARO
          I have, that's true...but my
          evidence is not strong enough
          to bring charges against you.

He glances over to the doctor.

                    TARO (Cont'd.)
          What is your opinion, Dr. Viet?

50   MED. CLOSE ON VIET

He turns around and gets up.

                    VIET
          Klaas van Gelder died of shock
          and suffocation caused by snake
          poison. He was a sick man, Taro.
          It might well have been that he
          had a fainting spell in the garden,
          and that that snake attacked him.
          Anyhow, that's my official report.

He looks over to Dina.

51   CLOSE ON DINA

as she stares motionlessly ahead.

                    TARO (o.s.)
          And your private opinion?

Now she slowly turns to look at Viet.

52   MED. CLOSE ON VIET

He hesitates.

                                        (CONTINUED)

52   CONTINUED:

                         VIET
                My private opinion is of no
                value.

DOLLY SHOT as she slowly walks to the table and sits down.
Taro looks toward Al Long.

53   MED. CLOSE ON AL LONG

       as she stands, quietly, without expression.

54   MED. CLOSE - THE TABLE

       Taro stares at Barney and ponders, then looks at Viet and
       back at Barney.

                         TARO
                It might also have been that
                during a quarrel Mr. Chavez
                knocked down Mr. van Gelder, and
                the snake bit him. These animals
                attack anything that frightens
                them.

55   MED. FULL - BARNEY AND DINA

       Barney looks at Dina, who does not look up, her face
       betraying agony.

                         BARNEY
                The doctor told you that van
                Gelder died of suffociation caused
                by snake poison. This is the
                official coroner's report.

                         TARO
                True. But the mark on the dead
                man's head was produced by a blow...
                of a fist.

He points with his glasses at Barney, then puts them on.

                         TARO
                Your cheek is discolored.
                You've been in a fight.

                         BARNEY
                I had a fight with a worker.

                         TARO
                What about?

                                              (CONTINUED)

55   CONTINUED:

                              BARNEY
                        (heatedly)
                   Nothing that has anything to do
                   with Van Gelder's death. Why
                   don't you stick to the point? Why
                   don't you arrest me?

56   CLOSER SHOT - ON TARO

       He picks up the leaves of the Pe De Guine tree.

                              TARO
                   I would but for one thing,
                   Mr. Chavez. These leaves...
                   they belong to a plant called
                   Pe de Guine - the foot of the
                   god. Do you know about such
                   a plant?

                              BARNEY
                   No.

                              TARO
                        (to Viet)
                   These leaves worry me, Doctor.
                   They are used to put a magic
                   spell on people.

                              BARNEY
                   Now listen, Taro, don't accuse
                   me of using magic!

                              TARO
                   I don't!

       He looks up toward Al Long.

57   MED. CLOSE ON AL LONG

       standing near the door, watching.

                              TARO
                        (o.s.)
                   Al Long, please come over here.

       The old woman slowly walks toward CAMERA.

58   CLOSER SHOT AT THE TABLE

       As Al Long walks into the SHOT Taro holds out the leaves
       to her on the flat of his hand.

                                             (CONTINUED)

58   CONTINUED:

                              TARO
                    I want you to answer me
                    truthfully...do you know where
                    those leaves come from?

Al Long does not answer.

                              TARO
                    You know that it is against the
                    law to own a plant of this kind...
                    it's dangerous poison.

Al Long does not answer. Taro waits,then with a sigh he
puts the leaves on the table. Viet walks into the SHOT.

                              VIET
                    You can't make her talk, Taro.
                    You know that.

59   MED. CLOSE - OTHER ANGLE

                              TARO
                         (resigned)
                    I sometimes think I don't even
                    talk the language of my own people
                    anymore. Since I became an official,
                    I'm standing outside THEIR code of
                    law.

He turns to the native stenographer.

                              TARO
                    Don't put that down, Miss Cypriano!

The girl looks up and smiles at him. Taro sits down and
taking off the glasses, studies the different medicines
which stand on the table.

                              TARO
                    It must've been Al Long who put
                    the leaves on Mr. Van Gelder's
                    eyes. But why?

Viet pulls a chair and sits down.

                              VIET
                    Knowing the people as I do, she's
                    put a spell on somebody.

                              TARO
                    Yes. On the murderer.

He looks at Barney.

60   MED. CLOSE FAVORING BARNEY

                    BARNEY
              (slowly, dangerously)
          We have a saying in English, Mr.
          Taro - shut up or put up!

Taro disregards him as he turns to Dina, CAMERA PANNING.

                    TARO
          Do you expect to sell the
          plantation, Mrs. Van Gelder?

                    DINA
          I haven't thought of it.

                    TARO
          It isn't going to be easy for you
          to manage. Or is Mr. Chavez staying
          here to help you?

                    BARNEY
          Let me answer to that, Dina. Yes.
          I am staying.

                    TARO
          I see.

He plays with his glasses, but as Dina answers, he puts them
on, watching her intently.

                    DINA
          But I don't see what business it
          is of yours.
              (she gets up enraged)
          To put an end to your suspicion:
          Mr. Chavez has a perfect alibi
          for last night.

61   MED. CLOSE - FAVORING DINA

as she stands, glowingly, staring at Taro. Viet is
turning to her, and the stenographer looks up. Barney perks
up, taking the cigar out of his mouth.

                    TARO
          I'm interested to hear it, Mrs.
          Van Gelder.

                    DINA
          He was in my room last night -
          from the moment Klaas left the
          table...until his body was found.
          Is that enough evidence for you?

                                        (CONTINUED)

61   CONTINUED:

                         TARO
                I am satisfied. Thank you, Mrs.
                van Gelder.

62   CLOSE ON VIET

       as he looks startled and crushed at Dina, he dries his
       forehead with his handkerchief, then downs his drink.
       Suddenly he looks old and worn.

                         VIET
                Is that the truth?

       Dina does not answer him, but she looks at him quietly,
       her mouth tightening.

63   CLOSE ON BARNEY

       as he grins. He gets up and walking over to Dina takes
       her in his arms. CAMERA DOLLIES WITH HIM.

                         BARNEY
                Thank you, darling! I didn't
                want to tell them...

       Dina submits to his embrace listlessly. Suddenly she
       embraces him tightly, hiding her face on his shoulder.
       Barney turns to the people at the table.

                         BARNEY
                We're going to get married as
                soon as possible. You may fill
                out the license, Mr. Taro...

       As he smiles the CAMERA pulls into FULL, as Taro picks up
       the papers, and the stenographer gets up.

                         VIET
                     (listelssly)
                Congratulations...

                         TARO
                My best wishes too...

       CAMERA still moves further.

                         BARNEY
                You are invited to our marriage...
                all of you!

                                        DISSOLVE TO:

64   INT. LIVING ROOM - DAY - DULL SHOT

Wedding day. The room is decorated gaily with flowers.
The large table is laden with food, and the mestizo
servants, dressed in white, carry trays with drinks.
Taro, the native commissioner, is present in his dress
uniform. A few plantation owners and their wives and
daughters, Al Long in her best native dress, stands near
the door leading into the servants quarters. She is
directing the staff. Barney, Dina, Viet, and Van Heussen,
a plantation owner are conversing.

65   MED. CLOSE ON BARNEY

He stands, an empty glass in his hand, talking to Van Heussen.

> VAN HEUSSEN
> Is this your first marriage,
> Mr. Chavez?

> BARNEY
> My father used to say: try
> everything once... When I get
> married, I want to stay married!

> VAN HEUSSEN
> Well, I think a man can make a
> marriage last - but it's not up
> to him to keep it happy.

> BARNEY
> (suspiciously)
> What do you mean?

> VAN HEUSSEN
> I've been married for twenty-six
> years... I keep my marriage going -
> my wife has to do the rest! And
> believe me, she has to work at it!

He points to:

66   MED. CLOSE

near the phonograph, which Dina is just changing, an enormous
fat lady is talking to her. Beside her is her young daughter,
Stella, a thin, anemic looking girl.

> STELLA
> Is it really true you have been
> a dancer...

(CONTINUED)

66   CONTINUED:

                          MRS. VAN HEUSSEN
          Stella! It is not polite to ask
          questions!

                          DINA
          Why not, Mrs. Van Heussen?
                    (to Stella)
          Yes, dear, I worked in night
          clubs - in Paris - London - New
          York - and Rio - I was quite an
          attraction!

                          STELLA
                    (awed)
          Oh - I've never been to a night
          club! It must be exciting! Oh,
          Mrs. Van Gelder, will you dance
          for us?

                          MRS. VAN HEUSSEN
          I don't understand that child -
          she never opens her mouth at home -
          and here - in your house...

                          DINA
          Of course I will dance for you...
          Now, let me see, what record shall
          we put on?

CAMERA DOLLIES with her to the record cabinet. Stella
goes with her, and as Dina opens the cabinet, the girl
eagerly starts picking out a record.

                          STELLA
          Let me find one for you...here...
          this one... The Dance of the
          Candles...

As Dina takes the record to put it on the machine:

                          DINA
          Yes - that's my favorite...

67   MED. CLOSE - ON AL LONG

       at the door. A servant walks by, carrying a glass with
       a transparent liquid on a small silver tray. Al Long
       stops him for a moment, he nods and walks off. CAMERA
       DOLLIES with him a few feet, moving into CLOSE. An
       odd-shaped leaf is submerged in the highball glass, like
       a mint leaf in a julep.

68   MED. CLOSE

on Taro, as he stands, glass in hand, beside Dr. Viet.

> VIET
> Enjoying yourself, Taro?

> TARO
> No, I am not.

He looks around, bored and disgusted.

> VIET
> You aren't?

> TARO
> I wouldn't have come here if
> it weren't my duty to perform
> the marriage ceremony...I
> still consider signing the
> papers a ceremony...but you
> see...

He adjusts his glasses and shrugs.

> VIET
> I know what you mean. You
> policemen are only happy
> when you can put a rope
> around a man's neck. Just
> consider this occasion not
> a marriage - think of it as
> a wake.

> TARO
> (he has never
> heard that
> word)
> A wake? What is it?

> VIET
> An old Irish custom -- making
> merry at somebody's funeral.

> TARO
> Thank you, Doctor. You've put
> me in the right frame of mind!

69   MED. CLOSE

on Barney and Van Heussen.

(CONTINUED)

69   CONTINUED:

>   BARNEY
>   May I drink to you as your
>   new neighbor. Yes, we're
>   only forty miles apart...
>   and that's practically door
>   to door in this part of the
>   woods.

He lifts his glass to drink - finds it empty. The very
moment the servant with the highball glass (in which the
leaf is submerged) stands beside him, offering him the
drink.

>   VAN HEUSSEN
>   Well - I see you're getting
>   service in your house!

Barney lifts the glass.

>   BARNEY
>   To good neighborliness!

They drink, while the servant quickly leaves the SHOT.
MUSIC of the phonograph is HEARD. Barney has emptied the
glass and seems to sway, but he gets hold of himself.

>   VAN HEUSSEN
>   Your wife is going to dance?

>   BARNEY
>   Yes. She's the most graceful
>   dancer you have ever seen!

>   VAN HEUSSEN
>   (with conviction)
>   But it's bad luck to dance be-
>   fore the wedding.

>   BARNEY
>   (amused)
>   Superstition! You've been in
>   the jungle too long, Mr. Van
>   Heussen! Come along - have
>   a good look at her!

70   MED. CLOSE

on Dina, as she starts to dance, CAMERA PULLING BACK.
She dances gracefully, dressed prettily for her wedding
in a wide, embroidered skirt. The guests walk closer
to watch her.

71   REVERSE SHOT

      on the guests, Dina in f.g. The guests are standing in a
      half circle. CAMERA FOLLOWS Dina, until the dance ends.
      Scene intercut by MED. CLOSE or CLOSE SHOTS:

72   Al Long, indifferently watching.

73   Barney, pleased with Dina, but somehow dazed, slightly
      squinting as if to have to adjust the focus. Beside him,
      Van Heussen.

74   Stella Van Heussen, all eyes and next to her mother.

75   Taro, contemplatively, now taking another drink from a
      tray a servant offers to him.

76   MED. FULL

      The dance is ended, the phonograph played out. The guests
      are applauding. Barney walks quickly up to Dina, takes
      her in his arms and kisses her. The people applaud again.

77   CLOSER SHOT

-     on Barney and Dina.

                         DINA
                 This is your last unlawful
                 kiss, Barney Chavez! Why
                 don't you sign the papers
                 and make it legal?

                        BARNEY
                   (turning to Viet)
                 Doctor! Lead the bride!

      As Viet moves forward and Dina stretches out her hand,
      with a smile,

                                          DISSOLVE TO:

78   MED.FULL TO MED. CLOSE

      CAMERA is standing behind the refectory table. Taro steps
      into the SHOT, opens a brief case. He takes a document out,
      and from his coat pocket a fountain pen, which he opens.

79   MED. CLOSE TO MED. FULL

       from his angle; Barney and Dina as they step toward the
       table. She is holding his hand and smiles expansively.
       Behind them the guests are following.

80   MED. CLOSE

       on Al Long as she slowly steps forward to watch the cere--
       mony.

81   MED.CLOSE THE TABLE

       Taro puts on his glasses.

                         TARO
                I've prepared the papers,
                Mr. Chavez. All you have
                to do is sign them and pay
                for the government stamp.

       CAMERA MOVES slowly into CLOSE.

                         BARNEY
                I see - every new step in
                life starts with paying out
                money.

       Taro passes the pen to Barney.

                         BARNEY
                     (continuing; to
                      Dina)
                No, you sign first. I'm
                afraid you might change
                your mind.

       Dina smiles at him and taking the pen from him sits down.

                         DINA
                How shall I sign? My maiden
                name?

                         TARO
                No, your legal name: Van
                Gelder.

       Dina signs the document, then gets up. Barney now sits
       down, and CAMERA moves closer. He picks up the pen.

                         BARNEY
                May I first read what I'm
                signing? I've never done
                this before!

                                           (CONTINUED)

81   CONTINUED:

                              DINA
                    You know very well what you're
                    getting into!

       CAMERA MOVES still closer, as Barney signs the marriage
       certificate: BARNEY ALBERT CHAVEZ. CAMERA STAYS on his
       hand as he puts down the pen.

                              BARNEY
                    Now let me read what I've
                    signed!

       CAMERA follows his right hand as he puts it on his lap.
       Suddenly the hand changes - the fingers curl and become
       claws.

82   CLOSE

       on Barney's face, as he looks down at his right hand, his
       face contorting as if in pain.

83   CLOSE

       The hand, which can be seen only from his angle: it has
       changed into a gorilla's claw.

84   CLOSE

       on Barney as he stares at his hand. He jumps up, pushing
       the hand into his pocket.

85   MED. FULL TO FULL

       Taro in f.g. Barney jumps up and runs away from CAMERA,
       pushing Viet aside with his left.

86   MED. FULL - REVERSE SHOT

       seen from the door, where Barney runs toward CAMERA and
       disappears. Dina stands, startled, Viet walks up to her.
       Van Heussen cleans his coat with his hand -- th drink he
       is holding, spilled.

87   CLOSE

       on Taro, as he stares toward the door, startled.

88   CLOSE

on Al Long, as she looks into the same direction, a faint
smile on her face.

89   MED. CLOSE

as Dina stretches out her hand toward the doctor.

                    DINA
                 (weakly)
          Viet...

                    VIET
                 (taking her hand)
          Stay here - let me find out!

As he turns to walk out,

                                        DISSOLVE TO:

90   INT. BARNEY'S ROOM - MED. FULL TO MED. CLOSE - DAY

This is the same room where Klaas had lived. Barney comes
rushing into the room, the hand still in his pocket. He
slams the door and bolts it. Then he turns, upset,
frightened, leaning against the door.

Steps come closer - and a knocking is HEARD.

                    VIET
                 (o.s.)
          Barney!

A hand is trying the handle.

                    VIET
                 (o.s.; continuing)
          Open up!

Barney stands breathing hard, still shocked, the hand in
his pocket.

                    VIET
                 (o.s; continuing)
          Open up!

Barney slowly turns and unbolts the door. He steps back
as Viet enters.

                    VIET
          What happened?

                                        (CONTINUED)

90   CONTINUED:

                              BARNEY
                    Close the door!

Viet closes the door, Barney steps back further, looking
at Viet. Viet steps over to him and lifts his face.

                              VIET
                    You're sick!

                              BARNEY
                    Doctor...

He stops again.

                              VIET
                    What is it?

                              BARNEY
                    My hand...my right hand...

He looks down at the pocket, where he had hidden the hand.

                              VIET
                    What's the matter with it?

CAMERA MOVES CLOSER as he takes out his hand.

91   CLOSE SHOT ON HIS HAND

It is normal - human. Barney moves his fingers, staring
at it unbelievingly.

                              VIET
                         (continuing)
                    Show me your hand...I can't
                    see anything wrong with it.

He takes Barney's hand and moves its fingers.

                              BARNEY
                    It's all right - yes - it's
                    all right...it...did hurt...
                    suddenly, hurt terribly!

The words tumble out of his mouth, hesitatingly, then
fast again.

                              VIET
                    What hurt? The fingers?
                    What hurt you?

                                        (CONTINUED)

91   CONTINUED:

                    BARNEY
          I'm all right -- don't worry,
          I'm all right!

Viet looks at him disturbed, searchingly.

                    VIET
          Let's go back.

                    BARNEY
          No! Tell them - I - I sud-
          denly got sick. I got a
          fever...tell them anything
          you want --

                    VIET
          You better lie down. I'll
          send Dina in...

Barney sits down on the bed, his hands limply in his lap.

                    BARNEY
          No. I don't want to see
          anybody.

92   MED. CLOSE

CAMERA at door. Viet walks to the door.

                    VIET
          Are you sure you don't want
          to see her?

                    BARNEY
          No - not now...Just leave me
          alone, will you?

                    VIET
                  (hesitatingly)
          I'll look after you later on!

He leaves, closing the door, as CAMERA MOVES CLOSER to
Barney. He stares at his hand and touches it, still
numb and shocked.

                                        FADE OUT.

FADE IN:

93   INT. AL LONG'S ROOM - DAY

The small Pe de Guine plant. It had a dozen leaves when

                                        (CONTINUED)

93   CONTINUED:

we saw it first - now no more than eight are left -- fat,
egg-shaped leaves. Al Long's hand comes into SHOT and
breaks off one. As CAMERA PULLS BACK into MED. CLOSE, Al
Long takes the leaf between her fingers and twists it.
A few transparent drops fall into a small glass. Al Long's
lips move silently as she stares into the container and as
CAMERA MOVES INTO CLOSE her whispering voice becomes dis-
tinct:

                    AL LONG
          Cursed shall be his mind...
          he shall be restless like a
          hunted beast...he shall be
          without peace forever.

                                   SLOW DISSOLVE TO:

94   INT. DINA'S BEDROOM - NIGHT - MED.FULL DOLLY

Dina is wearing a thin, transparent, silk dressing gown.
She stands in front of the large mirror at her dressing
table, painting her lips. Barney is seen in the mirror,
walking up and down, like an animal behind bars.

Her bedroom leads - like the other rooms - into the garden.
The French windows (doors) are closed. Barney walks up to
the door. Dina turns to him.

                    DINA
          Do you like me?

                    BARNEY
          Of course.

He pushes open the door, and at once the jungle noises are
HEARD prominently.

                    DINA
          Why don't you open the bottle
          of champagne?

She points at the bottle which stands in an ice container.
Two glasses are standing on the tray.

                    BARNEY
          I never liked that stuff - I
          was brought up on moonshine.

                    DINA
          Then pour a glass for me,
          will you?

                    BARNEY
          Sure...

                                        (CONTINUED)

94   CONTINUED:

He steps over to the dressing table, and opens the bottle.
Dina watches him as he fills her glass, and then, reluctantly, his. Dina embraces him. Barney puts back the
bottle.

                    DINA
          Tell me...

CAMERA MOVES into CLOSE TWO SHOT

                    BARNEY
          Yes?

                    DINA
          Something is bothering you
          - since the day we married
          ...are you sorry you married
          me?

Barney shakes his head, and as she kisses him, he frees
himself slowly.

                    BARNEY
          No...why should I be? I
          never thought I'd have such
          a beautiful wife - and a large
          plantation - I never was rich
          in my life...now I am...

                    DINA
          But you have changed so much!

CAMERA PULLS BACK into MED. CLOSE. Dina withdraws, she
picks up her glass with champagne, but does not drink it.
Barney steps back to the window and listens.

95   CLOSER SHOT AT THE WINDOW

                    BARNEY
          I haven't changed...No...
          I...
                    (his face is
                     strained)
          Listen, Dina, listen...

                    DINA
                    (entering the
                     SHOT)
          What is it?

                    BARNEY
                    (pushing the door
                     wide open)
          The jungle...

96   CLOSE

on Dina as she listens and watches him uneasily.

> DINA
> Close the door -- I don't
> want to hear it!

97   CLOSE ON BARNEY

> BARNEY
> It's like music...listen...
> that high voice, that's a
> bird...with long red feathers
> ...it flies without making a
> noise...but its voice gives
> it away.

Dina walks into the SHOT.

> DINA
> I know it - it's a Vicuna
> bird.

> BARNEY
> And that other one - the "O
> Ferreiro", doesn't it sound
> as if it were hammering iron
> rails with all its might?

> DINA
> But Barney - what's so special
> about that bird?

> BARNEY
> (listening in-
> tently)
> I can hear the snakes, too...

> DINA
> (shocked)
> The snakes...

> BARNEY
> Yes..the Surucurus and the
> green Cipos which chase
> horses...
> (he turns to her)
> I have to go...I need a gun...

98   MED. SHOT

He looks around in the room.

(CONTINUED)

98   CONTINUED:

                         DINA
                    (shocked, des-
                    perate)
             Barney!

She holds on to him, embracing him, and puts her hand on
his forehead.

                         DINA
                    (continuing)
             You've got a fever?

Barney angrily frees himself.

                         BARNEY
             No - of course not...but
             where is that gun?

DOLLY SHOT as he walks over to her dresser, opens it and
takes out the gun; he breaks it open and looks at the
bullets, then loads it.

                         DINA
             You can't go out into the
             jungle at this time of the
             night...

Barney puts the gun into his pocket, and walks back to the
door, pushing it wide open.

                         BARNEY
                    (hastily)
             Go to bed, Dina...I'll be back
             soon...

He listens to the thousand noises.

                         BARNEY
                    (continuing)
             Hear it?

Suddenly as if Barney had ordered it, the whole jungle
seems to come to life; the thunderous voices of the jaguars
is HEARD in the distance, and a ROARING emanates from the
different bands of howling monkeys. The SHRIEKING of
birds, and the hollow BARKING of the peccaries are HEARD.

                         BARNEY
                    (continuing)
             I won't be long!

Dina steps into his way. The glass falls out of her hand
onto the floor. She holds on to Barney.

                              (CONTINUED)

98   CONTINUED (2):

                         DINA
                 If you love me - don't go...

                         BARNEY
                 I must!

He tries to free himself but Dina holds on to him. The
pumas roar is HEARD closer.

                         DINA
                 Barney! You can't leave me
                 alone!

Barney pushes her back and she stumbles. He disappears
into the night. Dina gets up again, and runs to the
screen door.

99   CLOSE

       at the screen door, CAMERA facing the room. Dina stops in
       CLOSE.

                         DINA
                       (continuing)
                 Barney - Barney!

She listens. Suddenly the noises die out, only Dina's
echo is HEARD mockingly.

                         ECHO
                 Barney - Barney!

Dina listens to the thousand jungle noises which descend
upon her.

The she closes the door, and stands motionless, listening.
CAMERA MOVES into CLOSE; she looks frightened, mixed up,
and unhappy.

                                   DISSOLVE TO:

100   INT. JUNGLE - NIGHT - MED. LONG

       on Barney as he breaks through the underbrush into scene.
       He stops and listens, then goes on toward CAMERA.

101   MED. FULL

       as animals scurry away. Then Barney breaks into SHOT,
       walking on as if feeling his way.

102   MED. CLOSE BOOM SHOT

as seen through Barney's eyes as he walks on: The lianas,
their giant leaves, the small animals running away into the
trees (STOCK). Slowly the picture changes:

103   MED. CLOSE BOOM SHOT

photographed through a sheet of glass which has been covered with oil or vaseline in such a way that the edges are
blurred, but the middle is free and clear like an iris in
an eye - the impression is given that Barney sees the jungle
as an animal would see it.

The whistling of the gorilla is HEARD, shrilly, penetratingly. CAMERA DOLLIES as branches snap and are bent back
as Barney (unseen) walks on.

104   STOCK SHOTS
to
107   of animals scurrying away. Intercut with Barney (O.S.) as
he walks on.

108   CLOSE (STOCK)

the head of a puma, hissing, showing its fangs, retreating.

109   CLOSE (STOCK)

A giant Iguana running away.

110   DOLLY SHOT

as CAMERA lumbers on, the secne seen through the ANIMAL'S
(Barney's) eyes.

Suddenly the CAMERA stops, as though Barney had stopped,
and into the close range of the CAMERA stretches an arm -
Barney's arm - changing into that of a gorilla. As the
CAMERA is stationary, a sigh is HEARD, of terror, then the
gorilla's voice is HEARD, and CAMERA MOVES quickly through
the brush and undergrowth as if Barney were running to
escape himself.

DOLLY SHOT as CAMERA breaks through the brush and stops at
a small clear pool, which mirrors back a round bright moon.
It is a small clearing in the bushes. A few animals (STOCK)
are scurrying away, then as CAMERA (being Barney) arrives
at the pool, Barney kneels down to look at himself in the
water. At first his hands and arms are seen: those of a
gorilla. Then slowly, out of the misty sight of the Gorilla's eyes, a head bends over the pool. It is a gorilla's

(CONTINUED)

110   CONTINUED:

head - its eyes beady. It blows through its nostrils, and
now its WHINE is heard again, pitiful, frightened, then
the picture slowly fades away, but at the same time the
edges of the picture become sharp again as CAMERA TILTS up
toward the trees - as Barney regains his human sight.

SLOW DISSOLVE TO:

111   EXT. GARDEN IN FRONT OF THE PLANTATION BUILDING - NIGHT -
      LONG

The house is still fully lighted -- yellow beams falling
through the window into the garden. The jungle's voice is
HEARD - its multitude of animal cries.

                    DINA'S VOICE
          Barney -- Barney...

Then Dina comes into SHOT, followed by her servants.

112   MED. CLOSE DOLLY

on Dina, as she quickly comes into SHOT, behind her Al Long
and two servants. Dina is in her dressing gown. She now
stops.

                    DINA
          Where is he?

                    AL LONG
          Over there - near the hibiscus
          bush...

113   MED. FULL AS SEEN FROM DINA'S ANGLE

Under a flowering bush lies Barney, unconscious, as if he
had collapsed going home. CAMERA MOVES CLOSE: his coat
is torn, his shirt hanging out in shreds. Dina enters the
SHOT and kneels down beside him, while one of the servant
lights the scene with a large lamplike flashlight.

CAMERA MOVES CLOSER: Dina lifts his head, holding her hand
close to his lips.

                    DINA
          He is breathing...
               (she turns)
          Let's take him inside...
          quickly...

(CONTINUED)

113   CONTINUED:

The servants step into the SHOT and as Al Long lifts up
the electric lamp (or oil lamp) the two mestizo boys lift
up Barney's heavy body.

                                    DISSOLVE TO:

114   INT. BARNEY'S BEDROOM - DAY - MED. FULL

The shutters are closed, and the sharp sun throws the
shadows of the bamboo screen across the bed and the room.
Barney is lying on his bed, his eyes closed, breathing la-
boriously. Dina sits near him on a stool, watching him.
Barney whispers in his sleep. Dina bends down to him.

115   CLOSER SHOT

                        BARNEY
                These are not my hands...
                these are not my arms...this
                is not my face...no...it isn't
                my face...

He turns his head away from CAMERA and Dina wipes his forehead, straightens out the pillow.

                        BARNEY
                     (continuing)
                This is not my voice...no...
                it is not my voice...

                        DINA
                Barney...

                        BARNEY
                These are not my hands...
                this is not my face...no...

His voice dies out in a murmur. Dina, frightened, looks
up, as the door o.s. opens.

116   MED. CLOSE

as seen from her angle, where Viet enters. He carries his
doctor's satchel. CAMERA GETS UP as though Dina were getting up and DOLLIES to the doctor.

117   MED. CLOSE VIET AND DINA

                        VIET
                Hello, Dina!

                                    (CONTINUED)

42.

117   CONTINUED:

Dina puts her hand on his arm.

                    DINA
          I thought you'd never come!

Viet puts his satchel on a table and opens it.

                    VIET
          I was a hundred miles away...
          I think I'll have to get my-
          self a small airplane...that
          would accelerate matters -
          landing in your front yard...

He turns to the bed as CAMERA DOLLIES. Walking over to
Barney he picks up his arm, feeling his pulse.

                    VIET
                 (continuing)
          How long has he been like
          this?

                    DINA
          Since I found him - in the
          garden.

                    VIET
          How long ago was that?

                    DINA
          Six hours ago...

Viet nods,and drops Barney's hand.

                    VIET
          It's the fever!

118   CLOSER SHOT

on Barney, Viet. Barney tosses his head.

                    BARNEY
          My hands - they hurt -- they
          hurt...

Viet turns and walks over to his satchel, and taking out a
hypodermic, he fills it.

                    VIET
          He complained about his hands
          before...

                              (CONTINUED)

118   CONTINUED:

                  DINA
           But what he says doesn't make
           sense!

                  VIET
           The things he says in his
           fever? Of course not...

                  BARNEY
           The gorilla - watch out!

Viet looks at Dina who turns away and walks over to Barney.
Without a word, Viet too steps over to the bed, and (away
from CAMERA) injects the needle in Barney's arm.

                  VIET
           That's all we can do - at the
           moment.

He has finished injecting the hypodermic and straightens
up.

                  DINA
           He is unconscious...see...

                  VIET
           I gave him a shot of barbituric
           acid. He's asleep...give him
           quinine when he wakes up.

Then returning to his satchel he takes out a box of quinine.

                  VIET
               (continuing)
           How's your supply of quinine?

                  DINA
           Thanks, I have enough left.

                  VIET
           From Klaas?

                  DINA
               (resentful)
           My own, you gave it to me,
           remember...the last time I
           had an attack of fever...

119   MED. CLOSE

at the table. The mirror behind, reflecting the bed.
She sits down, near Barney, and looks defiantly at Viet,
who pulls a chair close to her.

120   CAMERA PULLS INTO CLOSE TWO SHOT

Viet puts his hand on hers.

                    VIET
          Happy?

                    DINA
          Very.

                    VIET
          Klaas loved you...

Dina takes her hand away.

                    DINA
          Barney too loves me - and I
          love him. That's the differ-
          ence between my two marriages!

Viet gets up.

                    VIET
          Klaas was my friend.

                    DINA
          What do you want me to say?
          I told you how unhappy I am
          he had to die - such a hor-
          rible death!

                    VIET
          At such a convenient time!

Dina too gets up, angry, tensely, offended.

                    DINA
          Yes. At such a convenient
          time. Klaas died of heart
          failure - and shock - or do
          you want to change your di-
          agnosis?

                    VIET
          I knew the cause of his death
          -- but not the -- motive!

Dina looks coldly at him.

                    DINA
          An accident!

                    VIET
          It must have been -- since
          Barney was in your room that
          night.

                                        (CONTINUED)

120   CONTINUED:

                    DINA
          You wish that wasn't the
          truth, isn't that it?

                    VIET
          Yes.

                    DINA
          A woman always knows a man's
          feeling for her. Sorry, Viet
          - Barney is my husband, for
          better or for worse!

                    VIET
          Dina...

                    DINA
          You never had the courage to
          do anything about your feel-
          ings for me...but you're
          blaming Barney -

                    VIET
                 (shocked)
          You know what you're saying?

                    DINA
          Yes - nothing but everybody
          thinks!

Viet picks up his satchel, unhappy, frustrated.

                    VIET
          Whatever happens, Dina --
          remember I'm your friend.
          You can always call on me.

                    DINA
          I will remember it.

Viet walks to the door as CAMERA PANS.

                    VIET
          Barney's going to be all
          right. I'll look in again
          in a few days - you know
          where to find me in case of
          an emergency.

                    DINA
          Yes. Thank you, Viet.

121   MED. CLOSE

favoring Viet. He looks as if he wants to say something to
her. Then he leaves and closes the door. Dina turns toward CAMERA. She walks over to Barney's bed and sits down
on the small stool, drying his forehead with a white hand-
kerchief. CAMERA MOVES INTO CLOSE as she watches him,
tenderly, lovingly.

                                        DISSOLVE TO:

122   TARO'S OFFICE - DAY

The office is almost bare but for a couple of wooden chairs,
a file cabinet, a row of books on a stand, a telephone on
the plain desk. The window is open, and the street noises
come in plainly.

Taro is sitting behind his telephone, his coat hanging over
the back of his chair. The collar of his shirt is open,
and he telephones, his glasses in one hand, in the other
the receiver. The heat in the room is extreme.

The pretty native secretary is sitting close by, listening
to the conversation on a second phone, taking it down in
shorthand.

                    TARO
                (into the phone)
            You've got a couple of stowa-
            ways on board, captain? No -
            you can't dump them here --
            I'm not interested in feeding
            them. You want to throw them
            overboard? I wouldn't do that,
            Captain! Too many things
            clutter up our little port
            already!
                (he chuckles)
            Good day, captain, and have a
            safe trip home!

He hangs up, and the secretary, too, puts down the phone.

                    TARO
                (continuing)
            Have you got that, Miss Cypri-
            ano? In case we pick up those
            people, despite the captain's
            promise not to smuggle them on
            land - we'll make his shipping
            company responsible!

The stenographer picks up her pencil and note book.

123   CAMERA MOVES CLOSER

as Taro turns, putting on his glasses and looking out of
the window.

                    TARO
                  (continuing)
          If they were bundles of hay
          or stalks of bananas - any-
          thing negotiable - but humans!
          Who wants human beings!

He turns toward CAMERA as the door opens o.s.

124   MED. CLOSE - FAVORING VIET

He puts down his satchel, and takes out his pipe. The
stenographer leaves the room through a second door.

                    VIET
          Hello, Taro...

                    TARO
                  (getting up)
          Come in, Doctor.

                    VIET
          Am I interrupting important
          affairs of state?

                    TARO
          No. Come right in and make
          yourself comfortable.

125   MED. CLOSE TWO SHOT - VIET AND TARO

Viet sits down with a sigh and dries his forehead.

                    VIET
          Have you heard about that
          big cat that's supposed to
          be around?

                    TARO
          Of course. Some say it's a
          puma -- some say it's a giant
          ape - some - it's the succarath!

                    VIET
          The succarath? What's that?
          That's a new kind of animal
          to me!

                              (CONTINUED)

125   CONTINUED:

                         TARO
                    (lightly)
          It's a demon that feeds upon
          living animals, and tears them
          up with his claws. Sometimes
          it also attacks human beings!

                         VIET
          It hasn't so far, I hope!

                         TARO
          Not yet., But I'm sure it will.

                         VIET
                    (shocked)
          You are SURE?

                         TARO
          Somebody will use that talk
          to kill somebody he wants to
          kill - and then blame it on
          the succarath.
                    (he shrugs)
          It happened before!

126   MED. CLOSE OTHER ANGLE

        As Viet, pipe in hand, looks speculatively at Taro, who
        picks up a file, opens it, looking at the papers.

                         TARO
          I closed the Klaas Van Gelder
          case officially -
                    (he reads)
          death due to suffocation due
          to snake poison.
                    (he closes the
                     file and puts
                     it aside)
          That's your report, Doctor.
          It isn't my opinion. But my
          opinion in this case, doesn't
          carry much weight!

                         VIET
                    (chuckles)
          Well - you're only the police
          official - who would be in-
          terested in YOUR opinion!

127   MED. FULL DOLLY SHOT

        Taro gets up and walks up and down in the room, finally

                                        (CONTINUED)

127   CONTINUED:

stepping over to the window, looking down into the street
below (o.s.). He now closes the window and the street
noise is subdued.

                    TARO
          I was born in this little
          town, Doctor.

                    VIET
          I know.

                    TARO
          I have many law books in my
          office as you can see. But
          sometimes those books are no
          good at all - in this part of
          the country!

128   MED. CLOSE - FAVORING VIET

                    VIET
          Sometimes they don't help
          much either in the part of
          the world where I come from.

Taro stops in front of Viet, playing with his glasses he
now puts on.

                    TARO
          I often regret that I went
          to universities, made my
          Ph.D. -- studied law...I
          only became confused.

                    VIET
          You never gave me that im-
          pression, Taro.

Taro walks back to his desk and sits down as CAMERA MOVES
CLOSER on him.

                    TARO
          But how can I help being
          confused? My native mind
          is filled with so-called
          superstitions - and my legal
          mind has to rely on knowledge
          put down in books by people
          without emotion.

                              (CONTINUED)

50

128   CONTINUED:

                    VIET
          You have to suppress your
          emotions and follow the
          books - this is the first
          duty of anybody who has to
          be a judge!

                    TARO
          True. But only our logic
          makes mistakes, our emotions
          never.

He looks at a paper in front of him, picks it up, puts
it down again.

                    VIET
          Justice must detach itself
          from emotion!

                    TARO
          I know - but I also know that
          Barney Chavez murdered Klaas
          van Gelder. I know it -
          emotionally. I ought to ar-
          rest that man and charge him
          with murder...but...

He shrugs, gets up again, walks over to the window and
looks out.

129   MED. SHOT - FAVORING VIET

Viet looks thoughtful and worried.

                    VIET
          But what, Taro?

Taro turns to him.

                    TARO
          I haven't got a tight enough
          case to have him convicted
          by human law...But I know
          he won't escape punishment...
                    (he smiles at
                    Viet, apolo-
                    getically)
          The succarath will get him!

Viet gets up, and shakes his head.

                              (CONTINUED)

129   CONTINUED:

> VIET
> The jungle demon? Taro -
> you're joking. You don't
> mean it!

Taro steps closer to Viet and looks at him, thoughtful,
unsmiling.

> TARO
> Barney Chavez will be brought
> to justice. The jungle will
> see to it!

> VIET
> (dumbfounded)
> The longer I live here, the
> less I understand you people.

> TARO
> We cannot fight the jungle -
> we can only keep its powers
> in chains - for a while...
> sooner or later Barney Chavez'
> guilt will break through the
> chains of his mind...and punish
> him. I can wait!

Viet shrugs, he gives up understanding Taro. He sighs and
pockets his pipe.

> VIET
> I give up! A policeman who
> waits for the accused to break
> down by the weight of his own
> guilt - it doesn't seem to be
> a very efficient way of deal-
> ing with justice!

He turns, taking his satchel to leave.

> VIET
> Thanks for the lecture on
> ghoolies and ghosties!

The telephone rings. Taro picks it up. He puts his hand
over the mouth piece.

> TARO
> All right -- drop in again,
> Doctor.
> (into the phone)
> Hello? This is Commissioner
> Taro speaking...

130   MED.CLOSE

at the door. The doctor is just leaving when Taro beckons
him to wait. The doctor closes the door again.

                    TARO
                 (continuing)
          Yes. Mr. Van Heussen?

131   MED. CLOSE -- FAVORING TARO

He sits down, playing with his glasses, then putting them
on again. He beckons Viet to sit down.

                    TARO
                 (with a grin)
          Where?   At your plantation?
          Three people have seen it?
          I bet you, Mr. Van Heussen,
          in a few days a hundred people
          will have met it somewhere...
          and then the stampede will be
          on! It killed a cow? That's
          serious - if it starts kill-
          ing. Of course I will be
          over at your place as soon
          as possible...Good day, sir.

He hangs up, and sighs humorously.

                    VIET
          What is this all about?

                    TARO
          Rubber tappers at Van Heussen's
          plantation have seen the succar-
          ath!

                    VIET
          They have?

                    TARO
          Yes. I told you somebody will
          see it sooner or later - and
          here it is, like a jack-in-
          the box. But the case is
          rather grim: it has killed al-
          ready...an animal this time -
          next time it might be a human!

                    VIET
          What does it look like, that
          mystical animal?

                              (CONTINUED)

131   CONTINUED:

                              TARO
                    It takes various shapes.
                    Last time it had the head of
                    a woman, the forelegs of a
                    tiger, the hind legs of a
                    wolf, and a voice like a
                    broken trumpet!

                              VIET
                    I wouldn't miss having a look
                    at it for anything in the
                    world!

                              TARO
                           (seriously)
                    It will enlarge your entomo-
                    logical knowledge and besides,
                    we might need a medical man
                    like you around.

        Viet nods as Taro rings a bell.

132   CAMERA FACING DOOR IN MED. CLOSE

        as the secretary enters. Taro passes her going to the door.

                              TARO
                           (continuing)
                    Watch the telephone, Miss
                    Cypriano. And in case of an
                    emergency you'll find me at
                    the Van Heussen plantation.

        As he and Viet leave the door,

                                        DISSOLVE TO:

133   INT. BARNEY'S BEDROOM AT THE PLANTATION - MED. CLOSE

        The door leading into the garden flies open, and the cur-
        tains billow.

134   DOLLIE SHOT

        The CAMERA is the gorilla. Care should be taken that
        Barney sees him as an animal, but nobody else. Barney would
        look at himself in any mirror, believing he is the ape.
        Anything and any part of his body within his vision is part
        of the GORILLA. But when other people look at him, the
        picture would change into that of Barney.

                                        (CONTINUED)

134   CONTINUED:

CAMERA DOLLIES INTO BARNEY'S BEDROOM THROUGH THE OPEN DOOR.
for a moment it stops, as though it were listening, then
it turns and faces the mirror: the picture shows a large
gorilla. He now lifts his hand and smashes the mirror.
At once the picture disappears and CAMERA MOVES ON.

DISSOLVE TO:

135   INT.LIVING ROOM

CAMERA MOVES ON, and the tapping of the gorilla's large
feet is HEARD, as he slowly walks on, now stopping, then
walking on.

DISSOLVE TO:

136   INT. DINA'S BEDROOM

CAMERA FOCUSES on the door, leading into the garden and the
bed. Dina lies on the bed, dressed in riding outfit. Lying on her tummy, her arms outstretched, her hair spread
over the white covers. The door opens slowly. Dina does
not hear it -- she is fast asleep. The mirror above the
dressing table repeats the picture.

137   REVERSE SHOT (CAMERA IS THE GORILLA)

Room as seen from the gorilla's point. For a moment the
ape's long arm enters the shot in close, then CAMERA TRAVELS
on, slowly approaching the bed. As the gorilla comes within the vision on the mirror, the gorilla is seen, as he
looks at himself, his long arms dangling, he approaches
the bed.

138   CLOSE SHOT

on Dina as she lies on the bed. The gorilla's hands enter
the shot. Dina sighs and turns on her back. The gorilla's
hands disappear out of shot.

His shuffling feet are HEARD. Dina opens her eyes. CAMERA
PULLS BACK as she sits up. For a moment she covers her
face. Then she listens. The shuffling of feet is HEARD.
Dina jumps up.

                            DINA
                Hello - who's there?

For a moment it is quiet then the feet shuffle on.

139   INT. LIVING ROOM - LONG - MED. CLOSE DOLLY SHOT ON DINA

as Dina appears in the large room. She waits and listens,
frightened by the ominous quiet. Then as she walks on,
toward the centre of the room she pauses at the Chinese
screen, which hides part of the dining room area.

                              DINA
                 Al Long!

CAMERA MOVES CLOSER: she listens, suddenly behind her the
hairy hands of the ape enter the shot, but as they almost
touch her, Dina walks out of shot, while CAMERA PULLS BACK.
The hands disappear.

CAMERA PANS as Dina quickly runs to the gun rack which is
hidden in a wall closet. She opens it and takes out a
thirty-thirty gun.

CAMERA CLOSER as she breaks the gun open and inserts a magazine. She cocks the gun and looks around:

140   LONG - AS SEEN FROM HER ANGLE

The door to the garden is open and the cries of the animals
are HEARD loudly, frightened, and then the deep angry voice
of the gorilla.

141   DOLLY SHOT - ON DINA

as she lifts the gun and shoots toward the door, into the
garden, then she reloads the gun and shoots again, in
mounting panic. She turns as a thunderous noise is HEARD
at the entrance door.

142   CLOSE

the door leading into the living room from outside. It
bursts open.

143   CLOSE

Dina, gun in hand, ready to shoot stares terrified toward
the door. She lifts the gun.

144.   CLOSE the door where Taro and Viet enter. They stop,
startled seeing Dina and the gun pointed at them.

                              VIET
                 Do you always shoot your guests?

                                        (CONTINUED)

144   CONTINUED:

Dina runs into the shot. Taro takes the gun from her,
while she clings to Viet.

                  DINA
          I'm so glad you came...

She takes him by the arm and leads him toward CAMERA.

145   INT. LIVING ROOM

near low tea table. Dina and Viet enter the shot. Taro
puts down the guns.

                  VIET
              (kindly)
          What's the matter, Dina?

                  DINA
          I'm scared...

                  VIET
          What about?

He holds her at arm length and looks at her.

                  DINA
          I don't know...Somebody was
          here...

                  VIET
          Who?

                  DINA
              (desperate)

          I don't know - I don't know...

She suddenly hides her face.

                  VIET
          What did you shoot at?

                  DINA
          I don't know...

                  VIET
          Your nerves are slightly on
          edge -- it's the coming rain.

CAMERA PANS as Viet takes her by the hand and makes her sit
down. He looks at her with sympathy. Taro sits down too.

              (CONTINUED)

145   CONTINUED:

                         TARO
               Where is Mr. Chavez?

Dina takes the hands off her face and looks at him, controlling herself.

                         DINA
               I haven't seen him since last
               night.

                         VIET
               Where is he?

Dina shakes her head; she is lost and unhappy.

                         DINA
               Out in the jungle...

                         VIET
                    (disbelieving)
               The jungle?

                         DINA
               Yes.

                         VIET
               It doesn't make sense to me.
               What is he doing in the jungle?

                         TARO
                    (sipping his tea)
               Hunting!

                         DINA
               Hunting? He didn't take a
               gun along!

                         TARO
               He doesn't need to.
                    (he turns to
                    Dina)
          -    We just came by to warn him
               ...the rubber tappers have
               put up traps...

                         DINA
               Traps? What for?

                         TARO
               There is a wild animal around.

                              (CONTINUED)

145   CONTINUED:

> VIET
> It has killed quite a number
> of cattle.

> DINA
> (worried)
> What kind of animal is it?

> TARO
> Not an ordinary one...It -
> walks on his hind legs and
> is red in color...Don't for-
> get to tell your husband to
> be careful of traps - out in
> the jungle!

> VIET
> (upset)
> Come, come, Taro, don't con-
> fuse Dina. I know you'll end
> up saying Barney is the jungle
> demon.

Taro smiles mysteriously, and shrugs his shoulders.

> TARO
> The jungle is only a symbol.

He takes a long thin cigar from his pocket and lights it.

> DINA
> What are you talking about?
> (to Viet)
> Barney's still got a fever.
> That's why he doesn't want to
> stay in the house.

> VIET
> You better take him away from
> here!

> TARO
> (with a curious,
> knowing smile)
> And if he doesn't want to leave?

> DINA
> Of course he will, when I ask
> him!

She gets up, mixed up and uncertain.. Taro gets up.

> TARO
> The next time he leaves for
> the jungle, why don't you go
> with him?

> DINA
> I will.

146   MED. FULL

Taro walks over to his gun and picks it up.

                        TARO
            Come on Doctor. We have to
            leave before night fall.

Viet rises too.

                        VIET
            Yes. We better go. Sorry,
            Dina, I can't do much about
            Barney. It's up to him to
            take care of himself.

CAMERA DOLLIES with Dina, as Viet and Taro walk to the
door.

                        TARO
            When you leave for the
            jungle - don't forget to
            take your gun, Mrs. Chavez.
            Good day.

                        VIET
            Goodbye, Dina...

                        DINA
            Come back soon.

                        VIET
            You know I will.

Dina watches the men go out. Then CAMERA DOLLIES with
her as she walks to the wall, opens a tall closet, and
picks up a slender but powerful rifle, which stands on
the rack.

                                    DISSOLVE TO:

147   EXT. JUNGLE - CLOSE ON POOL OF WATER (Shot through oiled
        glass)

The gorilla's face is seen in the water. It looks ferocious
and terrifying. His arms now enter the shot and disturb
the surface of the water in a

                                    DISSOLVE:

148   A LEOPARD SNARLING (as seen through the gorilla's eyes)

                                    DISSOLVE TO:

149   MED. CLOSE

       seen through Barney, the animal's eyes; a strange creature
       is sitting on a giant leaf. It is the blowup shape of an
       insect, frightening looking.

                                                    DISSOLVE TO:

150   CLOSE

       A giant tadpole toweringly fills the screen.

151   CAMERA MOVES ON again to stop in CLOSE - at the terrifying
       face of a toad.

152   The following shots depend on the material that can be
thru   produced; tiny animals blown up to giant size, revealing
156   their frightening shapes.

157   CAMERA TRAVELS ON

       in boomshot, up into a tree.

158   CUT IN different SHOTS of animals scurrying away. The
thru   different animal voices change into echolike sounds,
161   hollow, as if not a human ear but that of a strange crea-
       ture was listening to them. The VOICE OF THE GORILLA is
       HEARD.
                                                    DISSOLVE TO:

162   MED. FULL - (STOCK)

       Other part of the jungle, where a leopard roars and dis-
       appears in flight.

163   MED. CLOSE - JUNGLE

       The bushes in f.g. move, then Dina appears, gun in hand.
       She looks around, then walks on.

                         DINA
                  Barney - Barney...

                         ECHO
                  Barney - Barney...

164   MED. CLOSE - (STOCK)

       A group of tiny monkeys scurry away.

165   MED. CLOSE

on Dina as she makes her way through the jungle. Again
she calls out:

                        DINA
             Barney - Barney...

                        ECHO
             Barney - Barney...
                   (then overlapping)
             Dina - Dina...

Dina stops in her tracks, and listens and calls:

                        DINA
             Barney...

                        ECHO
             Barney - Dina, Dina...

                        DINA
        Where are you?

                        ECHO
        Where are you - here - here...

Dina walks out of shot toward the sound.

166   MED. FULL

Other part of the jungle, as Dina enters the shot, gun in
hand. She now shoots it off. The sound reverberates.

                        BARNEY'S VOICE
                   (closer now)
             Dina - Dina...
                   (echo)
             Dina - Dina...

                        DINA
        Where are you?

She looks toward a group of small trees.

                        BARNEY'S VOICE
             In here - but I'm caught in
             a trap!

Dina walks toward the voice.

167   MED. FULL

near a tree trunk. Barney lies on the ground, his legs

                                        (CONTINUED)

167   CONTINUED:

caught in a steel trap. His face is contorted with pain;
he tries to free himself. He is wearing high boots, which
have saved him from having his leg crushed. Near the trap
is a young goat, fastened to the tree trunk. Dina steps
into the shot and rushes up to Barney.

                        BARNEY
                I can't open it!

He raises on his knees.

                        DINA
                    (kneeling near
                      him)
                Your leg...

                        BARNEY
                Give me that gun...

He takes the gun from her, and pushes the barrel between
the teeth of the trap, prying it open. Dina looks helpless at him.

                        BARNEY
                    (wildly)
                Don't stand around! Push a
                rock between the teeth of
                the trap...

Dina picks up a flat rock, and as Barney, his face con-
torting pulls the trap apart, Dina pushes the rock between the sharp teeth. Barney extracts his leg, and the
trap snaps shut again.

168   MED. CLOSE

on Barney as he stands up, on one leg. Blood oozes through
his broken boot.

                        DINA
                Stay here - I'll get help!

                        BARNEY
                No!

His voice is so wild, that Dina stops in her tracks.

                        DINA
                You're hurt - let me cut off
                the boot!

                        BARNEY
                No - let me hold on to you...

                                        (CONTINUED)

168   CONTINUED:

She steps over to him as he puts his arm over her shoulder
and uses the gun as a walking stick. His face shows his
suffering.

                    DINA
          Lean on me - don't be afraid
          ...

169   MED. CLOSE

CAMERA behind the young goat - Dina and Barney in b.g.
The goat, frightened, bleats in fear and tries to free
itself.

                    BARNEY
          Let's get out of here...

While the animal strains miserably, Dina and Barney walk
OUT OF SHOT.

                                        DISSOLVE TO:

170   INT. BARNEY'S BEDROOM - SAME EVENING - CLOSE TO MED. CLOSE

Barney is sitting in a chair, his leg being bandaged by
Al Long who is kneeling in front of him. The boot, cut
off, lies on the floor. Barney's head is bent back, his
face betraying his exhaustion.

Al Long leaves the room. Barney slowly, painfully gets
up. He stands on his bad leg, trying it. CAMERA MOVES
INTO CLOSE as he stares at his hands, in disgust and fear.
Then CAMERA DOLLIES WITH HIM as he looks into the mirror.

171   CLOSE MIRROR SHOT

on Barney. His face is lined and drawn. Now Barney sees
Dina enter, and turns around.

172   MED. CLOSE

as Dina enters. She has changed into a dress - and looks
very feminine, and lovely. With brisk steps she walks
over to Barney.

                    DINA
          You mustn't get up!

Barney looks at his leg and shakes his head.

                                        (CONTINUED)

172   CONTINUED:

                    BARNEY
          I'm all right. That old
          woman really knows her stuff -
          the bleeding stopped right
          away after she put some of
          her jungle medicine on the
          wound. I have no pains...
          she's much better than your
          doctor! The quack!

But he sits down and pulls her closer.

                    DINA
          I better call Viet - the
          quack! Just to make sure!

                    BARNEY
          I don't want to see him. I
          told you nobody should know!

                    DINA
          Why not? It wasn't your
          fault - anybody could've
          stepped into the trap!

CAMERA MOVES CLOSER as Barney looks at her, silently.

                    BARNEY
          No - anybody but me would
          have known! But --
                    (he stops, think-
                    ing hard)

                    DINA
                    (mystified)
          What do you mean?

                    BARNEY
          I heard that goat - it...
          called me!

                    DINA
          It called you?

                    BARNEY
          Yes - it wasn't exactly a
          goat's voice...it was...
                    (he thinks hard)
          ...it was something I had
          never heard before...some-
          thing -- beautiful -- com-
          pelling...I just couldn't
          resist going there...I didn't
          seem to walk - I flew - I

172   CONTINUED - (2)

> BARNEY (Cont'd)
> think I did...then I saw it
> - and the next thing I knew
> was that trap closing
> around my leg!

Dina watches him with growing apprehension.

> DINA
> Let's go away from here!

> BARNEY
> (shaking himself
> free from his
> thoughts)
> Yes. Let's get rid of the
> plantation - and never come
> back...

He embraces her and she hides her head on his shoulder.

> DINA
> Van Heussen will buy it - he
> always wanted it...

> BARNEY
> Yes. And we will make the
> price so attractive for him
> that he cannot refuse...

> DINA
> Where are we going to go?

> BARNEY
> Home - where I came from --
> New Mexico!

> DINA
> Anywhere, Barney...I always
> hated the jungle. I never
> was really happy here!

She gets up and looks around apprehensively, disturbed.

> DINA
> (continuing)
> This was Klaas' bedroom...
> this furniture...he sat on
> this chair - slept in this
> bed...everything reminds me
> of him...I hate him more now
> since he is dead...I don't
> think he has left us!

(CONTINUED)

172   CONTINUED - (3):

Barney gets up and takes her in his arms while the CAMERA
MOVES CLOSER.

                    BARNEY
          I wanted to leave right
          away after Klaas' death -
          but I didn't dare...the
          people...

                    DINA
                 (interrupting
                  him)
          I don't care about the
          people - what they talk or
          think about us...The past
          can't hurt us anymore as
          soon as we are out of here!
          Nothing can hurt me if you
          don't leave me!

                    BARNEY
          Nothing can ever part us, -
          nothing...

CAMERA MOVES INTO CLOSE on his face as he looks down at
her, disturbed, and uneasy.

                              DISSOLVE TO:

173   INT. AL LONG'S ROOM - DAY

CLOSE ON the PE DE GUINE PLANT - only four leaves are
left. A hand comes into the picture, picking one of
leaves. Then as CAMERA PULLS BACK into MED. CLOSE,
showing Al Long and the plant, the thin stem is almost
depleted.

                              DISSOLVE TO:

174   INT. LIVING ROOM OF PLANTATION - AFTERNOON - CLOSE

on Barney, as CAMERA DOLLIES into MED. FULL, revealing the whole room. Barney is standing near Van Heussen. He looks tired, nervous, his face is lined, as though he had not slept. Van Heussen is happy, sparkling with anticipation.

> VAN HEUSSEN
> I say, it was lucky that Klaas van Gelder died!

> BARNEY
> Lucky? For whom?

> VAN HEUSSEN
> For you - for me...I never thought I'd be able to move into this proud mansion...The van Gelder's were rather patrician...a little snobbish - you know. They'd never have put up this place for sale!

> BARNEY
> I didn't know them that well. I only worked for them.

> VAN HEUSSEN
> After Klaas married Dina he seemed to loosen up a bit - but then he became even more - like his father, Gontram van Gelder.

> BARNEY
> I know what you mean - stubborn, righteous, domineering - He could do no wrong!
>> (he looks around
>> as if looking
>> for the departed
>> family)
> Well - they don't exist anymore...not one of them!

> VAN HEUSSEN
>> (smugly)
> And the Van Heussen's will take over -

Dr. Viet enters the shot, as usual a drink in his hand.

> VIET
> Sorry to see you leave, Barney.

                           (CONTINUED)

174   CONTINUED:

Barney turns slowly, measuringly to him.

> BARNEY
> I haven't left yet, Doctor.
> I'm still around!

> VIET
> Where are you going to live?
> I hear Dina is mad about Rio.

> BARNEY
> I haven't made up my mind yet.

> VAN HEUSSEN
> Don't question him, Doctor -
> or he might reconsider sell-
> ing the plantation!

> VIET
> (with a laugh)
> I don't think so - the papers
> are already drawn. Taro will
> be here any moment to notarize
> them!

> VAN HEUSSEN
> You can rely on Taro - he's
> around when you need him - or
> when he thinks he should be
> around!

> VIET
> He has an intuitive sense for
> people - it's quite uncanny...

> BARNEY
> There he is - just talk about
> him...and he'll pop up! It
> never fails!

175   MED. LONG SHOT

Toward door, where Taro and his colored secretary enter.
Al Long stands, as usual, near the door - and as it is
a hot day, she passes Taro a long drink from the tray
that stands on a small table beside her. Taro walks
toward Barney and Viet, while the secretary steps over
to the refectory table. For a moment Taro stops to talk
to a servant.

176   MED. CLOSE

on Barney, Van Heussen and Viet. Barney turns his back

(CONTINUED)

176   CONTINUED:

on Taro as he approaches.

                    BARNEY
          How can you stand the jungle
          this long, Doctor?

                    VIET
          Not at all! But what can I
          do but like it? I signed a
          government contract for five
          years. That time will be
          over soon.

He looks sharply at Barney and turns him toward the light.

                    VIET
                 (continues)
          Say - let me have a look at
          you...

                    BARNEY
          What's the matter?...

                    VIET
          Your eyes - the pupils - they
          worry me!

Barney turns brusquely.

                    BARNEY
          There's nothing wrong with me...

As he turns, Taro has entered the shot.

                    BARNEY
                 (continues)
          Oh - here he is, the law - how
          are you, Commissioner?

                    TARO
          Thank you, very fine.

He dries his forehead.

                    TARO
                 (continues)
          But I hope the rains will
          start soon!

                    VAN HEUSSEN
          Yes, it's unbearably hot! I
          think I'll have this place
          air conditioned as soon as I
          take over!

                                   (CONTINUED)

176   CONTINUED - (2):

> TARO
> I have got the papers all
> drawn up for sale.
>   (he smiles at
>   Barney but his
>   eyes are observ-
>   ing, and sharp)
> The last time you put your
> name on a document, I too,
> was instrumental in a way...

> BARNEY
> I hope I don't have to sign
> any more papers you've drawn,
> Taro.

> TARO
>   (smiling)
> The final papers are never
> signed by us...

Viet laughs loudly.

> VIET
> They are signed by me! I am
> the coroner!

Taro slowly turns to him.

> TARO
> Exactly! That's what I meant!

                              DISSOLVE TO:

177   INT. DINA'S ROOM - SAME AFTERNOON - MED. CLOSE PAN SHOT

Dina is sorting out her clothes. The door to the closet
is open, its contents spilled over the bed. Dina looks
happy as she goes through her things. Al Long is helping
her, taking the clothes out of moth-proof bags.

> DINA
>   (throwing a dress
>   on a heap in the
>   corner)
> All that stuff in the corner
> is for you, Al Long.

> AL LONG
> Thank you, Madame - but I
> have so many things left from
> my former mistress - I never
> wore them.

                              (CONTINUED)

177   CONTINUED:

                              DINA
                    Then give them away -

She looks up as Viet enters.

178   MED. CLOSE ON VIET

        as he comes closer. He looks uneasy and unhappy at the
        heap of dresses.

                              VIET
                    Now I'm sure you're going to
                    leave! I didn't quite believe
                    it before...

                              DINA
                    You didn't!

                              VIET
                    No - words often don't mean
                    much...but when you see it...

                              DINA
                    You'll come to visit us in
                    Rio. Didn't you tell me you're
                    going to quit the government
                    services?

                              VIET
                    Yes, in a few months...

        He sits down, watching her sorting out clothes. Dina
        holds up a white dress, and then quickly throws it on
        the heap in the corner.

                              DINA
                            (hastily)
                    That's for you, Al Long.

                              VIET
                    Wasn't that the dress you wore
                    when you got married to Klaas?

                              DINA
                    Yes, that's why I want to get
                    rid of it...the past is dead -
                    Viet - stone dead! I don't
                    even want to be reminded of it!

        She looks at him for confirmation. But Viet only stares
        at her thoughtfully.

                                        (CONTINUED)

178   CONTINUED:

                         VIET
                    I'd like to talk to you --
                    alone for a minute.

He looks at Al Long.

                         AL LONG
                    May I take those clothes out
                    of your room, Madame?

                         DINA
                    Please.

Al Long takes an armful of clothes and walks to the door.

                         DINA
                         (continuing)
                    I will call you when I need
                    you.

                         AL LONG
                    Yes, Madame!

She leaves. Viet waits until the door is closed.

179   MED. CLOSE - OTHER ANGLE

as Viet walks over to Dina who sits down on the bed, tired
and weary.

                         DINA
                    What's the matter with you?
                    You look serious!

                         VIET
                    I'm worried!

                         DINA
                    About me?

                         VIET
                    About Barney! He doesn't
                    look healthy to me.

                         DINA
                    It's the fever - he never
                    really got over it. He'll
                    be all right as soon as we
                    get out of here.

                                        (CONTINUED)

179   CONTINUED:

                    VIET
          Dina tell me --
                    (he hesitates)
          Does he take drugs?

                    DINA
          Quinine, that's all.

Viet shakes his head, he picks up a perfume bottle, reads
its label, puts it down, picks up another one, smells at it,
to put it down again.

                    VIET
          I watched him today...his
          eyes...
                    DINA
                    (alarmed)
          What is the matter with his
          eyes?

                    VIET
          Dilation of the pupil - cer-
          tain drugs cause optical
          atrophy, sympathetic irrita-
          tion - or weakness of the
          ocular nerve...

Dina shakes her head confused.

                    DINA
          I don't understand a word!

                    VIET
          He looks like a man that's
          been poisoned!

Dina is startled.

                    DINA
          Poisoned!

                    VIET
          I'm pretty sure. I'd like
          to examine him.

                    DINA
          Examine him? He wouldn't
          like it.

                    VIET
          I know...it's almost impos-
          sible to make a sure diagnosis
          of a living person without a
          chemical examination...but the
          symptoms...

                              (CONTINUED)

179   CONTINUED - (2):

Viet shrugs again. Dina thoroughly frightened, walks to
the door.

                        DINA
              Wait here! I'll get him!

Viet nods, and Dina leaves.

180   MED. CLOSE

on Viet alone. He walks to the door which leads into the
garden and opens it. The sun is sinking. The jungle
noise comes in at full force.

181   CLOSE ON VIET

as he turns, and picking up one of Dina's dresses caresses
it for a moment then throws it back on the bed.

                                   DISSOLVE TO:

182   INT. LIVING ROOM - MED. FULL - EVENING

The lights are on. Dina enters the room in b.g. Taro is
sitting at the table - at the same spot where he was during the marriage ceremony. The secretary puts some documents in front of him.

183   CLOSER SHOT

On Van Heussen, standing beside Taro, reading a document.
He now puts it on the table.

                        VAN HEUSSEN
              Here I am, with a hundred
              thousand in cash in my
              pocket, looking for a man to
              pick it up!

He sees Dina walking toward table.

                        TARO
              There's Mrs. Chavez - now
              we'll get some action!

Dina enters the shot.

                        DINA
              Have you seen Barney?

                                   (CONTINUED)

183   CONTINUED:

                    VAN HEUSSEN
                    (surprised)
           Have WE seen Barney? We
           thought he was with you!

CAMERA QUICKLY PULLS BACK as Taro gets up.

                    DINA
           No - the last time I saw him
           he was talking to you!

She looks around, then calls:

                    DINA
                    (continuing)
           Al Long!

184   MED. CLOSE DOLLY

on Al Long as she walks over to Dina.

                    VAN HEUSSEN
           Where is Mr. Chavez?

                    AL LONG
                    (quietly)
           He went away.

                    VAN HEUSSEN
           Went away!

                    AL LONG
           I saw him crossing the gar-
           den - for the jungle.

                    VAN HEUSSEN
                    (nervously)
           Well, it's almost dark! He
           won't be long - he CAN'T be
           long!

185   MED. CLOSE

Door leading into the garden from living room. Dina
enters the shot, and pushes open the door. She stops in
the doorway, and calls out:

                    DINA
           Barney...Barney...

The noise of the animals increases at once as if in reply.

                                        (CONTINUED)

185   CONTINUED:

                              ECHO
                    Barney - Barney...

She turns, listening, as CAMERA PULLS INTO CLOSE at her
unhappy face.

                                        SLOW DISSOLVE TO:

186   MED. FULL - LIVING ROOM - NIGHT

The lamps are lighted, and the same people are sitting
around. Van Heussen is playing cards with Taro at the
table. Dina is standing near the door leading into the
garden. Viet walks up to her. CAMERA DOLLIES WITH VIET
as he stops in MED. CLOSE.

                              VIET
                    Dina!

She turns slowly. Her eyes are dry and unhappy.

                              DINA
                    He won't be back tonight.
                    You better tell Van Heussen
                    it's no use waiting.

                              VIET
                    You must make it possible for
                    me to see him -
                         (he shakes his
                          head, worried)
                    What is he doing in the jungle
                    at night? It's suicide!

                              DINA
                    It's suicide for me too -
                    waiting for him!

187   MED. CLOSE

on Van Heussen, as he throws down the cards and gets up.

                              VAN HEUSSEN
                    It's silly! I can't concen-
                    trate!
                         (he looks at his
                          wrist watch)
                    Ten o'clock! I think we
                    should send the servants out
                    to find him! Something must've
                    happened to him!

                                        (CONTINUED)

187   CONTINUED:

Dina enters the shot.

                    DINA
        No - it's no use. He will be
        back late!

Van Heussen turns to her, controlling his temper.

                    VAN HEUSSEN
        Then you tell him if he wants
        to sell his plantation, he can
        see me at my house! Tell him
        this is no way to behave!
        Running away...without an ex-
        cuse!

                    TARO
        Mrs. Chavez could sign the
        papers. She is the owner.

                    VAN HEUSSEN
        She could?

He looks at her with new hope.

                    DINA
        My husband is the boss in the
        house.

                    VAN HEUSSEN
        I wish my wife could hear that.
        Tell Barney to show up tomorrow,
        or our deal is off!

188   MED. CLOSE - ON TARO

as he puts the papers together, and puts them into his
brief case. Then he studies Dina and looks toward Al
Long, thoughtful, knowingly.

189   MED. CLOSE ON AL LONG

as she stands at the door without an expression on her
quiet native face.

                                    SLOW DISSOLVE TO:

190   EDGE OF JUNGLE AND GARDEN - EARLY MORNING

This is a 'mood' SHOT: slowly the daylight comes up, and
the animal voices die down - the birds voices increase in
strength.

191   CLOSE (STOCK)

a giant gorilla slowly walks back into the undergrowth.

192   Barney stands silently underneath a broad-leaved tree,
almost blending with the background. He now walks forward toward the CAMERA. He looks at his hands and puts
the into his pocket. Then he walks toward CAMERA
blocking it.

DISSOLVE TO:

193   INT. LIVING ROOM - FULL - MORNING

The morning sun falls through the large French doors.
The lights are still on. CAMERA DOLLIES to Dina, who
lies in a large chair, her feet pulled up, as if she had
fallen exhausted asleep. She now wakes up and looks
toward the door leading into the garden.

194   MED. FULL

from her angle. Barney enters the room quiet like an
animal. He closes the door behind him.

195   MED. CLOSE

as Dina gets up and pushes her hair off her forehead.
Barney steps into the picture. His shirt is torn, and
his face smeared with dirt and dust. Dina has waited
silently.

                    BARNEY
                (looking around,
                 his voice hoarse)
        I'm glad they've left.

                    DINA
                (coldly)
        They left the day before yes-
        terday!

                    BARNEY
        I've changed my mind. I'm
        not going to sell the planta-
        tion. I - like it here!

He walks past her to go to his room.

                    DINA
        Barney!

(CONTINUED)

195   CONTINUED:

He stops and turns.

> BARNEY
> It's no use arguing. I've
> made up my mind.

> DINA
> Your mind is sick!

> BARNEY
> I never felt better and
> clear in my head.

> DINA
> I won't stay here.

> BARNEY
> If you want to leave - I won't
> hold you.

Dina walks close to him, CAMERA MOVES CLOSER as she looks
into his eyes, unhappily, searchingly.

> DINA
> Barney. Viet told me - it's
> some poison...

> BARNEY
> Poison?

> DINA
> Yes - you're being poisoned!
> Viet is sure of it!

> BARNEY
> He's lying to you. Don't tell
> me he doesn't. I have my eyes
> open!

> DINA
> But why should he...

> BARNEY
> He's in love with you...

> DINA
> There is nothing between me
> and Viet and you know it.

> BARNEY
> It doesn't matter - I don't
> care! I'm happy. But not
> here.

(CONTINUED)

195   CONTINUED - (2):

He looks around in the room.

                    BARNEY
                  (continues)
            Not in this place! I'm happy
            out there - in the jungle!

196   CAMERA AT THE DOOR

Leading into the garden. As Barney walks toward it, Dina
follows him. He pushes the door open. The jungle noises
are HEARD prominently, and then the high whistling noise
of the Lizard.

                    BARNEY
                  (continuing)
            Listen! Hear it? It's call-
            ing me again!

                    DINA
                  (embracing him
                   in fear)
            Barney - please...

He pushes her away, holding her at arms length.

                    BARNEY
            Why shouldn't I tell you...

He lets go of her and looks at his hands.

                    BARNEY
                  (continuing)
            There, in the jungle - I
            change...my hands...they grow
            ...in size...in strength! My
            eyes! I can see much further
            than I can see now - the small-
            est leaves on the top of the
            highest tree! I can climb the
            trees as if I had wings! I can
            smell a thousand smells - of
            flowers and plants and animals
            ...I'm powerful; the jungle is
            my house! It belongs to me!

                    DINA
                  (desperate)
            Please - listen to me! It
            isn't true - listen, Barney!
            I love you!

                                        (CONTINUED)

196   CONTINUED:

                         BARNEY
               Out there - in the jungle -
               I can hear voices, miles away.
               The animals talk to me - I
               understand what they are say-
               ing. They are afraid of me.
               I am their king!

Dina steps back, her arms limp.

                         DINA
               Yes. You are...

She touches his face, tenderly.

                         DINA
                       (continues)
               Now go to sleep. You are
               tired.

                         BARNEY
               Yes.

                         DINA
               I too am tired. Very tired.
               Please go to sleep.

                         BARNEY
               I will. Until tonight.

She takes his arm and leads him away from the door, while
CAMERA DOLLIES WITH THEM.

                         BARNEY
                       (continues)
               I'll let you see the jungle
               as I see it at night. Then
               you'll know that I am telling
               the truth!

A noise at the door o.s. is seen. Barney wheels around:

197   THE GARDEN DOOR - DAY

AS SEEN from Barney's and Dina's angle. Three men are
looking through the glass door into the room. They stand
motionless, their faces pressed against the glass. One
of them is Ferrero, the foreman, the other two rubber
tappers. Dina walks to the door and opens it.

                         DINA
               Come in.

                                        (CONTINUED)

197   CONTINUED:

The three men enter shyly, slowly, frightened. Barney
walks INTO THE SHOT as CAMERA MOVES CLOSER.

                    BARNEY
            Why didn't you use the front
            door?

                    FERRERO
            We saw you leaving the jungle
            - and we followed you, Mr.
            Chavez.

                    BARNEY
            What do you want?

                    FERRERO
            We can not go on working for
            you.

                    BARNEY
            You can't?

Dina walks out of the shot, unnoticed by the men.

                    FERRERO
            No - nobody wants to work
            around here anymore. It isn't
            safe.

                    BARNEY
            It isn't safe?

                    FERRERO
            There's an animal around - we
            are afraid of. We almost
            caught it in a trap - but it
            got away. Now none of my men
            will go to the jungle anymore
            - as long as it is alive!

                    BARNEY
                (with a smirk)
            What does it look like, that
            - animal?

Ferrero looks at his men who stand silently.

                    FERRERO
                (hesitatingly)
            We - don't know. We just came
            to get our pay. I think we're
            going to move away from here,
            to find work somewhere else.

                                    (CONTINUED)

197   CONTINUED - (2):

                        BARNEY
             Sure, you can have your money.
             I won't hold you.

198   MED. CLOSE - OTHER ANGLE

        Barney walks to a desk and opens it, taking out a bundle
        of money. Ferrero steps closer.

                        FERRERO
             You own us two weeks pay --
             that's all.

                        BARNEY
             Okay...

        He counts off some bills, and passes them to Ferrero.
        The man takes them hesitatingly.

                        FERRERO
             Your hands...

        CAMERA MOVES INTO CLOSE AT BARNEY'S HANDS.

                        BARNEY (O.S.)
             What's the matter with them?

                        FERRERO'S VOICE
             It looks like - dry blood!

                                              DISSOLVE TO:

199   INT. VIET'S OFFICE - DAY - CLOSE

        on a hand passing a glass with a white foaming liquid - it
        is a man's hand - and as CAMERA PULLS BACK, Viet and Dina
        COME INTO THE SHOT. Viet's office is simple; the usual
        enameled white furniture of a doctor's equipment is stand-
        ing about. A desk - two chairs. The window shutters
        are closed, and the strong sun falls through the shutter
        opening into the room. Viet is passing the glass to Dina.

                        VIET
             Drink it down!

                        DINA
             What is it?

                        VIET
             Take it, it will calm you.

                                              (CONTINUED)

199   CONTINUED:

Dina is dressed in tropical white, wearing a tropical
helmet; she takes the drink and empties the glass. Her
face shows her disgust. Then she takes off her helmet,
and shakes her hair. Viet walks up and down, in thought,
then he stops in front of her.

                    VIET
                (continuing)
            It's a pretty grim picture
            you're painting, Dina.

Distressed he looks at her, as CAMERA MOVES CLOSER,
favoring Dina.

                    DINA
            I would be frightened if I
            weren't so unhappy!

                    VIET
            He thinks he is a jungle
            animal - what kind of animal?

                    DINA
                (tortured)
            He said he can - kill. The
            jungle is afraid of him.
            Viet - I've known Barney for
            more than a year! He always
            was sane!

                    VIET
            No. He wasn't.

                    DINA
            To me he behaved rationally
            until the last few days.

                    VIET
            You know that's not true.

He pulls a chair close to her and sits down, taking her
hand.

                    VIET
                (continuing)
            You must face the truth, Dina.
            There's no use hiding from it.

                    DINA
            What do you want to say?

                    VIET
            Taro is convinced Barney mur-
            dered Klaas.

                                        (CONTINUED)

85.

199   CONTINUED - (2):

Dina at once pulls her hand away, and leaning back looks
at Viet.

                    DINA
          You, too?

Viet gets up and CAMERA PULLS BACK. He walks to the window, then he turns and looks at her, distressed.

                    VIET
          Yes. I'm certain. He killed
          Klaas - and it was no accident!
          It was premeditated murder.
          Only because you are in love
          with him, you don't want to
          see it!

                    DINA
                 (simply)
          Yes. I am in love with him.

200   MED. CLOSE - OTHER ANGLE

                    VIET
          He has to be put away, you
          know he has! He is danger-
          ous! Dina!

He is searching for words.

                    VIET
                 (continues)
          It's his conscience that
          drives him out of his mind.
          He likes the jungle - be-
          cause thinking himself an
          animal gives him the right
          to kill - animals have no
          conscience - that's his way
          out. He will finally turn
          against you!

                    DINA
          I am not afraid!

                    VIET
          But don't you see - as long
          as you are alive - he will
          be reminded of his crime...

                    DINA
          I told you - I am not afraid!

                              (CONTINUED)

200   CONTINUED:

                       VIET
            I won't let it happen...I
            will see to it...it's my
            duty as a doctor...to get
            him behind bars.

He stops, his face angry, menacing.

                       DINA
            Even if I tell you not to...

                       VIET
            Yes!

There is a pause, then Dina gets up and picks up her helmet. Viet stops her.

                       VIET
               (continues)
            You know I love you...since
            the day Klaas brought you to
            the house. I think of you -
            all the time. You're before
            my eyes...

                       DINA
              (with a thin
               smile)
            Did you tell Klaas?

                       VIET
            He was my friend - but I
            hoped...

He stops, overcome by his emotions.

                       DINA
            May I finish the sentence for
            you? You hoped you would
            have a chance after he died
            ...isn't that...?

He stands, helplessly.

                       VIET
            I gave up when you married
            Barney. I knew what had
            happened - but I had no proof
            - no real proof...

                       DINA
            Or you'd have had Barney
            arrested for murder, wouldn't
            you?

200   CONTINUED - (2):

                         VIET
          If you had helped me...yes!
          But that won't be necessary
          anymore. He is sick -
          mentally deranged. You're
          going to be free very soon...

                         DINA
          You might as well give up
          hope, Viet. I love Barney.

                         VIET
          You will forget him soon!

                         DINA
          My fate - and his, cannot be
          separated. I know he killed
          Klaas...we never talked about
          it. but he knew I was on his
          side when I protected him
          that night...I lied to Taro.
          Barney had not been to my
          room - before Klaas had died.

                         VIET
          You know what you're saying?

                         DINA
          Yes. You might think I have
          no morals, because I don't
          feel badly about Klaas' death
          - I wanted him to die. If
          Barney had not done it, I
          might - one day - I hated
          him, since the day Barney
          came to us.

                         VIET
          Klaas was kind to you!

                         DINA
          I hated even his kindness!

                         VIET
                    (stunned)
          Dina - Barney is irresponsible
          for his actions...If you leave
          him, nobody ever will know...

     Dina walks to the door, and turns.

                                        (CONTINUED)

200   CONTINUED - (3):

                              DINA
                    Don't you understand? I
                    can't live without Barney.
                    We belong together. Nothing
                    will ever part us- not even
                    - that jungle! We are bound
                    together forever through our
                    guilt!

                              VIET
                    Yes. You are. But you know
                    what I have to do...

                              DINA
                    I don't care. Goodbye, Viet.

        She leaves the room.

201   CAMERA MOVES INTO CLOSE

        on Viet, as he stands, helplessly, hopelessly...

                                        DISSOLVE TO:

202   INT. AL LONG'S ROOM - AFTERNOON

        CLOSE ON the Pe de Guine plant. It has only one leaf
        left which now Al Long's hand picks. The stem now is
        bare, as CAMERA PULLS BACK, revealing Al Long.

                                        DISSOLVE TO:

203   INT. LIVING ROOM - EVENING - CLOSE

        on Barney's hands, as he pulls out the bullet from the
        cartridge, which contains the powder, shakes out the
        powder, then puts back the bullet. As his hands take
        a few of the 'doctored' bullets to put them back into
        the magazines, CAMERA PULLS BACK revealing Barney at the
        table, the rifle lies on the table. He now pushes the
        magazine back into the rifle, and as CAMERA PANS, puts
        the rifle back on the rack.

                              BARNEY
                    The servants have run away!

        Dina walks into the shot.

                              DINA
                    They have?

                                        (CONTINUED)

203   CONTINUED:

Her voice is toneless, tired. Barney steps up to her and
looks at her pale face.

                    BARNEY
          The workers have quit - Al
          Long's gone...why don't you
          leave me too?

                    DINA
          I can't.

                    BARNEY
          You better go...

                    DINA
          Why?

                    BARNEY
          You can go wherever you want
          - you got money...you will
          forget me soon!

                    DINA
          That's what Viet told me. I
          can go wherever I want, I am
          free...

She now turns as CAMERA PULLS BACK.

                    BARNEY
          He's right.

                    DINA
          I told him that I belong to
          you. I told him that only
          death can us part.

                    BARNEY
          Death!

He sits down now, looking toward the door leading into the
garden. Dina walks up to him.

                    DINA
          Yes, that's what I told him
          - and what I am telling you!

                    BARNEY
          Death cannot touch me. I
          just started to live - out
          there, in the jungle!

                    DINA
          Barney...

                              (CONTINUED)

203   CONTINUED - (2):

She kneels down, close to him as CAMERA MOVES CLOSER. She
looks at him tensely, her face unmoved.

                    DINA
                 (continues)
          Should you ever be unfaithful
          to me, I'm going to kill you.

                    BARNEY
          You will? I'm flattered.

He laughs.

                    DINA
          Yes. I thought of another
          woman...it never entered my
          mind it could be the jungle.

                    BARNEY
          You don't know the jungle...

                    DINA
          Now I do - and I hate it. I
          hate it more than I could
          ever hate a woman who took
          you away from me.

                    BARNEY
          Well - you can't fight the
          jungle!

                    DINA
                 (soberly)
          That is true. I cannot fight
          the jungle.

Barney gets up, looking down at her.

                    BARNEY
          What else did you tell the
          doctor?

                    DINA
          He knows you killed Klaas.

She gets to her feet and faces him, quietly, determinedly,
to clear her relation to him. Barney watches her with
curiosity.

                    BARNEY
          How smart of him. He has no
          proof.

                              (CONTINUED)

203   CONTINUED - (3):

                         DINA
             I told him I protected you
             that night. I told him I
             lied when I said you had
             been with me!

                         BARNEY
             I see. That's your revenge!
             Now Taro will arrest us both.

                         DINA
                   (determinedly,
                    quietly)
             He won't.

                         BARNEY
             You can go wherever you want.
             I won't hold you back!

                         DINA
             You mean I'm standing in your
             way?

                         BARNEY
             He won't find me in the jungle.

He turns and walks to the door.

204   MED. CLOSE

at the door.

                         DINA
             Take me with you.

                         BARNEY
             To the jungle? You wouldn't
             like it there. You haven't
             got the eyes to see - nor the
             ears to hear what I can hear.
             It wouldn't protect you - that
             jungle. You hate it, that's
             why it hates you.

                         DINA
             You can't stop me from going
             with you.

Barney watches her, trying to read her thoughts.

                         DINA
             I'm coming with you, there is
             no way out!

                                        (CONTINUED)

204   CONTINUED:

                          BARNEY
              No?

                          DINA
              No, there is not.

Barney walks to the door.

                          DINA
                     (continuing)
              I'm coming with you!

Walking over to the rack, she picks up the rifle, breaks
it open, to make sure it is loaded. Then she walks up
to Barney.

205   MED. CLOSE

Barney waits for her, watching her handle the gun. A
faint smile is on his lips.

                          DINA
                     (continuing)
              Don't you take a gun along?

                          BARNEY
              I wouldn't know what to do
              with it.

He turns to go.

                          DINA
              Barney...

As he stops again, waiting, with controlled impatience,
she makes a last appeal.

                          DINA
                     (continuing)
              Don't go - let's stay here...
              don't go tonight. Tomorrow
              we will leave the country and
              never return. Please Barney!

Without a reply he turns and walks away. Dina follows him.

                          DISSOLVE TO:

206   EXT. JUNGLE NIGHT

CAMERA focuses on a clump of trees. The jungle noises are
HEARD distinctly. Steps come closer - then Barney and Dina

                          (CONTINUED)

206   CONTINUED:

walk into shot. Dina is holding the gun. Her jacket is
half open. She is wearing no hat, her hair falling into
her forehead. She listens to the wild cries of the animals.

                    DINA
          Barney!

He stops and turns to her.

                    BARNEY
          Do you like my jungle?

                    DINA
          Let's go back, Barney --
          please...

                    BARNEY
          I will never go back, never...

He walks on, when Dina calls him again.

                    DINA
          Stop - or I'll shoot...

He stops and looks at her, as she stands the gun raised.

                    BARNEY
          Why don't you shoot?

As she stands, helpless, the gun in hand - he laughs.

                    BARNEY
                 (continuing)
          Go on, you can't miss...But
          you can't make me go back.
          We don't belong together...

Dina drops her gun.

                    BARNEY
                 (continuing)
          Goodbye...Dina...

He turns and walks off.

207   MED. FULL

as Barney disappears in the underbrush out of sight.

208   MED. CLOSE

on Dina, as she runs after Barney.

                                        (CONTINUED)

208   CONTINUED:

                                DINA
                    Barney! Barney...

        But he has disappeared.

209   MED. CLOSE

        on Dina as she makes her way through the underbrush. The
        large leaves obscure her vision. She stops and listens,
        in fear.

210   THE TOP OF A TREE - (STOCK)

        The mess of lianas, the eyes of a nightbird shining like
        candles. It now flies away on silent wings.

211   MED. CLOSE

        on Barney in a dense part of the jungle. He stands
        silently, listening. The jungle noises rise as if his
        presence had enraged the animals; the sharp scream of
        birds, the howling of monkeys, the distant cry of pre-
        datory animals. Barney rips open his collar then stares
        at his hands. His face contorts in pain, as he looks at
        them.

212   CLOSER SHOT

        as seen through Barney's eyes. (Oiled glass shot) Look-
        ing at his hands which loom large in f.g. the picture
        slowly changes as if Barney's focus were changing into
        that of an animal; the edges of the picture become blurred,
        the middle stays sharp, then the hands change into claws.
        NOW THE CAMERA BECOMES BARNEY'S EYES. The hands are seen
        in f.g. as he walks on. The voices of the jungle become
        funneled and echo-like, distorted. CAMERA MOVES ON.

213   FULL - (STOCK)

        as a flock of monkeys take off in flight.

                                            DISSOLVE TO:

214   CLOSE

        at a tree trunk in f.g. Dina comes into shot, staggers,
        stops, turns, to go on. As soon as she is out of CAMERA
        ANGLE the Gorilla's arms come into the shot in f.g. as if
        he had watched Dina.

215   MED. CLOSE

        on Dina as she enters another shot, stops, looks around
        lost. She stands petrified.

216   MED. CLOSE - (STOCK)

        A leopard takes off roaringly, as the gorilla's snarl is
        HEARD.

                                        DISSOLVE TO:

217   INT. LIVING ROOM - NIGHT

        The large room is empty. Now the light is being switched
        on. Viet's voice is HEARD.

                                VIET (O.S.)
                        Dina - where are you...?

        Viet walks into scene, toward CAMERA. He carries a gun.
        He stands lost, looking around.

                                VIET
                        Dina!

        Taro enters from the servant's quarters. He carries the
        potted plant - the Pe de Guine. But only the stem is
        left, the leaves gone.

218   MED. CLOSE

        as Taro walks up to Viet.

                                VIET
                        Not a soul around! The ser-
                        vants have left too.

                                TARO
                        I expected it. See what I
                        found!

        He holds the bare stem up to Viet for inspection.

                                VIET
                        What is it?

                                TARO
                        A Pe de Guine plant. That
                        old woman, Al Long had it
                        all that ime...that's the
                        poison she used on Barney
                        Chavez.

                                        (CONTINUED)

218   CONTINUED:

He puts the plant down, worried, thoughtful.

                    VIET
          Dina must've followed Barney
          into the jungle.

                    TARO
          Yes. Come on, let's find
          them!

                    VIET
          How can we - at night!

                    TARO
          I know my jungle, Doctor.
          Out there my senses are closer
          to that of an animal than to
          a human being!

He cocks his gun and pushes it under his arm, and as he
walks toward the garden door, and Viet follows:

                    DISSOLVE TO:

219   EXT. JUNGLE

on Dina as she runs through underbrush, and disappears.

220   CLOSE

tree in f.g. as the gorilla's arms appear, and stop, as
if he were listening.

221   MED. CLOSE

on Dina as she enters shot, and stops in CLOSE AT CAMERA.
Exhausted, half out of her mind; the gorilla's snarl is
HEARD.

                    DINA
          Help!--help!

Dina turns; she lifts the gun as she sees. She shoots -
but the gun does not respond.

222   MED. CLOSE TO CLOSE

The gorilla, walking toward her, rearing on his hind legs.

223   She again presses the trigger - in vain - then faints as
       the big ape enters the shot.

224   MED. CLOSE

       on Viet and Taro, as they stop and listen.

                         ECHO
                 Help - help...

                         VIET
                 Did you hear it?

       They listen as the echo repeats:

                         ECHO
                 Help - help...

       Viet lifts the gun and shoots. The echo of the shot rolls
       on a thousand fold.

225   MED. CLOSE

       on Dina, as she listens, then collapses in a faint, while
       another shot and its echo is HEARD.

                         ECHO
                 Dina - Dina...

226   CLOSE

       on Dina's face. She lies unconscious on the leaf-covered
       ground. Now the gorilla's arms come into shot and scoop
       her up. CAMERA DOLLIES revealing only Dina and the gorilla's
       arms and claws. Her hands and head are hanging limply.
       Her eyes are closed, her shirt torn.

                         ECHO
                 Dina...Dina...

       Echo of shots follows.

227   BOOM SHOT CLOSE NEAR POOL

       Dina's face IN CLOSE, as she lies in the monster's arms.

                         VIET'S VOICE
                      (closer now)
                 Dina...Dina...

       Dina opens her eyes, and her face distorts in terror.

228   CLOSE

as she sees the gorilla's face bent over her.

229   AS SEEN FROM HER ANGLE

The gorilla's huge face bent over her, his fangs exposed.

230   The claws of the monster's right hand closes around her throat.

231   MED. CLOSE - OTHER PART OF JUNGLE

Taro and Viet listen to a terrifying shriek, and the gorilla's triumphant cry.

                    TARO
         Over there...

He runs away followed by Viet.

232   NEAR POOL AND TREE (BOOM SHOT)

CAMERA HIGH FOCUSING Taro and Viet as if seen from a high tree. As Taro and Viet come running into shot.

                    TARO
                 (continuing)
         It's in there...

233   FULL SHOT

seen from their angle. A large tree, completely covered with leaves and lianas - a mass of verdage. The leaves shake as if a large animal (hidden to the eye) were climbing up the tree.

234   MED. CLOSE

on Taro as he lifts his gun and shoots. Viet too empties his gun in a rapid volley.

235   BOOM SHOT - THE TREE

The leaves suddenly stop moving, then a heavy body tumbles through the leaves, and breaking branches, ripping off lianas, crashes to the ground. CAMERA FOLLOWS THE FALL.

236   CLOSE - AT POOL

as Taro runs forward toward the body OUT OF SHOT, which
has fallen to the ground.

237   PAN SHOT - CLOSE

on Dina, as she lies, broken, her face turned away from
CAMERA, and as CAMERA PANS to the water, the gorilla's
ugly snout is seen in the mirror of the pool. Its eyes
break - its head sinks down and as the head comes into
the sight of the CAMERA - it is Barney's.

CAMERA QUICKLY PULLS BACK - showing Barney and Dina lying
at the edge of the pool. Barney is hanging over a rock
which protrudes from the pool, his upper body is naked.
CAMERA PULLS BACK FARTHER and shows Taro and Viet, looking, guns in hand, silently, stunned, at the two bodies.

DISSOLVE TO:

238   EXT. JUNGLE - DAY - (STOCK)

as CAMERA MOVES BACK OVER JUNGLE

                    KLAAS' VOICE
          ...something out of prehis-
          toric age - something that
          haunted the world a million
          years ago...the jungle itself
          arose to avenge my death...

DISSOLVE TO:

239   INT. LIVING ROOM - DOLLY SHOT - (SAME AS AT BEGINNING)

The large room, its windows broken, plants wind their
creepers around the decaying furniture. As CAMERA MOVES
QUICKLY BACK,

FADE OUT.

SETS:

Klaas plantation:

        The living room
        Klaas' bedroom
        Dina's bedroom
        Al Long's small room

The town:

        Taro's office in town

        Viet's office in town

The garden

The jungle

FUN FACTS

By Tom Weaver

During my 1984 interview with Curt Siodmak, he called *Bride of the Gorilla* "one of the pictures [his own pictures] I like most for some reason. It was a marvelous idea. ...It had real characters, and a story. Today's horror film directors, they have a mattress with 250 gallons of blood coming up out of it [1984's *A Nightmare on Elm Street*, a new movie when I talked with Siodmak], and *that* they call a picture! *This* was development of a character."

Herman Cohen's job responsibilities weren't confined to Broder's offices and the sets of Broder's movies: Cohen told me,

When Jack and his wife Beatrice would go out of town (Jack had to go to New York a lot because the headquarters of Realart were there), he'd have me come over to this magnificent home they had in Beverly Hills, 810 North Camden, just a couple of blocks from the Beverly Hills Hotel. He'd have me move in there when he went out of town, to supervise the help. I didn't take offense to it because Bessie, his cook, was from Detroit, and once she knew *I* was from Detroit, she made anything I wanted her to make. Then they had the housemaid, and then they had the valet, they had a pool and a basketball court...and the minute they went out of town, I would call up my buddies and girlfriends and invite 'em over for the day. A lot of my friends would say, "I wouldn't take that from him! You were hired as an assistant! He's *using* you!" But I was *happy* with that arrangement! I had a small one-bedroom apartment in Hollywood, paying $100 a month—I was very happy to go live at 810 North Camden for the week!

It's a touch that's easy to miss: Notice that Al Long's Pe de Guine plant has less leaves on it every time we see it, the old witch obviously making the juice of "the plant of evil" a regular ingredient in Barney's potent potables.

Something about *Bride of the Gorilla*—the presence of Barbara Payton? the title?—brought out the "wit" in *Variety* columnists, who ran "funny" one-liners before, during and after production. George E. Phair, who had the humor column "Retakes," joshed on July 23, "As the prospective 'Bride of the Gorilla,' no doubt Barbara Payton will be the recipient of a coconut shower." On August 2, "Just for *Variety*" writer Mike Connolly came out with "BOINGG-G-G DEP'T: the wisp of pure nothing worn by Barbara Payton in *Bride of the Gorilla*." On August 16, Phair was back with another knee-slapper: "Jack Broder's *Bride of the Gorilla* wound up in seven days. Evidently gorillas believe in short honeymoons."

When screenwriter-producer Nunnally Johnson noticed the name Gisela Werbiseck Piffle in the phone book, he was intrigued, dialed the number and asked the woman who answered, "Is this Gisela Werbiseck Piffle?" She said it was, and asked who was calling. "Nunnally Johnson," he replied.

"Sorry, I don't know you," she said. "Could it be that you have the wrong Gisela Werbiseck Piffle?"

Hollywood columnist Erskine Johnson heard the above anecdote and thought it was a gag, so he too contacted Gisela Werbiseck Piffle and then wrote about her in a June 1946 column. "She's a charming, gray-haired lady who once starred on the Vienna stage, fled to the U.S. with her husband when Hitler took over Austria, and has worked in the movies ever since. 'In Europe,' Gisela told us, 'my name was not funny.'"

"She was the Marie Dressler of Europe," Gisela's husband told Johnson. "She was a female Charlie Chaplin."

It's difficult to take one look (and one listen) at this ogress and imagine her as an on-set funster, but Johnson's column gives that impression. He writes that whenever she

In the 1940s, the Universal horror flicks and RKO's Val Lewton spine-tinglers were poles apart—but their respective poster boys Lon Chaney and Tom Conway make a good team in *Bride of the Gorilla*.

was paged on a set ("Gisela Werbiseck Piffle!"), she always replied, "Who, me?"—and it never failed to get a howl.

Chaney occasionally wears glasses in *Bride*. The script specifies that he needs them for distance, not for reading, a piece of information that's not only useless but incorrect: The two times he wears them in the movie, it *is* for reading. The actor also had four eyes in the 1950 crime drama *Once a Thief*…

In *The Wolf Man*, Larry Talbot's (Chaney) backstory is that he left his home in Wales and ended up in California, where he was employed at an optical company and got to be proficient with astronomical instruments. We get the impression that he's become a handy, practical Joe Lunchbox, utilitarian perhaps to a fault—and quite unprepared to now return to the family hearth in Wales, a land of superstition where "in a great many ways, we *are* a backward people" (according to Sir John Talbot, his father). Siodmak must have liked crafting a character caught between

two cultures, or he liked the way Chaney played those *Wolf Man* scenes, or both, because in *Bride of the Gorilla*, Lon's Commissioner Taro is faced with the same sort of dilemma. He vents to Dr. Viet:

> You know, doctor, I was born in this little town. …I sometimes regret that I went to university, and then returned to this jungle with its super-stitions. It only served to confuse me. …How can I help being confused? My native mind is filled with these superstitions. My *legal* mind was developed through books, written by people without emotion.

Producer Val Lewton's *Cat People* (1942) is another chiller where viewers decide for themselves whether Simone Simon's protagonist morphs (into a large killer-cat) or not. Another reason *Bride* brings *Cat People* to mind is the presence of Tom Conway as a doctor in both. Lewton's follow-up *I Walked with a Zombie* (1943), co-written by Siodmak, is set, like *Bride*,

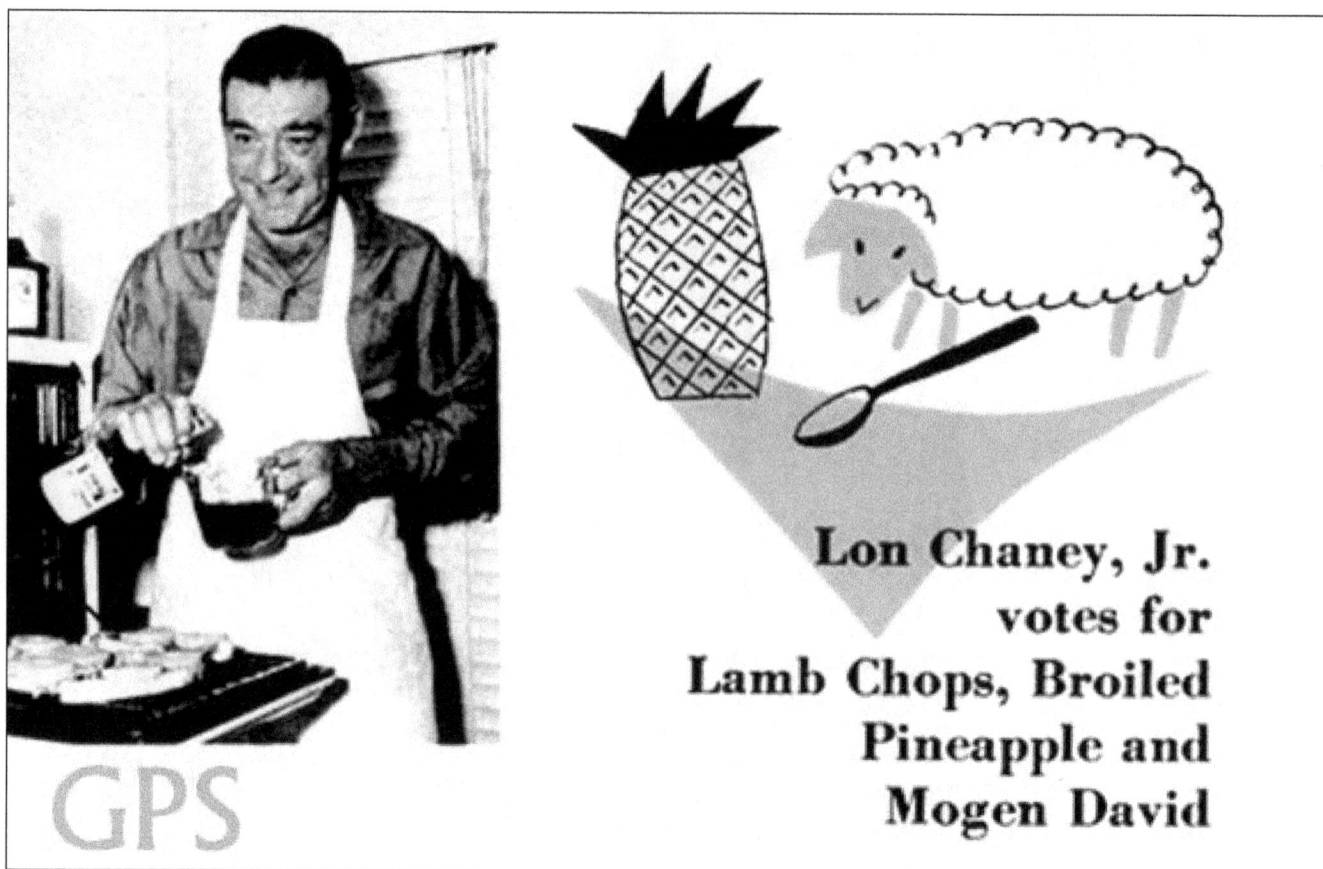

Lon Chaney, Jr.
votes for
Lamb Chops, Broiled
Pineapple and
Mogen David

One day Lon prepared lamb chops for his castmates—and according to *Bride* publicity, "His unusual recipe proved to be so successful that Chaney found himself drafted to job of cook for the remainder of shooting on the movie."

on a back-of-beyond plantation where supernatural forces may be in play, and with two half-brothers (James Ellison and Conway) proving once again that two men for one woman is a recipe for mayhem.

Tom Conway (1904-67), like Payton and Chaney, was another barstool barnacle whose fast times caught up with him. After he did his last acting in a *Perry Mason* opposite the succarath himself, Raymond Burr, it was publicized that he was living in a $2-a-day Venice, California, hotel room, a slave to John Barleycorn, and burdened with impaired eyesight. Offers of help came in from fans and fellow actors alike. Stints in a county hospital and a convalescent sanitarium cleared his brain and he was rarin' to get back into the biz, telling reporters, "It will be more or less a cold start, but acting-wise, I think I'm at my peak." A short time later, he lost his battle with cirrhosis of the liver in a Culver City hospital.

Or maybe he *didn't* die in a Culver City hospital. Zsa Zsa Gabor and Conway's actor brother George Sanders married in 1949 and were man and wife for several years; in her 1991 autobiography *One Lifetime Is Not Enough* she shared some memories of her onetime brother-in-law Conway:

George contacted [me with] the tragic news that Tom had cirrhosis of the liver and that he was dying. I was very fond of Tom and we had a family reunion. At the end of it, George said, "Here, old boy, take this $40,000. Go to Capri and die there happy."

Tom did exactly as George said, except that he didn't die. On Capri, Tom met a German scientist who had discovered a new serum that he wanted to test. He told Tom, "Let me try it out on you since you're dying anyhow. It may kill you or it could, conceivably, cure you." He persuaded Tom to try it and miraculously, he was cured.

George, however, was now in a difficult situation—particularly when Tom asked him for money. His voice ringing with determination, "I'm sorry, old boy," said George. "You're my brother but you are supposed to be dead. I never want to see you again."

After that, Herbert [Zsa Zsa's then-husband Herbert Hutner] and I supported Tom every

Curt Siodmak liked to blow smoke.

time he was broke. One day, his ex-wife called and said that this time Tom was, in earnest, on his deathbed. Francesca [the daughter of Zsa Zsa and Hilton Hotel founder Conrad Hilton] and I visited him at the hospital in downtown L.A. and when we left, I gave him $200, telling him, "Tip the nurses a little bit so they'll be good to you."

The next day the hospital called me and informed me that Tom had disappeared. I found out later that he had taken my $200, had gone to see his girlfriend, had gotten drunk, and then went to bed with her. Then he died, right there in her bed. I contacted George, but he was still so livid about his $40,000 and Capri that he wouldn't help me or even show up at the morgue to identify Tom's body.

Herman Cohen recalled Lon Chaney as unhappy during production, but according to *Bride* publicity he was quite convivial, invading the commissary kitchen and preparing for other cast members one of his favorite dishes, lamb chops with broiled pineapple slices in Mogen David wine (see photo on page 154). To

Filmfax interviewer Dennis Fischer, Siodmak recalled, "When the picture was finished, he cooked a moose stew. He shot a moose, and he baked it for the whole crew. Ray Burr came to me and said, 'What does *she* think she is, *cooking for the whole crew?*'"

How much faith should we place in Curt Siodmak's comments about…well, *anything?* The details of his anecdotes tended to change drastically from one interview to the next; you get the impression some of them were concocted out of thin air. So "Caveat emptor!" when it comes to many of the Siodmak assertions in this book; also his statement that Lon Chaney had "a terrible death wish," a claim he made to interviewer Patrick Sierchio of *Written By* magazine. "They say as a kid he tried to commit suicide," Siodmak told Sierchio, backing it up with an anecdote: He said he wrote *Frankenstein Meets the Wolf Man*'s (1943) Festival of the New Wine song on the set the day it was to be shot and, because the song included the line "May you live eternally," Chaney had a meltdown: "He blew up; he really blew up: 'I don't want to live eternally.' [He] rejected it."

Sigh. First of all, the song lyrics are in the *Frankenstein Meets the Wolf Man* script, written many months before production began, so Siodmak's claim to have whipped them up on the set is loco. And as for Chaney's outraged reaction to "May you live eternally" (actually "May they live eternally"), Siodmak is surely remembering *Larry Talbot's* (Chaney) outraged reaction to the line *in the movie*: "'Eternally'! I don't *want* to live eternally!" In fact, he's probably ascribing *Larry Talbot's* "terrible death wish" to Chaney!

Moral of the story: It's probably a good idea to always take the salty Siodmak with an additional pinch (or fistful) of salt.

A big scoop in the September 26, 1951, issue of *Variety*: "Lon Chaney Jr. will be billed henceforth without the 'Jr.'" It would have been an even *bigger* scoop if they'd run that item ten years earlier, around the time the actor dropped the Jr. starting with *The Wolf Man*!

Lon Chaney must have minded his ps and qs on *Bride of the Gorilla* because he was brought back to play a villainous role in Jack Broder's *The Bushwhackers*, and worked for Broder a third time the following summer in *Battles of Chief Pontiac*. Years later, Chaney told Bob Burns that he liked his role as Chief Pontiac.

Lon's co-workers from the 1940s regularly recalled him as a sometimes out-of-control actor who'd brawl with Broderick Crawford just for fun, taunt and try to pick fights with other actors, torment Evelyn Ankers with silly pranks, break a vase over the head of director Robert Siodmak, choke a fellow actor during a *Mummy's Ghost* scene, etc. But his 1950s colleagues tended to call him a nice guy. Chalk it up to older-and-wiser, probably.

In the spring of 1951 RKO made the comedy *Behave Yourself!* in which an assortment of Damon Runyon-esque gangsters try to get their hands on a dog unwittingly adopted by a young accountant and his wife (Farley Granger and Shelley Winters). The cast's sole survivor Marvin Kaplan told me,

I thought Lon was wonderful. He was a very gentle, sweet man, the son of a very great actor. I played a gangster, and Sheldon Leonard [another gangster] and I had a falling-out. They gave me a huge gun which I had to hold with two hands, and to Sheldon they gave a little toy pistol [*laughs*], and we shot each other. The mistake I made was, I fell down first. *Never* fall down first—because other people are gonna land on *top* of you! So Sheldon laid down on top of me, and then later in the scene Chaney laid down on top of *both* of us [*laughs*]! And

Chaney was a very heavy man! Then Bill Demarest, who played the cop, stepped on *all* the corpses' hands! It was a very funny scene.

Now, Lon, I only saw him lose his temper once. Shelley Winters caused a lot of delays and a lot of nonsense on the picture. Shelley had a lot of problems at that time. She never came prepared. It was a comedy and she didn't know what the hell to do with it. My first experience on the set of *Behave Yourself!*, I came on the set and the first thing I heard was [Shelley yelling], "*Virginia!* Get me my slippers!" I guess I was standing next to Virginia, and she said, "Let the bitch get her *own* slippers!" [*Laughs*] Shelley cried all the time, she was always crying, and we were doing a farce comedy! Constantly crying and emotionally upset, and it did not help the movie!

Anyway, Lon had another job lined up, something he was gonna do right after *Behave Yourself!*, and he had to lose it because she caused us to go way over-budget and over-schedule. So he was very angry about that, and rightly so. [*Tom Weaver: Lon got mad at her to her face, or did he just vent to you and the other actors?*] I don't think he ever told her directly. But we found out. There were so many delays on that picture. After one o'clock, she would find some reason to leave the set.

I remember Lon as a very gentle, very quiet, very private man. I liked him very much. And a very good actor.

Behave Yourself! and *Bride of the Gorilla* were double-billed in some theaters, giving Lon fans a double dose of the lovable lug.

Wellll…maybe even in the '50s, not *every*body found Lon lovable. In *The Bushwhackers*, Chaney was a ruthless landowner and Myrna Dell his equally ruthless, gunslinging daughter. "He was horrible," interviewee Dell says in the Boyd Magers-Michael G. Fitzgerald book *Western Women*. "That son of a bitch wouldn't read off camera for my closeups. He was an alcoholic, or a recovering one. He had a mean manner, like alkies often have. On the closeup shots, I read my lines offstage for him. When it was my turn, the dialogue director started to do Chaney's part. I told him to tell Lon to get his ass over here or I wouldn't do any more readings for him. He was not very likable, a lush, hung over."

🍌 Joseph Breen did what he could to keep suggestions of bestiality out of *Bride of the Gorilla*, but the poster ad lines undid all his work, and in spades (see the ads in the *Bride* pressbook starting on page 222). One pressbook article's title calls the movie an "Exiting [*sic*] New Adventure Film." Another article includes the plausible-sounding tidbit that Chaney had his house trailer on the set and used that as his dressing room.

🍌 According to the October 11, 1951, *Hollywood Reporter*, Lon Chaney and his wife were currently in Detroit "for public appearances at yesterday's premiere of *Bride of the Gorilla*, opening day-and-date in three theaters." The trade also announced that he was lined up to make p.a.s with the picture in Boston, Newark, Philadelphia and New York.

🍌 One scene in the Civil War drama *Drums in the Deep South*, made a few months before *Bride*, is good for a snicker for Payton fans who know she was fickle and faithless to the power of infinity: At the start of the movie, Payton, a married woman, re-encounters James Craig, a beau from years before. As Craig drops the first hint that he's still interested in her, she keeps her back to him and responds with high-and-mighty Dixie dignity and perhaps a touch of offense: "I'm Braxton's wife—nothing can change that." Craig turns on the charm, and exactly 64 seconds after "I'm Braxton's wife—nothing can change that," she and Craig are in a lip lock.

Sixty-four seconds. One wonders if Payton ever held out that long in real life!

🍌 In 1951, it was probably next to impossible for movie fans following the seamy Barbara Payton saga *not* to think of Tone and Neal while watching *Bride of the Gorilla*'s confrontation scene between Barney and Klaas. The two men stand in the garden just outside the house at night and argue over Dina, just as Tone and Neal did at Barbara's apartment. Then, as in Neal's version of what happened at Barbara's, the unimposing, smaller, older Klaas starts the fight (landing a blow that the tough, muscly Barney barely feels) and Barney effortlessly finishes it, laying out his opponent with a single shot.

🍌 In his 2008 memoir *In Spite of Myself*, actor Christopher Plummer recalled Tone as a man

Payton and Tom Neal toured in a 1953 stage production of *The Postman Always Rings Twice* that a *Variety* critic caught in Pittsburgh: "[The] whole thing's third-rate from every angle."

with "a penchant for domineering, glamorous women—Joan Crawford was one spouse among many—need I say more? …None stayed with him for long. He seemed to search for this kind of self-destructive alliance, an alliance that could not but help inflict certain pain. Indeed, Franchot Tone was motivated and driven by pain." In a stage production of *The Petrified Forest*, Plummer was gangster Duke Mantee and Tone the failed poet Alan Squier, and in the last act Squier begs Mantee to kill him. "Franchot directed this [speech] to me every night and every night his conviction was extraordinary," Plummer continued. "Here was a man already dying it seemed—still praying to be snuffed out. I no longer was convinced it was Squier, but Franchot himself pleading for his death. It was eerie, too close, almost too real, and shattering, shattering."

🍌 **Imagine**…: Part 1: Imagine lying on the ground with boxer-weightlifter Tom Neal sitting on top of you, you eat his punches 'til you slip

Which was the first horror movie release of the 1950s? It's hard to say for sure but we'd like to think that the *Bride* came before the *Son*. Just to make things very respectable, quite proper, as Boris Karloff might say.

away into Dreamland, then wake up from your semi-coma in a hospital with a pulped profile—*and discover that newspaper accounts of the attack had been written humorously!* That was the Tone of the Franchot coverage in some papers, for instance one where **WINNAH** was the bold-faced start of the caption of a photo of Neal! Parts of that same article were written in the style of a sports-page boxing story. Various theaters had fun pairing Payton's *Bride of the Gorilla* with a Tom Neal movie, and Bob Hope made Franchot Tone jokes part of his regular routine, as the busted-up Tone got a coast-to-coast horse laugh from some newspaper writers and segments of the entertainment industry.

Imagine…: Part 2: Imagine being a regular Joe with an interest in juicy Hollywood gossip, and getting to hear about the Tom Neal-Franchot Tone rumpus *from Payton herself.* Apparently many Chicago denizens did: Viola Swisher wrote in "Just for *Variety*" on December 14, 1951, "[T]he Windy City house where La Payton's holding forth is Minsky's Rialto, whose *Chicago Trib* ad reads: 'On Stage All Shows—Barbara Payton—Hear Lowdown on Tone-Neal Battle.'"

Now imagine being able to see a *recreation* of that battle. Wellll, keep imagining, because probably nobody ever did. But Payton and Neal did tour with a stock production of *The Postman Always Rings Twice* and, if it was like the 1946 MGM movie, one scene in this romantic triangle tale would have had Neal murderously clobbering an older man (playing Payton's husband) with Payton an eyewitness.

A perfect *Bride of the Gorilla* co-feature for fans with a fascination for the Payton-Tone-Neal fireworks: *Dangerous*, the 1935 Bette Davis vehicle. Tone is her leading man, bland and full of boring speeches in his role of a prominent architect who recognizes his all-time stage favorite (Davis) down-and-out in a dive and tries to pull her up out of the gutter and put her back on Broadway. Somewhere along the line, he starts to fall for this snarling bottle baby. Davis thinks of herself as a jinx because so many of the men in her life came to bad ends, not realizing that her reckless, supremely selfish behavior was the cause of their downfalls; *she's* the author of her own misery, and the misery of the men around her. The spectacle of Tone irresistibly and irresponsibly drawn to this blonde train wreck certainly brings Tone and La Payton to mind.

In a December 9, 1951, United Press story, Payton said that a group of producers wanted her and Tom Neal "to make a picture about a Marine who returns to his girl from Korea. I think Tom is interested in making it but I don't think I am." Two days later, December 11, columnist Erskine Johnson revealed more about the proposed picture: It was the next movie on the slate of producer Ed Levin (no doubt Edward *Leven*, *Bride*'s associate producer) and it would feature Payton and Neal in the story of a Marine returning home to find that his wife hasn't been faithful. "There's no part in it for Franchot Tone," Johnson quipped. He ended with, "Hollywood would

'Twould appear that Franchot Tone "celebrated" the ten-year anniversary of The Fight—with another fight! According to Marc Scott Zicree's *The Twilight Zone Companion*, Tone worked one day on the 1961 *TZ* episode "The Silence"—and then no-showed on Day 2. Turns out he was in a clinic with the left side of his face a mess. Tone spun a cockamamie story about bending to pick a flower, falling over and tumbling down a hillside; but the way Rod Serling heard it, the actor had approached a girl in a restaurant parking lot, and her boyfriend saw red. The *Twilight Zone* folks also saw red—Tone's scraped-raw fist-magnet kisser—and from then on photographed nothing but his undamaged right side. The identity of "Franchot Tone Slugger #2" is not known.

rather not admit it, but Barbara's last film *Bride of the Gorilla* is racking up staggering box office grosses."

Another item to add to the files of "Bullshit... or not?": In Payton's autobiography *I Am Not Ashamed*, she writes of coming to New York City as part of her *Bride of the Gorilla* promo tour and encountering six drunken cowboys in town for a rodeo. They all ended up back at the cowboys' room at a Greenwich Village hotel, where Payton's antics prompted the men to begin brawling. "I just leaped on the couch and yelled—rooting them on," she wrote. "They were mad as hell—and drunk, so they were really out to maim each other." The hotel manager hollered cop, all the cowboys were lassoed by the law and Payton wasn't. *But*, she added, "the rodeo boys got the last laugh. [*Bride of the Gorilla* was] showing at the Rialto Theater and they picketed it with, 'Don't see Barbara Payton.' It was a private joke that got me some extra publicity. A month later I met

one of the boys at a cocktail party and he told me they had spent the night in jail but it was great fun. They weren't even mad at me."

Bride of the Gorilla was occasionally co-featured with Realart reissues of the Universal Westerns *Frontier Badmen* (1943) and *The Daltons Ride Again* (1945), creating Lon Chaney double-bills. Another Western with which it shared theater screens: *The Daltons' Women* (1951) with Tom Neal. In September 1951 when Neal's knuckles were probably still scabby from hitting Franchot Tone, the Pix theater in Minneapolis showed *The Daltons' Women* and ran newspaper ads calling attention to the fact that Neal was "The Franchot Tone Slugger." Front-of-house displays at the theater itself also played up that fun fact.

(This entry was written by Dr. Robert J. Kiss.) Which came first: Jekyll's son or the gorilla's bride? Both *Bride of the Gorilla* and Columbia's *The Son of Dr. Jekyll* can stake a fair claim to being the first American horror feature of the 1950s. *Son* went into production first, shooting taking place between March 13 and March 30, 1951. *Bride* did not start until July 26, but was then rushed into release, premiering in Highland, California, on October 8. *The Son of Dr. Jekyll* was not be seen by a paying audience at a regular theater until the week of October 10. However, a special *Son of Dr. Jekyll* press preview had already taken place in Hollywood on September 28, on the basis of which trade journals including *Film Bulletin, Motion Picture Daily* and *Variety* published reviews. Thus, the question of "which came first" depends entirely on the criteria applied. Of course, even though *Bride* reached a small number of movie theater patrons in California first, this is not indicative of the nation as a whole, with numerous communities getting to see *Son* well in advance of *Bride*, in particular due to the latter being given a staggered release. Within the sample of around 900 movie theaters across the U.S. during the period from October 1951 to August 1952, around 1.5 percent opened both features simultaneously as a double-bill!

Horror movie fans reading the November 7, 1951, *Motion Picture Exhibitor* (a bi-weekly publication) must have breathed a sigh of relief: After a near-total six-year horror movie drought, *Bride, Son of Dr. Jekyll* and *Strange Door* were all reviewed in the same issue!

Raymond Burr made only two '50s monster movies, *Bride of the Gorilla* and *Godzilla, King of the Monsters!* (1956), but both had significance: *Bride* was one of the first horror movies of the decade, *Godzilla* the first Japanese monster movie, and both were big moneymakers.

(This entry was written by Dr. Robert J. Kiss.) Jack Broder Productions entered into a multi-picture deal with Cheryl T.V. Corporation shortly after the latter's incorporation in November 1952. This resulted in its features coming to television within roughly a year of the end of their first run at theaters. *Bride of the Gorilla*, included in an initial package of six features, made its small screen bow during the week of July 12, 1953. The package was comprised of *The Basketball Fix* (making its TV debut in May 1953), *Two Dollar Bettor* (June 1953), *The Bushwhackers* (June 1953), *Bride of the Gorilla* (July 1953), *Kid Monk Baroni* (September 1953) and *Bela Lugosi Meets a Brooklyn Gorilla* (December 1953). A second package of four features followed in 1954-

55. One of the features was *Breakdown* (1952); in April 1956, its executive producer Theodore J. Ticktin filed a legal suit against Jack Broder Productions, Realart Pictures and Cheryl T.V., claiming loss of theatrical revenue due to the picture having been released to television "too soon." This package consisted of *Battles of Chief Pontiac* (making its TV debut in October 1954), *Breakdown* (December 1954), *Run for the Hills* (December 1954) and *Hannah Lee* (July 1955).

Another feature made by Jack Broder Productions, the Korean War picture *Combat Squad*, released by Columbia in 1953, was not seen on TV until February 1962.

Herman Cohen climbed the show biz ladder from working as Broder's schlepper (the broom up the ass, remember) to vice-president of Jack Broder Productions and Realart Pictures. But making the decision to leave the company was as easy as pie:

> Jack had six kids, and I was like a babysitter for the family, whenever he and Beatrice went out of town. I was quite close to the family because of the kids, the kids liked being with me. So we're having dinner and Bessie serves the dessert, she made great pies. And she made blueberry pie. Jack turns to Bessie, "Bessie! You *know* I hate blueberry pie. What did you make blueberry pie for?" Bessie says, "Because Herman likes blueberry pie!" [*Laughs*] And he gave me a dirty look and said, "*Herman?!*" And then I realized, I'm gettin' *too* close to the family! Time for my *exit*! [time to move on from Broder].
>
> I formed my own company at the same studio, General Service Studios on Las Palmas. I got a small little office there 'cause I knew everybody there and I knew the owner, James Nassour, a wonderful guy. He gave me a helluva deal, and I hired a secretary, and I started Herman Cohen Productions.

Cohen's first Hollywood movie, *Target Earth* (1954), featured gorilla guy Steve Calvert in a change-of-pace role inside a giant robot outfit.

Bride of the Gorilla was the first rung in Barbara Payton's descent into what Joe Dante calls (in his "Trailers from Hell" installment on *Bride*) "the B-movie jungle." It was followed by just five more credits: *Four Sided Triangle* and *The Flanagan Boy* (both 1953) from England's Hammer Films; Jack Broder's *Run for the Hills* (1953); the same year's *The Great Jesse James Raid*, described below; and *Murder Is My Beat*

RUN FOR A CAVE!..
...and be sure you take
a beautiful doll!

JACK BRODER PRODUCTIONS
present

SONNY   BARBARA
TUFTS and PAYTON
Run for the HILLS

with JOHN HARMON · BYRON FOLGER
VICCI RAAF · RICHARD BENEDICT
SIDE SLATE and PAUL MAXEY

Executive Producer TED LEWIS · Produced by MARK D. RICE and R. D. LEVIN · Directed by LEW LANDERS · From an Original Story by LEONARD NEUBAUER

The offbeat comedy *Run for the Hills* teamed Payton and Sonny Tufts, another casualty of the stardom-to-bardom syndrome. His career was a shambles after multiple arrests for public drunkenness and other antics.

(1955). *The Flanagan Boy* is interesting because it's yet another Payton movie based on that familiar bit of marital geometry, the eternal triangle, and it's obviously designed to make fans recall MGM's *The Postman Always Rings Twice* (1946) with Lana Turner and John Garfield. *How* obviously? Payton wears the same sort of white bathing suit that Lana famously wore in the earlier movie; and she and the actor playing the equivalent of the Garfield role have the character names **Lorna** and **Johnny** (as in **Lana** Turner and **John** Garfield).

For American release *The Flanagan Boy* was retitled *Bad Blonde* and, if that wasn't enough to make 1950s moviegoers remember Payton's recent off-screen sexploits, howzabout the large block of text smack-dab in the middle of the poster: "[The Bad Blonde is] not a pickup or a prostitute…she's more dangerous than either!" The name BARBARA PAYTON is right underneath this ad line, almost as though she had signed it, so that no one could possibly miss the connection.

Payton and Neal did eventually appear together in a movie, 1953's *The Great Jesse James Raid*, but her character is so utterly dispensable that you have to wonder if it was written into a fully finished, existing Western script just so Payton could be *in* it. As Kate, the dance hall girlfriend of badman Bob Ford (Jim Bannon), she sings "That's the Man for Me," a line that probably passed through Payton's mind about 20 times…a week. The movie was shot in April 1953, about a year after she and Tone divorced, but she's already full-faced and chunky, quite unappealing compared to the way she looked in her earlier movies. Ford, Jesse James (Willard Parker) and others plan to hijack a gold shipment, and make preparations to do so throughout much of the running time, but there's a double-cross and most end up dead. In fact, the *Raid* promised in the title is not even attempted! In his last

The way she walked was thorny. Barbara Payton in the early 1950s (far left) was sought by the majors; a few years later, she'd be lucky to be picked up by a buck private. On the left is Tailspin Payton in a Hollywood police station in the early 1960s. (*Bride* photo courtesy Ronald V. Borst/Hollywood Movie Posters)

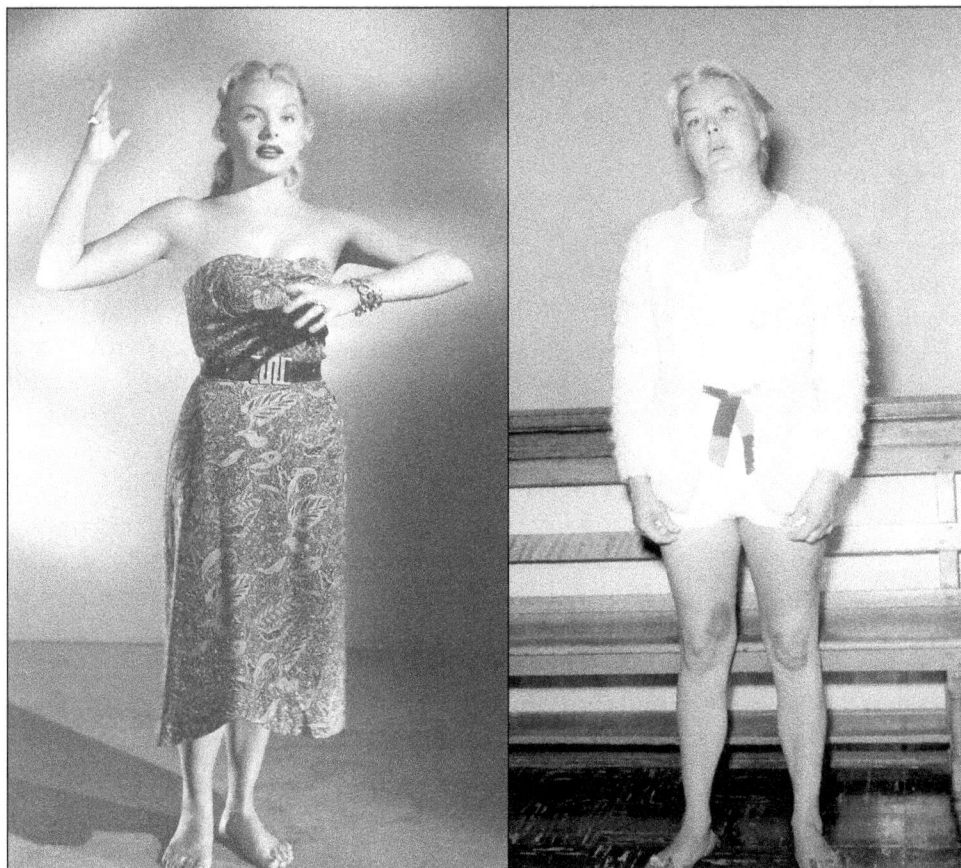

movie, Neal plays one of the would-be hijackers, Arch, a gunman with a morbid streak; he's always pawing Kate, who hates every minute of it.

Realart came to the end of the road in their relationship with Universal in 1957, with Universal's Milton R. Rackmil confirming in March that the studio was not renewing its deal with Realart to handle their oldies "because we feel we can do better on TV than by reissuing them." And, as so often happens in Hollywood, what begins in good faith ends in contention: On February 13, 1958, Universal slapped suit on Realart, claiming the defendant still owed in excess of $46,000. "Realart was to give periodic written reports about revenue derived, which Universal now asserts were incorrect and did not reflect the true figure of gross receipts," *Variety* reported.

Andrew Dowdy wrote about *Bride of the Gorilla* quite entertainingly, and at surprising length, in his 1973 book *Movies Are Better Than Ever* (aka *The Films of the Fifties*):

Realart's promotion of [*Bride*] included special Halloween previews, one of which was my first experience at a midnight movie. The appearance of Barbara Payton on the screen was greeted with instant verbal approval, accompanied by whistling, stomping, and the ecstatic tribute of flying popcorn boxes, many of them sacrificed unemptied. It reminded me of a similar testimony rendered the previous year during Marilyn Monroe's brief scenes in *The Asphalt Jungle*. Marilyn, of course, went on to render her fragile talent to more exacting demands. But for Barbara Payton our popcorn enthusiasm was too late. She already was on the downward path, proof that the mostly mythical ethos of the Hollywood starlet occasionally touched living flesh.

…Only months before the Tone-Neal fracas, Fox and MGM were interested in her. Within a few years she had made her last Hollywood movie.

…She drifted around, down to Mexico where she put on weight, back north to stucco anonymity. …Police photos of her arrest for prostitution revealed a plump blonde, eyes red from crying, her puffy face a reminder that the body treats alcohol as a fat. Nobody could believe she was the starlet who once looked like Lana Turner.

No stranger to Hollywood's gorilla guys, Raymond Burr appeared in *Bride of the Gorilla* with Steve Calvert; in the 3-D murder mystery *Gorilla at Large* (1954) as the owner of a carnival that features the dangerous Goliath (George Barrows); and in the 1965 *Perry Mason* episode "The Case of the Grinning Gorilla" where in one scene Mason is followed in a darkened mansion by one of the owner's pet gorillas (Janos Prohaska). Even when the pursuing gorilla knocks a door off its hinges, Mason keeps his cool. (*A la Bride of the Gorilla*, there's a shaky subjective shot as the gorilla comes toward Mason.) Between the gorilla, the absence of courtroom scenes and a Mason whose temper noisily flares several times, it's quite the offbeat episode. And not once does the gorilla grin!

"I knew Raymond…and ran fast!" This according to actor William Swan, who played the rescue boat seaman scared to death by *The Monster That Challenged the World* (1957), played Olivia de Havilland's son in *Lady in a Cage* (1964), etc. Swan told me, "I did a couple *Perry Mason*s, and he had roving hands. He said, 'I've made some changes in the script. Come to my dressing room after we wrap today, and I'll give them to you.' I did as instructed, and for the full time I was there, he paraded around in his underwear. And…it was not a pretty sight [*laughs*]. I know *exactly* what he was up to, because he kept stroking my head, my hair. I thought, 'I've got to get *out* of here. Quickly!' He was a nice man otherwise, it seemed to me. But as a Lothario, he lacked any subtlety!"

By 1965 Tom Neal's Hollywood career had long faded in the rear view mirror of history. On April Fool's Day of that year, he shot and killed his wife Gail; he needed a better lawyer than he could afford so friends like auto dealer Glenn Austin came to his aid, taking out a local newspaper ad soliciting contributions. Neal's punches *must* have scrambled Franchot Tone's brains: Reportedly even *he* kicked in with a few bucks!

Or maybe not. Lisa Burks, who's been working for years on a Tone biography, read about Tone's contribution in a book called *Palm Springs Confidential* by Howard Johns, perhaps the first and only source ever to mention it. "I didn't find anything in Franchot Tone's papers to confirm it, like a letter or a cancelled check," she told me. "The auto dealer has since died and the author couldn't give me anything past what he put in the book. So at this point it's hearsay and alleged."

Found guilty of involuntary manslaughter, Neal served seven years, was paroled in December 1971 and died of heart failure in North Hollywood several months later. He was 58. While he was in the pokey, Barbara Payton—just 39—died of liver failure in her parents' San Diego home, and Franchot Tone succumbed to liver cancer in New York at age 63. In the space of just five years, these three scandal-scarred souls had all died way before their time.

Raymond Burr starred in *Perry Mason* telemovies right up until 1993 when the ravages of cancer confined him to the bed in the all-white bedroom of his Northern California home. At one point near the end, he spent 30 hours, without a break, sitting upright on the edge of that bed, "willing himself to fight the excruciating pain, refusing to take his pain-killing morphine drip and settle back into the mound of eight to ten pillows he normally slept upon semi-recumbent,

A few months before Raymond Burr's passing, 65,000 *TV Guide* readers put him third on the list of TV's Best Dramatic Actors (behind James Garner and Richard Chamberlain) and put *Perry Mason* in the top spot on the Best Drama list.

Perry Mason fans may know Robert Benevides' name from his Production Consultant credit on *Perry Mason* telemovies but you, gentle reader, are apt to know him better as an actor: He played Morty, the sailor who disappears while swimming with his girl in *The Monster That Challenged the World* (1957), and a victim of the alien in the 1963 *Outer Limits* episode "O.B.I.T." (see filmstrip on right).

because of his size," Mary Murphy wrote in *TV Guide*. "What he thought during this final battle is not known. What he said to his friend, long-time companion and business partner Robert Benevides, was, 'If I lie down, I'll die.' Eventually, he did lie down, and 48 hours later, he died."

Less than six weeks after Burr's September 12, 1993, passing, friends and fellow actors sang his praises on prime-time TV in *The Defense Rests: A Tribute to Raymond Burr*, a one-hour NBC special followed by a Perry Mason telemovie on an all-Burr night. In the

interim, his obits had told the tear-streaked tale of a tragic romance, a marriage that also ended in heartache, and a dead son, but all this info was bogus; fact-checkers could find no basis for them, and unearthed the fact that Burr actually was gay. His friend and publicist George Faber denied it vigorously: "I chuckle when people say he was gay. ...There are certain people who want to believe the worst in people." These were probably the things Burr would have *wanted* Faber to say, maybe *instructed* him to say. In a deathbed interview, Burr told *TV Guide* that his one big regret was accepting the role of the courtroom telehero: Perry Mason came to dominate his life, and without it, he perhaps "could have been married again, had more children, led a normal, everyday life." Burr was also in the process of writing an autobiography in "an attempt to get back at the tabloids he felt had smeared his name with accusations that he'd fabricated his marriages and in fact had a decades-long homosexual relationship with Benevides."

Curt Siodmak probably could have reduced the amount of stress in his life, maybe lived to be 99 instead of just 98, if he'd never become a director. In the spring of 1950 it was announced that he'd been hired to direct *Fire Island, N.Y.*, to be shot in New York; at first, Ilona Massey and Helmut Dantine were set for the leads; later, Dane Clark, Charles Korvin, Hildegarde Neff and Hope Miller were slated to star. Nothing came of it. His directing debut *Bride of the Gorilla* was compromised, *spoiled* really, by his bosses' insistence on an on-screen gorilla. Siodmak was hired to direct *The Magnetic Monster* (1953) but the job quickly became too complicated for him and he got quietly bounced during production. It was announced that he would direct the 1953 *Donovan's Brain*, based on his novel, but this time he was shunted aside before production even *began*. In our 1984 interview Siodmak said that the movie's producer Tom Gries ("meanest son of a bitch I had ever seen") took a dislike to him and wouldn't let him direct.

That same year he was the announced director of *Crosscut* with Bruce Bennett, a Bennett-scripted story of the Washington lumber industry, set to be financed by lumberjacks(!); that one also got chopped down. In 1954 Columbia's Sam Katzman hired him to write and direct a sci-fi movie; Curt wrote Katzman movies but never directed one. Making the terrible *Curucu, Beast of the Amazon* (1956) and the even-worse *Love Slaves of the Amazons* (1957) in South American jungles affected his health; he told me in 1984 that he'd never physically recovered. In my interview with *Love Slaves* star Don Taylor, he said that Siodmak didn't know how to direct

and that co-star Eduardo Ciannelli belittled the inept helmsman, telling him to go back to school and other rude comments.

In 1958 Siodmak directed Screen Gems' pilot for the proposed *Tales of Frankenstein* teleseries and it went nowhere. In 1959 and '60, for a Hollywood company called Herts-Lion, he hiked back and forth to Sweden to direct the Lon Chaney-hosted teleseries *13 Demon Street*, which also came a-cropper. *Variety* reported in December 1960 that Siodmak was suing Herts-Lion for $12,875 in writing-directing back pay. Several days later *Variety* printed a letter from Herts-Lion veepee Leo Guild who claimed that they did not think Siodmak was entitled to it but at the request of the Writers Guild and the Directors Guild had offered to pay him; but then Siodmak's attorney upped the amount to $18,000 which included his legal fees "[and] we made known our intention not to pay this additional sum."[22] Herts-Lion decided to turn three *13 Demon Street* episodes into a theatrical feature and, on a Hell set in some cheap Hollywood studio, they had Herbert L. Strock direct new framing

Beginning in 1948, Lon Chaney occasionally announced that he and Curt Siodmak were becoming partners in moviemaking, but nothing ever came of this. They worked together one last time on episodes of *13 Demon Street*, a spooky Swedish-made teleseries hosted by a rather dilapidated-looking Lon.

sequences with Lon Chaney as the Devil. (Strock told *Monster Bash* magazine that Chaney "seemed very relieved not to be working with Curt Siodmak again!") This feature, titled *The Devil's Messenger*, was released in 1962, with Siodmak's name nowhere to be found in the credits.

In 1966 Siodmak trekked to Prague to direct *Ski Fever* because when you think Swinging Sixties, ski resorts and young people romping on the slopes and in the sack, you think Curt Siodmak. *Variety* mocked this "carelessly made" attempt to attract the teen market with its shots of the ski lodge surrounded by bright green grass, and its process work which "appears to have been done in a department store display window."

After all this, Curt in his 1997 autobiography surmised that his brother Robert's efforts to convince him *not* to direct were prompted by Robert's fear that Curt would have "a big success."

"Curt has many negative feelings," Herbert L. Strock told me. "He always had a chip on his shoulder because of the fact that he could never follow in the footsteps of Robert, his brother, who *was* a fairly good director. Curt just couldn't get his own projects going the way he wanted to do them."

From the "You gotta love it!" department: In 2005 a DVD company called Vidtape released a double-bill of *Bride of the Gorilla* and *Invisible Avenger* (1958). On the cover are head shots of Chaney and Barbara Payton, so close together that it looks like a single two-headed person. And if this Manster-iffic layout isn't bad enough, the Chaney half isn't Lon Jr., it's his dear old dad, in a goofy grinning shot from 1923!

"My little seven-day-shooting picture [*Bride of the Gorilla*] was shown for many years on TV," Curt Siodmak wrote in *Even a Man Who Is Pure in Heart*. "Every time it was played, Gisela [Werbisek] sat in front of the TV set, admiring herself."

Never once does *Bride of the Gorilla* rise much above second feature status; its story was stamped out from a familiar die, and elements of excitement aren't there. To derive *any* pleasure from it, you have to be a card-carrying Monster Kid satisfied with an exotic rehash of *The Wolf Man* enacted by players we happen to like. It did make its presence felt in the 1951-52 cinemarketplace, doing quite well considering what it cost and what it *was*, but that probably had more to do with Barbara Payton, and the well-publicized mauling of Franchot Tone, than anything contributed by Curt Siodmak.

In short, Curt hadn't accomplished anything as a director with *Bride* that would cause sleepless nights for brother Robert, who apparently wanted only one Herr Director in the family. But Curt could still take pride in his accomplishment, and *did*, in *Even a Man Who Is Pure in Heart*: "I shot this full-length picture in seven days, a shorter time in which a TV sitcom is produced today."

From a bank book perspective, however, he hadn't done quite so well: "I broke even on this deal, since I received $2000 for the screenplay and direction, and paid $2000 to [join] the Directors Guild."

Imagine a Lewton-esque *Bride of the Gorilla*. A *Bride of the Gorilla*…or, better yet, *The Face in the Water* (Siodmak's original title)…with no gorilla, but *with* subjective shots of weird succarath claws (*not* gorilla hands), and an imaginatively made succarath face seen just once, **very** *vaguely* discernible in a climactic subjective shot of rippling pool water.

I think maybe *that* movie coulda been a contender.

GORILLA MY THEMES
The Music of *Bride of the Gorilla*
By David Schecter

Raoul Kraushaar's name has appeared on a few hundred feature films and television episodes, and for science fiction fans, he's probably best known because he's credited with composing the music for *Bride of the Gorilla* plus *Prehistoric Women* (1950), *Invaders from Mars* (1953), *Back from the Dead* (1957) and *The Unknown Terror* (1957). He also used the pseudonym Ralph Stanley, and that's who's credited on the 1948 dinosaur movie *Unknown Island*. Over his career,

Kraushaar's credits covered a range of job descriptions: music supervisor, music director, music consultant, conductor, composer, etc. Unfortunately, exactly what Mr. Kraushaar did on many of these productions cannot be known for certain, since the first two titles are catch-all positions for various tasks that might or might not have included creative responsibilities beyond the business ones.

Kraushaar has often been referred to as a music packager, the term describing a person who provides music for productions, with the sources generally or exclusively being written by other composers. Like a number of other composers or businessmen in the film music industry at that time, Kraushaar operated a music

Early and final version of cues sheets for *The Unknown Terror*, showing how the music credits pertaining to Paul Sawtell and Bert Shefter and their publishing company were replaced with credits for Raoul Kraushaar and *his* publishing company.

library that supplied pre-existing music tracks to film and television projects that didn't have the time or money to have original scores composed. Such music from Kraushaar's library wound up in many 1950s and '60s television series, including *Death Valley Days, The Gumby Show, Hopalong Cassidy, The Huckleberry Hound Show*, the original *Lassie, The Thin Man* and others.

In some cases, other composers would write new music expressly for a project, but Kraushaar would sometimes be credited with sole authorship of the works, or else co-authorship along with the actual composers. Kraushaar's Omar Music company would occasionally be listed as the music publisher that owned the copyright of the compositions. The advantage of being credited with writing or publishing film and TV music is that this information would be included on the production's cue sheets. Then, when the show played on TV or overseas, your performing rights organization (in Kraushaar's case, ASCAP) would pay writer or publisher royalties, presumably until the end of time. In addition, if any of the music was used for ancillary purposes, such as being re-used in a subsequent movie, TV show or commercial, the writer and publisher would receive licensing income as well as further royalties. There were a number of Hollywood music libraries doing roughly similar things, including Mutel and Gordon Music. The latter also owned a lot of music where Kraushaar was the credited writer.

When Kraushaar hired other composers to write new music, these jobs would probably be done as rights-free buy-outs. The composers would be paid for their actual work, but they wouldn't receive screen credit or credit on the cue sheets, meaning they would not receive any music royalties. Page 166 shows an early version of the cue sheets for *The Unknown Terror*, whose background score was largely if not exclusively composed by Dave Kahn. It's possible that Paul Sawtell and Bert Shefter, whose names are listed on the cue sheets as co-writers, also had a hand in it, although it's doubtful Kraushaar did. Sawtell and Shefter were pretty much the only composing team in Hollywood, writing countless film scores together (*The Cosmic Man, Kronos, It! The Terror from Beyond Space, Jack the Giant Killer, She Devil*). *The Unknown Terror*'s score is credited on the cue sheets as being published by their Bert Shefter Productions publishing company. However, in the revised version of the cue sheets that was submitted to ASCAP by 20th Century-Fox, only Kraushaar's name and his Omar Music publishing company are listed. What exactly

Raoul Kraushaar (standing) and Mort Glickman in the 1950s.

precipitated this alteration isn't known, but it illustrates how cue sheet and movie credits don't necessarily tell you who actually wrote the music.

When *The Unknown Terror* was released, the film credited only Kraushaar with writing the music, and to this day his estate and publishing company receive royalties when it plays. [Only the first page of each cue sheet version is shown here. Note that there are differences in some of the cue names and their timings, but they refer to the same music. Sir Lancelot, the other composer included on the cue sheets, was a Trinidad-born singer, songwriter, and actor (*I Walked with a Zombie, The Ghost Ship, The Curse of the Cat People, Zombies on Broadway*) named Lancelot Victor Edward Pinard. He wrote and performed a few songs in *The Unknown Terror* and is credited in the film as "King of the Calypsos"!

While Kraushaar probably had to pay the composers much of the money he received from production companies to provide music for their projects, given the low-budget nature *of* many of these projects, he would have known that future royalties would more than compensate him for what he paid the writers. When the buy-out included Kraushaar being able to publish the music through his own company, that would have doubled the royalties he'd receive. Plus, Kraushaar would end up with additional recordings that could be used in his library for future projects. When composers needed money in the here and now and they didn't care about future royalties or anyone knowing they had written the music, they could find work with Kraushaar and other music packagers and libraries operating out of Hollywood.

There was nothing illegal about using ghostwriters, and many famous and not-so-famous composers employed them, as do people in other creative fields. Some executives and music directors at studios and libraries would sometimes get their names on film, TV and music credits as being composers, thereby receiving corresponding royalties. Even an Academy Award nomination for Best Score did not necessarily mean you had everything—or *anything*—to do with writing that music. If you were an out-of-work composer, sometimes you had to go along with sharing or losing your writing credit if you needed the job. The history of pop and rock music is also replete with such "collaborations" done solely for financial reasons.

Exactly what Kraushaar's musical abilities were remain uncertain. He was born in Paris, France, on August 20, 1908, and studied at New York's Columbia University. After moving to California, he apparently crossed paths with Ted Fiorito, an orchestra leader, and Hugo Riesenfeld, one of the most important conductors and composers in the early years of motion pictures (the 1926 *Beau Geste, Peck's Bad Boy, Sunrise*, the 1923 *The Ten Commandments*). In the *ASCAP Biographical Dictionary*, Kraushaar's entry states that he conducted and wrote for various performers, including Gene Autry and Roy Rogers. A different biography lists him as having been some kind of assistant at both United Artists and RKO, as well as an assistant librarian at MGM, Warner Brothers and Los Angeles radio station KFWB.

Kraushaar is also credited with being a musical director at Republic, but his duties there are a bit of a mystery. Brigham Young University, which houses the Republic Pictures Music Archives, only shows his name in connection with about two dozen pieces of music, with the majority of them either being source music cues (non-dramatic music heard over a radio, phonograph, etc.) such as "Coronation March," "Jackson Swing," "La Cantare" and "Spanish Dance," or else collaborative pieces. Most of these "team efforts" appear to have been songs where at least one of the contributors provided lyrics, including "Daddy Dear," "I Fell in Love," "Just Between You and Me (Whadda Ya Say?)" and "Let Me Build a Cabin." The co-writers of these pieces included

incredibly skilled and prolific composers like William Lava, Cy Feuer and Mort Glickman (more about him later), whose music has been recorded and released on albums and CD. They all have many more writer credits in the Republic music archives than Kraushaar has.

In the world of film music, two composers were seldom co-credited with writing the same piece of music, with one rare exception being the aforementioned duo of Paul Sawtell and Bert Shefter. When you see two names associated with one piece of music, it's usually a song co-written by a composer and lyricist, or else an instrumental version of that song, as lyricists are still credited in such cases. If two names are on an orchestral piece of music that isn't a song, that often means that one of them got credited for a reason other than a musical contribution. If three names are on it, that probably means the person who didn't write the music had a friend. In his ASCAP biography, Kraushaar listed his chief collaborator as Minette Allton, with two projects they worked on being *Sixpack Annie* (1975) and *Children of Divorce* (1980). For whatever reason, he didn't mention any of the film composers who are listed as co-writers on many of his film and TV scores.

Whether Kraushaar was capable of composing complex film music isn't known. Many composers have archives housing their original music manuscripts; others' written scores can be found in studios' music libraries. However, to date, nobody in the film music business seems to have run across any of Kraushaar's written music in order to analyze it. None of his music seems to have ever been recorded or released for public consumption, the exception being one cue from *She Shoulda Said "No!"* (1949), which was lifted off the film's soundtrack, complete with narration.

Undoubtedly the most famous project that Kraushaar's name is associated with is the 1953 *Invaders from Mars*, whose score features some memorably haunting choral accompaniment, as well as chase passages that resemble Republic serial music. On January 10, 1953, the *Los Angeles Times* reported that Kraushaar "has obtained permission to have [his *Invaders from Mars* music score] published as a separate composition which will be called 'Music from Outer Space Into This World.'" This composition doesn't appear to have ever been performed. In reality, the *Invaders from Mars* music was ghostwritten by Mort Glickman, who worked on a number of projects that Kraushaar was involved with.

Born in Chicago on December 6, 1898, Glickman was educated in Chicago public schools, then moved to California and in 1939 began working in motion pictures. His music appeared in over 200 movies, although he didn't write entire scores for many of them, as other composers sometimes contributed to the soundtracks. In addition, much of Glickman's music was re-used in subsequent films. A lot of his music in the early 1940s was written for Republic serials, including *Adventures of Captain Marvel, The Black Widow, G-Men vs. the Black Dragon, Jesse James Rides Again, Jungle Girl, King of the Mounties, Mysterious Doctor Satan, Perils of Nyoka* and *Spy Smasher*. His music is also heard in low-budget Westerns and other film genres, including *Along the Navajo Trail, Campus Honeymoon, Thundering Trails* and *Whispering Footsteps*. The connection between Kraushaar and Glickman goes back at least to the beginning of Glickman's film career, as the two were co-credited on some music in *Jungle Girl*.

Mort Glickman was responsible for the music in *Bride of the Gorilla*, for which Kraushaar received the sole screen credit. The screenplays for both *Bride of the Gorilla* and *Invaders from Mars* are in Glickman's music archive at the University of Wyoming, showing he was definitely involved in both productions. Many other shooting scripts where Kraushaar was credited as the composer of record—but Glickman was not—also reside in Glickman's archive, among them *The Abbott and Costello Show, Hopalong Cassidy, The Longhorn, Maverick, Rose of Cimarron, The Sword of Monte Cristo, The Vanishing Herd* and *Waco*.

After Glickman died on February 27, 1953, Kraushaar then worked with composer Dave Kahn. Kahn was born in Duluth, Minnesota, on October 14, 1910, and studied with Ernst Toch and Ernst Krenek. After playing and arranging for dance bands, he wrote for movies and television, including *21 Beacon Street, Bachelor Father, Death Valley Days, Leave It to Beaver, Mike Hammer* and *Mr. Ed*. Kraushaar sometimes received credit for writing or co-writing Kahn's music, with two of their co-writing credits being for *Vigilante Terror* (1953) and *Back from the Dead*. In both pictures, Kraushaar was solely credited in the movie with writing the score, although Kahn was credited along with him on the cue sheets. A lot of Kahn's music from this era was published by Kraushaar's company, and some of it was also published by Gordon Music.

When Kraushaar passed away at age 93 in Pompano Beach, Florida, on October 13, 2001, a press release from Fort Lauderdale, Florida, was circulated stating, "Generations of American's [sic] grew up humming the themes to such classic television shows as *Lassie* and *Mr. Ed*, but few viewers realize that legendary composer, arranger and director Raoul Kraushaar composed those scores." One of the reasons few viewers realized that

A frame grab showing Kraushaar's *Bride of the Gorilla* screen credit.

was because it simply wasn't true. While Kraushaar supplied music to those series and many others, with the possibility being that he wrote some of it, he had no hand in writing the famous themes that viewers were familiar with.

The press release also mentioned that Kraushaar composed the music for "*Invaders from Mars*, one of the first Sci-fi flicks," and that "among his most famous musical scores and orchestrations for motion pictures are *Cabaret* with Liza Minnelli." In fact, *Cabaret*'s most famous musical score was written by John Kander and Fred Ebb, and the show was produced on Broadway in 1966, six years before the movie's release. In the film, Kraushaar is merely credited with being a music coordinator, serving as a music supervisor in post-production when the recorded tracks needed to be synched to the motion picture. It's likely that he got this job because the movie was produced by Cy Feuer, who worked with Kraushaar during their Republic days.

In addition, the press release claimed that *The Magnificent Matador* (1955) "was nominated for an Academy Award, partly due to its' [sic] masterful score done in Mexico in the 1950s" by Kraushaar. In reality, *The Magnificent Matador* was not nominated for any kind of award, either by the Academy of Motion Picture Arts and Sciences or anyone else. It's not known who wrote the press release or when it was written, but parts of it were reprinted in various versions of Kraushaar's obituary, so some of them are not an accurate assessment of his actual place in the history of film and television music.

Mort Glickman's *Bride of the Gorilla* score was composed for a moderately sized orchestra, probably numbering in the mid-twenties. Woodwinds, a smallish string section, and percussion are all efficiently used to take advantage of the orchestral forces on hand. Glickman knew how to benefit from the colors at his disposal, and these add a lot of variety to the score. His scaled-down accompaniment seldom sounds thin because he's always offering instrumental touches to keep things interesting, such as exotic woodwind figures and intriguing combinations of instruments.

Glickman's decision to avoid writing a lot of sustained, full-orchestral action passages was a wise one, as he didn't have sufficient brass or strings to effectively create music of this type. And it also helps that there's not much action in the movie, so his moderate ensemble offers enough variety to cover most scenes fairly well. Had there been a lot of action, he probably would have required more brass, which would have necessitated a further reduction in strings, and that would have made scoring the love scenes a little dicier.

Although strings are somewhat downplayed in the score, when the focus is on them, they usually sound surprisingly good, as the writing didn't stretch them beyond what their diminished numbers could properly handle. They're often played slowly and used to convey romance or atmosphere, rather than being featured prominently in what fast action music there is. Low strings are also employed where Glickman probably would have used brass if he had a larger orchestra. While brass adds impact to some appropriate moments in the score, it seldom dominates. The main difference between the orchestrations of *Bride of the Gorilla* and *Invaders from Mars* is that the latter film had a lot more action, and hence a much greater reliance on the larger brass section employed in that picture.

It's easier to use shortcuts and to repeat things than to have to come up with fresh musical material, and given the fact that *Bride of the Gorilla* was strictly a B picture, it would have been understandable had Glickman taken the easy way out by using some composing shortcuts. While the score contains a few ostinatos (repeated musical phrases) and trills (the rapid alternation between the same two notes), there's no reliance on these devices, which can sometimes be signs of laziness in a composer. Glickman does re-use a few musical ideas from time to time, such as a vibraphone shimmer and jungle drums, but these were done for thematic purposes rather than to make his job easier. In some programmers, composers would even use some of the actual recordings more than once in a picture—either due to budget and/or time constraints or lack of ingenuity. This wasn't the case with *Bride of the Gorilla*. That Glickman didn't seem to resort to any shortcuts is a testament to his work ethic and creativity.

Although there aren't any memorable musical themes in *Bride of the Gorilla*, that doesn't make the score any less successful. The film's simplistic plot is more than adequately served by Glickman's straightforward, yet multicolored, approach. After all, there isn't a lot of subtext in the movie that might have been helped by a musical accentuation of certain aspects of the story. The score is not terribly innovative, with tremolo strings creating suspense, Novachord or organ conjuring mystery, and other tried-and-true tricks of the trade. Glickman's music enhances scenes while they're unfolding and doesn't offer too much beyond that except reminding viewers that Raymond Burr's character is being taken over by the influence of the jungle. The music is prominently mixed on the soundtrack so it can easily be heard above the dialogue and sound effects.

The first minute of "*Bride of the Gorilla*—Main Title" opens with a series of repeated phrases with minor variations, and seems primarily designed to fill up the time it takes to display the credits. It sounds less like a through-composed piece than an assemblage of ideas, with some Miklós Rózsa influence thrown in for good measure. This might have been intentional, as Rózsa wrote the score for the 1942 Zoltan Korda-directed *Jungle Book*, where the Hungarian composer basically created the encyclopedia on how to score jungle-animal films. So it wouldn't be ridiculous to think that Glickman might have tried to emulate that approach. In fact, the second half of the "Main Title" is similar in execution to a cue Rózsa wrote for the beginning of *Jungle Book*, where montages in both films show various denizens of the jungle. Both Rózsa and Glickman scored these sequences by using different instruments and melodies to represent each beast, although the critters in *Bride of the Gorilla* are shown via stock footage. To be fair, though, it's an obvious way of tackling such a sequence. Rózsa's scene in *Jungle Book* was a lot longer, and while his melodic and orchestrational approaches were more sophisticated (and he had a much larger orchestra), Glickman does his best with the tools at his disposal, including a sliding effect on strings used to personify (serpentify?) a dangerous snake.

"Narration," the cue heard under Lon Chaney's introductory voice-over as Police Commissioner Taro, illustrates how Glickman used all the colors in his palette to create music that is beautiful, mysterious and forbidding at various points, as he juggles high strings, low strings, woodwinds, minimal brass, organ and other elements. It's an excellent composition that sets the tone for much of the music to follow.

Leslie Halliwell (*Halliwell's Film Guide*) called *Bride* "an incredibly inane two-bit shocker, a strong contender for any list of the worst films of all time" and categorized Payton, Chaney, Burr, Conway and Cavanagh as "a rare cast of non-actors." Here are four of the five (Conway, Payton, Cavanagh, Burr) plus Gisela Werbisek (standing) in the tense dinner scene.

When Barney arrives for dinner at the Van Gelder home and walks in on Dina as she's dancing, the source music "Rhumba El Perro" is a cut above similar music used in comparable scenes in such "crank 'em out" pictures. Nicely arranged for woodwinds, strings and percussion, it sounds like well-orchestrated gypsy music. The tune continues playing rather conspicuously even during the lengthy dialogue, and this is reflective of the overall respect with which the music was treated in the audio mix.

After the dinner table scene, the warm strings of "Don't Go Away" accentuate a potential romance between Barney and Dina, and when Larina professes her love for Barney, what could have been melodramatic or nondescript music in lesser hands instead has a few touches that illustrate how Glickman tried to go the extra mile (or at least a few hundred yards) when he didn't necessarily have to.

"The Snake Part #1" begins with an odd choice of music when Barney lectures Klaas Van Gelder outside

his home. Despite Barney and Klaas' accusatory tones, the music doesn't sound very threatening, and even though it darkens slightly as the conversation grows more ominous, it never comes close to the dramatic intensity of the dialogue. The sliding strings return when a deadly snake enters the scene, but the events leading up to and including Klaas' death-by-reptile could have been scored a little more potently, as not even the punches thrown by each man are musically emphasized. Instead, Glickman found a relatively simple and economical way of getting the musical point across with a reduced number of instruments.

After Barney enters Dina's bedroom without knocking, the scene is scored with more musical movement than one normally expects in a chatty scene like this, although that's partially due to the prominent volume the music has in the soundtrack. Despite this, the orchestral backing of "The Snake Part #2" doesn't interfere with the dialogue because Glickman chose instruments that have different timbres from the actors' voices, which both happen to be fairly low. When Al Long puts a pidgin English curse on Barney to turn him into a jungle beast, low brass, woodwind trills, vibraphone shimmers and other embellishments provide a suitable chamber music approach to this scene, with these sounds being used at other times in the score to evoke both her magical spell as well as the lure of the jungle, as the two are interrelated.

Exotic woodwinds and celesta highlight "Search the Room" when policeman Nado goes to Al Long's quarters to look for her "plant of evil," which she keeps in a chest. The music adds an appropriate mystical flavor, with strings and organ playing as Nado leaves. When Al Long places a curse on Barney in "The Poison," trilling woodwinds add a magical touch.

In "The Wedding," the background music combines light and frothy music befitting the happy occasion with some ominous underscore as Barney is served a drugged drink. As he swallows, woodwind trills and tympani accentuate the fact that he's drinking something much stronger than a boilermaker, reminding us that the sounds of the jungle are not far away, even in a gathering of such gaiety. When he and Dina meet outside, the cheery source music of "Honeymoon" plays, but as Barney prepares to sign the marriage certificate and his hand begins to blacken, prominent woodwind trills, brass and tympani sound. It's a powerful musical effect that adds a jolt of excitement to the sequence.

After Barney reveals to Dina that he loves the jungle and the critters in it even more than Tarzan does, he walks out alone into the foliage while the rich, warm strings of "He Turns" seem to conjure a romantic view of the jungle, an unusual but intriguing way of scoring such an idea. As Barney heads deeper into the soundstage undergrowth, low rhythmic sounds from brass and orchestra create a sense of some force driving him away from civilization. Glickman mixes in the musical themes of some of the jungle animals, and uses cymbal and vibraphone to add to the off-screen transformation of the beast that Barney's about to become. It's a complicated scoring approach, and while it's not flawlessly executed, the composer should be applauded for attempting more than a straightforward musical rendering of this event. Interestingly, the actual visual affirmation that Barney has achieved apedom is not musically emphasized.

"The Mirror" plays after an absence of music for almost seven minutes during some very talky scenes, with chiming celesta helping to enhance the bizarre sequence where Barney punches out a mirror after he sees a man in a gorilla suit staring back at him. A vibraphone shimmer ends the sequence, although even without music, this incident already belongs in the Cinematic Hall of Fame's Mirror Wing along with the reflective sequences in *The Lady from Shanghai* and *Duck Soup*. Foreboding low strings and brass raise suspense as Barney once again enters Dina's room without knocking, although he can probably be forgiven this time, as gorillas seldom knock. When Dina awakens and then leaves her room, the full orchestra provides some of the most intense music in the movie, mainly courtesy of the brass. Strings enhance the action, one of the few times they're used in such a fashion. What's surprising is that even though there's almost no dialogue and only a few sound effects, the music is mixed rather quietly in this sequence.

"The Trap" is heard when Dina looks for Barney, with flute runs bringing life to the jungle set, low strings again providing a sense of purpose in her search. Glickman strings together various motifs to keep things interesting until she finds him caught in an animal trap, when the music just seems a little unsure of what its purpose is supposed to be. In Glickman's defense, the sequence is a bit like a montage, with Dina's efforts being interspersed with shots of various jungle denizens, so the somewhat slapped-together nature of this music is understandable.

The sequence where Barney and Dina express their eternal love for each other despite a number of clunker lines and some less-than-believable acting was "scored" with crickets chirping in the background. Perhaps Glickman wanted jungle noises (assuming crickets can be considered jungle creatures) during their romantic interlude? Or maybe he didn't have enough time to score the scene, or else didn't think it required music? But given the lack of chemistry between the two leads and the absence of convincing dialogue, some amorous underscore might have helped evoke some of the deep romantic feelings that are missing from the presentation.

Vibraphone shimmers color Barney making his way "Out of the Fog," and then romantic and dramatic passages interweave as Dina tells him "You've Been Poisoned," whereupon Barney serves notice on his wife that he's decided to spend the rest of his life in the jungle, which at least means she wouldn't have to waste a lot of time dusting and vacuuming. Flute runs accentuate Barney's description of his heightened jungle senses, and some excellent string writing and the presence of drums leaves no doubt that the jungle is now Barney's home, the music accelerating to stress his crazed state of mind.

As Dina runs into the jungle after Barney, "Shoot Me" uses brass to help accentuate that his love for her has been replaced by his newfound love for foliage. When Dr.

Viet and Taro meet at the deserted Van Gelder home, some of the music that plays in "Shoot Me" is similar to that used two years later in *Invaders from Mars*, but it's more a case of both creations coming from the same artistic wellspring rather than being a deliberate act of copying. Another use of this music can be heard near the end of some *Alfred Hitchcock Presents* episodes, one being "Back for Christmas" (1956). What's interesting is that neither Glickman nor Kraushaar was credited with writing any music for that TV series, but Dave Kahn—Kraushaar's post-Glickman ghostwriter—was. Kahn's music in the show was published by Gordon Music, who would sometimes credit music to composers who didn't write it. The 1950s was definitely the Golden Age of Confusing Music Credits!

Bride of the Gorilla's climax ("The Gorilla Attack") is handled with the full ensemble as the chase is on to find Barney, who's probably out scrounging for bananas. Trills, repeated phrases and forceful strings sound while brass further builds the excitement. It's a well-conceived composition that builds throughout, and it manages to piece together sundry musical elements of the score without sounding disjointed. This assemblage wouldn't have been out of place in some of the serials Glickman scored near the beginning of his career.

A vibraphone shimmer in "Barney's End" accompanies the dying man seeing his image revert from simian to human—the musical effect connecting this to the earlier mirror scene. A sad oboe describes the lifeless body of Dina before the full orchestra brings the drama to a close, tympani hammering home the finality of the tale.

Despite the score being somewhat disposable and not "one for the ages," it was obviously made by a true craftsman. Well-conceived, composed and orchestrated, it serves the movie very well. It's one of the better ingredients in the film, and one wonders if, when Glickman presumably viewed the finished motion picture, he had any reservations that he wasn't credited for his fine creation.

SIODMAK'S BRAIN
By Scott MacQueen

The Siodmaks' beautiful home, Blossom Ranch.

One might joke about finding the writer of *Frankenstein Meets the Wolf Man* living near the fictive Mittel-European village of Visaria, stomping grounds of monsters, vampires and werewolves in the old Universal horror pictures, but I did not expect to pass through its homophonic sister city on my way to meet their author, Curt Siodmak.

What a difference a diphthong makes. A half-hour northeast of Visalia, California, Curt Siodmak made his home in Three Rivers, a sleepy little outpost of 2000 souls in the foothills of Sequoia National Park. It is eponymously named for being situated smack in the middle of three forks of the Kaweah River, though in truth there are *four* forks, making Three Rivers something of a misnomer. But twisting truth is an art in Hollywood, where Curt once made his living and reputation as a screenwriter and movie director.

On a bright, cloudless September morning in 1999 I threaded along Lake Kaweah a half-hour beyond Visalia. The desert and high desert of Southern California were behind me and the water table of the mountain region encouraged lush grasses and greenery so unlike the arid climate to the south. I turned my Toyota off Highway 198 and started up what seemed a small mountain. Under blameless azure skies the car chugged up a steep, badly paved roadway. What would I find at the top, a castle teetering over a precipice? A broken battlement of a bygone age? Horse-drawn caravans and gypsies huddled around campfires, muttering that there was a werewolf in camp?

Casa Siodmak came into view: a modest, one-bedroom yestermorrow house in post-World War II modernist style. "Blossom Ranch" was a charming, bygone product of the mid-20th century, the work of architect Frank Roberts who had been assistant to Frank Lloyd Wright. It was single story, redwood-faced with a cantilevered roof and windows that were more like glass walls wrapping around two sides.

The house was situated on 50 acres of rolling meadow sheltered by trees, ringed on all sides by mountain peaks, which on crisp nights glowed with phosphorescence when the moon was full and bright. The meadow behind the house was leased to an equestrian neighbor, and sociable horses gamboled down to the fence line to nod their heads and inquire of visitors for errant carrots or apples they might have hidden on their person.

Curt and his wife Henrietta had stumbled on Three Rivers in the late 1950s while searching for a rustic home for Henrietta's fickle mother. On sighting Three Rivers, Henrietta made up her mind. Just as she had moved them out of Nazi Germany and harm's way in 1933, she determined that they would decamp Hollywood for the Sierras. Curt was adamant that he would not leave Hollywood. His work was there. Henrietta knew better and smiled. They had known no other home since.

Forty-one years later I had come to whisk Siodmak back to the factory town he had left in 1958. I had been asked to shepherd the 97-year-old writer down to Los Angeles where he was to be a guest at Cinecon 35 over the Labor Day weekend.

Siodmak was a legendary figure. As a kid I positively doted on movies he wrote like *The Wolf Man, I Walked with a Zombie, Earth vs. the Flying Saucers* and *Donovan's Brain*. Six hours round-trip in his company would be enlightening for someone like me.

A reputation preceded him for being outspoken, a bit cantankerous and perhaps prone to embellishment, so I was expecting something of an überego. He had been interviewed so many times, with stories that seemed immutable. *Did Bela really sound like a Borscht Belt stand-up comic as a Hungarian Frankenstein Monster? Was Lon really a terrible drunk? Did you really write that werewolf jingle yourself?* I determined to avoid an inquisition but to meet him on his own terms and not dwell on questions about his past. It wasn't going to be that sort of encounter.

Curt welcomed me into the living room where he was holding court with the local postmistress and her husband. They had become good friends two years before when the Classic Monster Movie stamps had made the Three Rivers post office the official USPS "Wolf Man Station." The good folk of the Kaweah River region might not differentiate between a beast with five fingers and a creature with an atom brain, but they were not angry villagers. They knew a bona fide celebrity when they saw one and Curt Siodmak belonged to them.

The house had a Spartan aesthetic, repose for the

So *that's* how you say it!

spirit and clarity for the mind. It was typical modernism of the last century, stripped down and airy with natural materials and simplified geometric lines. You sensed that its occupants were contented people. The two walls of large windows opened up the house to the outdoors, admitting soft northern light. The differentiated spaces—a foyer, living room, dining area and kitchen—all flowed together in a continuum that still retained intimacy. The only segregated area with closed doors was the personal space, a small bedroom, bath and study. Curt had remodeled the attached one-car garage to create a guest bedroom.

Pots of live flowers and sprawling ivy, framed floral prints, simple oak furniture and comfy stuffed chairs added to a decor that would drive a pack rat or neurotic to distraction. No Siodmak career mementos cluttered the house. The sole token was a framed copy of Orson Welles' Grammy citation for "Best Spoken World Album" given for the 1982 release of Welles' *Suspense* radio adaptation of Curt's novel *Donovan's Brain*. Curt was not prideful about himself, but he was proud of Orson and proud of the award as it reflected on him as the author.

Curt was stooped and shrunken and bald as an egg but his eyes were keen and bright, his voice strong and forceful and his brain uncluttered and sharp. As we made our introductions and got to know each other, I could feel Curt's gaze on me. He was taking my measure, weighing me. He was keen to know what work I did and was interested that I was employed at one of the studios. That gave us a professional basis for conversation and he permitted himself to open up slowly to me. As the afternoon progressed, he became forthcoming enough to offer me advice, asking if I did any writing and encouraging me to pursue it so I could be my own boss and not beholden to "them."

"Your brain is your best friend. They can't take that away from you!" said the writer who had orchestrated many brain snatchings in his day. There was wicked tycoon Warren H. Donovan in *Donovan's Brain*, so indomitable that his malignant personality thrives even after his body has failed. There were the Ruritarian proles of *House of Frankenstein*, Strauss and Ullmann, low-class *dummkopfs* scheduled to become *dämonkopfs*. There was the hardboiled mobster of *Black Friday*, Red Cannon, a bad egg whose cerebrum gets scrambled with the erudite yolk of an egghead college professor, spouting poetry while bumping off his enemies. And of course, the *Creature with the Atom Brain*.

"My brain is my best friend—except for Henrietta," Curt stated with certitude.

I was ushered into the tiny bedroom to meet Henrietta, an invalid confined to her bed and wheelchair. Henrietta Siodmak retained her dignity and elegance. She was the Baroness de Perrot by birth, of Swiss nobility. She would have been heiress to a baronial legacy but for her father's indiscretion of marrying beneath his station. At 96 she still bore the stamp of beauty and the manner of European aristocracy. The flow of affection between her and Curt was tangible.

As we talked, there was a noise at the screened window and the final, most beautiful member of the household announced his arrival. Curt opened the window and a handsome, gregarious tabby tom cat sauntered in and nestled on the bed with Henrietta.

"This is Caruso," said Curt, stroking the little gray beast. As cats do, he had appeared one day, blasted to commemorate his arrival, and moved in. The tabby sang to Henrietta in tones of lyrical liquidity. Curt smiled. "Now you know how he got his name."

As the shadows began to lengthen I suggested to Curt that we should be on our way. It would be three hours to Los Angeles and dark when we arrived.

"Ah, but we are not going *tonight*! You will stay here and we will go *tomorrow*!" And that was that. No toothbrush or extra socks in my pocket. The bridge was out, so to speak, and I would stay the night.

The Siodmaks retained as part-time housekeeper a young Latina who came a few hours each day to attend to the shopping and cleaning and to arrange their meals, which Curt would later prepare himself. Having laid up salmon steaks, a salad and fresh vegetables for supper,

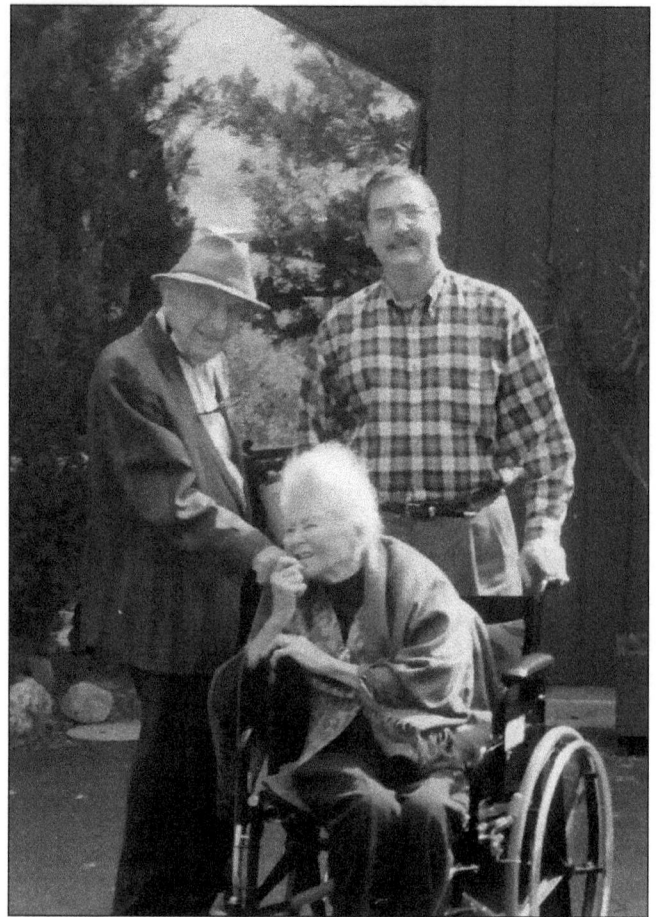

Scott MacQueen with Curt and Henrietta Siodmak. It was Henrietta who set her heart on a house in the Sierras in 1958, and it became their home until the ends of their lives.

she made final inquiries to their needs before leaving for the day.

The cocktail hour started at five. Curt brought down a sturdy silver plate martini shaker, an heirloom conspicuous by a creamy finish burnished by age. Would I like a martini, Curt asked? Scotch-and-water is my drink of choice, and I told Curt so. He looked at me incredulously, as if I had just told him I had an atom brain. "With *water*?" he barked in astonishment bordering on disgust, utterly disbelieving that anyone could be so barbaric as to dilute Scotch whisky. I relented and accepted a martini.

That was more to Curt's liking. When the drinks were shaken and poured, I noticed that the lip of the shaker top was engraved in German:

To my beloved Kurt from Henrietta —
FP1 — 1932

It was a gift to a writer from his muse. Henrietta had presented the shaker to him in Berlin 67 years before to commemorate his first literary success, *F.P.1 Does Not*

Reply, his novel about sabotage at a floating aviation platform in the mid-Atlantic.

I remarked on the shaker, which started Curt talking of the days before the war. "I was so stupid," he said. "You would think that a Jew would have known better and seen what Hitler was going to become, but I thought it would pass. Henrietta, the gentile, she was the one who saw clearly and said we had to get out—now! I would not be alive today but for this wise woman," and he kissed her hand, which made her glow.

As the martinis flowed, he spoke of Germany and Hollywood and the émigré experience. He talked about visiting the island location for *F.P.1*, Greifswalder Oie in the Baltic Sea (today a bird sanctuary) where the film of his book was made in German, English and French versions. He made no bones about the practicality of a work-for-hire writer concocting *Frankenstein Meets the Wolf Man* because he needed the money to buy a car.

I had determined to not play a round of *Jeopardy!* with Curt but my reason for being there, his upcoming appearance at Cinecon, lubricated by gin and dry vermouth, inevitably made him chatty. Soon his desire to reminisce was unstoppable. Two topics that recurred were his brother Robert and the actor Lon Chaney. Curt was indirectly responsible for launching both of their trajectories at Universal.

I once thumbed brother Robert Siodmak's shooting script for *Son of Dracula*, autographed by cast and crew. There were the usual homilies.

> To Robert—A swell guy to work for
> —Samuel S. Hinds

> Best wishes and appreciation for your swell direction!
> —Evelyn Ankers

Then came the besotted master of Dark Oaks, ham-fisted Lon Chaney Jr., who with characteristic sensitivity had written:

> I can't wish all foreigners luck, but I do for you.

Lon seems to have also made an exception for Curt. (Or *Curtis*, as he was billed on some of his Universal films.) They became friendly and when the horror picture boom went bust after the war, the two nearly

Siodmak wrote five Lon Chaney movies, starting with their most famous, *The Wolf Man*, and ending with *Bride of the Gorilla*.

started a production company together in 1948 to make the kind of pictures they specialized in.

"Lon Chaney was a close friend. He was a nice fellow but deeply troubled. He had a deep resentment of his father who, he told me, beat him as a boy and never gave him love or approval. This caused him to drink terribly. He was a tortured man and a secret homosexual. I had him on a picture I made called *Bride of the Gorilla* with Raymond Burr, who was also homosexual. They *hated* each other. You should have seen these two queens going at it, sparks shooting out of their eyes."

Lon had family issues and so did Curt. Sibling dynamics can be just as complex as the parent-child paradigm. Robert had given Curt his first typewriter in Berlin in 1929 and encouraged his writing. Years later with Weimar Germany a memory and the brothers thousands of miles away in Hollywood, it was Curt's turn to help his older brother.

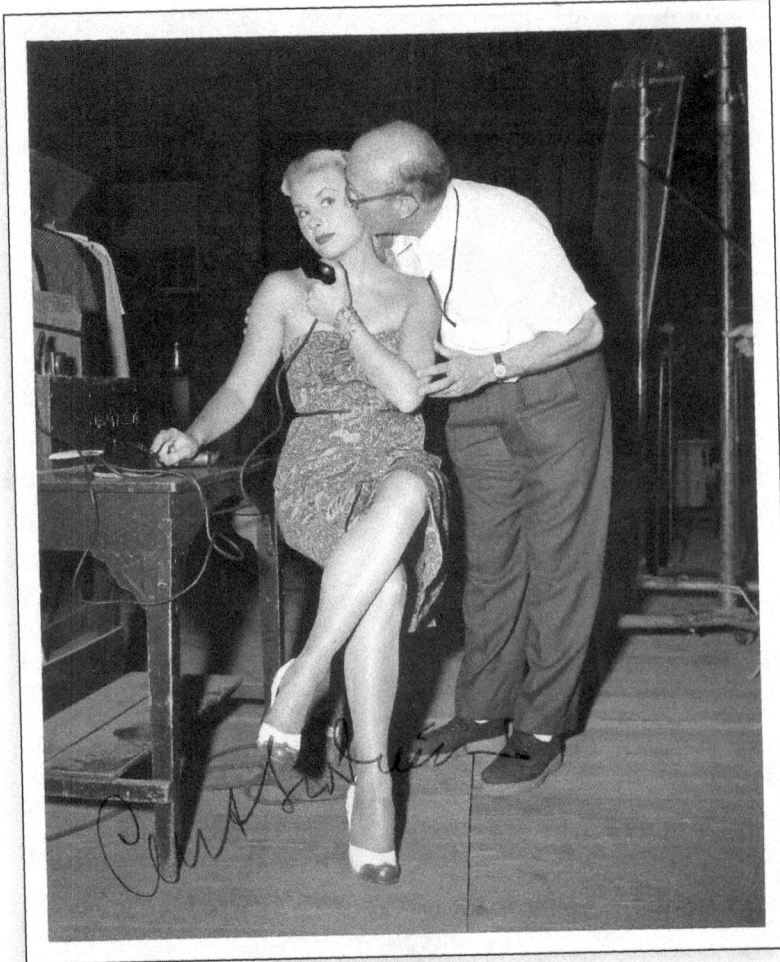

Siodmak felt that directing a movie was based "80 percent on public relations." He tests that theory with a peck to the cheek of *Bride of the Gorilla* star Barbara Payton. (Photo courtesy Ronald V. Borst/Hollywood Movie Posters)

"Jack Gross had me writing the story for Lon Chaney's picture *Son of Dracula* and Robert needed a job. I got Universal to hire him to direct it, and the first thing that son of a bitch Robert did was have me fired off the picture."

The following year Curt wrote *I Walked with a Zombie* for producer Val Lewton. The central plot is a contest of wills between two brothers. The elder one is a stiff-necked bastard married to the titular revenant. The kid brother is a sensitive softie deep in his cups. The boys' mother, as it transpires, has put the whammy on the errant wife to punish the daughter-in-law for diddling with the kid brother.

"That is Robert and me," said Curt. "No, we did not swap wives though Robert adored Henrietta. But we always fought, no question." I mentioned that Robert's famous thriller *The Spiral Staircase* (1946) was also about two brothers at loggerheads, the bad one a murderer, the good one suspected.

Curt just smiled and nodded his head. Robert had been dead a quarter of a century and Curt had yet to make peace with his brother's ghost.

Robert was a highly successful director of top-notch thrillers like *Phantom Lady, The Suspect* (both 1944) and *The Killers* (1946). I asked Curt why a successful writer in mid-life would decide to start directing. In my blockhead naiveté I suggested that perhaps he wanted to protect his screenplays?

Curt looked at me like my atom brain had just popped out of my head.

"I started to direct to show that *bastard* Robert that I could do it!"

If Curt had wanted to beat Robert at his own game, he was ill-advised. He was never a great shakes as a director. Discretion prevented me bringing it up, but Curt was removed from *The Magnetic Monster* after a few unproductive days. Producer Allan Dowling replaced him with Felix Feist on *Donovan's Brain* before he could shoot even a foot of Nancy Davis (later Reagan) wondering, "Where's the rest of Donovan?"

He was proud of making his two color features in Brazil. He wasn't proud of the movies. He knew they were terrible. But he had accomplished them against terrible odds and lived to tell the tale. "I directed *Love Slaves of the Amazons* on location in Brazil. It was a terrible experience. I had already done *Curucu, Beast of the Amazon* there, with Beverly Garland, and I should have learned from that. No resources, no facilities, just heat and incompetence and disease. It ruined my health making that picture. But I went back to do *Love Slaves*. Why did I do it? I bought this house with the money I made on that stupid picture, that's why."

The *Schwimmplattform ein Martini-Mixbecher* was shaken several more times. I asked Curt to autograph one of his books I had brought with me. Taking up a pen, he jotted on the flyleaf, "To Scott—*without water!*"

By the time dinner was served, my brain had been sabotaged by floating martinis decanted from the final days of the Weimar Republic. Curt showed absolutely no effect and was merrily broiling salmon filets in the kitchen. Wine was uncorked and candles were lit. Curt rolled Henrietta's wheelchair to the table and kissed her tenderly on the forehead as he served the excellent salmon filets. We dined by candlelight as through Frank Roberts' copious windows, night fell across the Sierras.

After supper, Curt went into the kitchen and took a canister (no, not the martini shaker) from the counter and beckoned me come outside with him. We stepped through sliding doors adjacent to the kitchen onto a patio slab and into the night. He snapped off the porch light so that only a small glow spilled from the kitchen into the yard. We settled into patio chairs.

"Just wait," he said with an air of mystery. Our eyes adjusted to the darkness and were soon met by the eyeshine of nocturnal creatures. From the canister Curt withdrew a handful of dog kibble and broadcast the hard brown nuggets into the darkness. To the perimeter of the brief circle of light came the cautious owners of the *tapetum lucidum*. Creatures of the night, masked, ring-tailed and determined. Dozens of them large and small, old and young. Creatures whose way of walking were thorny. Procyonid vagabonds on the prowl and on the dole.

The raccoons had come for their nightly handout. The Siodmaks had been subsidizing Three Rivers' nocturnal bandits for four decades.

By eleven o'clock we retired. Curt rolled Henrietta's chair into the small bedroom. Waving away my offer of assistance, he lifted her from her chair and placed her gently on the bed. Caruso bounded in trilling and purring and kneading the sheets as he prepared to bed down with his mistress. She smiled as Curt tucked her in and kissed her again on the forehead before escorting me to the guest room, the converted garage at the back of the house.

At six the next morning, Curt knocked on my door. Hollywood beckoned.

Actually it was Pasadena. Cinecon had recently departed the seedy charm of the Hollywood Roosevelt for the spacious efficiency of the Red Lion Inn. Chris Horak, former director of the Munich Film Archive, would interview Curt following a screening of the title-tells-all sci-fi drama, *Trans-Atlantic Tunnel*. It seemed an odd choice in that it owed very little to Curt. He had written the screenplay for this story of an extraordinary engineering feat in day-after-tomorrow style, very similar in tone to *F.P. 1*. It feels like Siodmak material though it is based on a 1913 Bernhard Kellermann novel in addition to being an English remake of an UFA picture.

Perhaps it was for the good. As his major assignment at Gaumont-British following his escape from Germany, *Trans-Atlantic Tunnel* positioned Curt, well, mid-Atlantic between Berlin and the new world, as good a starting point for conversation as an interlocutor could wish.

Curt's liason at Cinecon was an odd, potty little man named Robert Nudelman, invariably dressed in too-tight pants and a too-plaid, short sleeve polyester shirt buttoned at the neck. He was a "holy man" in film buff and recherché circles, a film geek with a reputation as a tireless champion of Los Angeles culture, history and architecture. Nudelman founded Hollywood Heritage and led the charge to preserve historic landmarks as diverse as the Cinerama Dome, the Lasky-DeMille Barn and the domed (and doomed) shell of the Hollywood Bowl.

Monomaniacal in his efforts to turn back the clock, Nudelman never had a job *per se* and subsisted on handouts from his parents and, it was whispered, from the *sub rosa* pilfering of Hollywood memorabilia he had cadged for the museum. Remarking on his premature death in 2008 at age 52, the *Los Angeles Times* called him "the conscience of Hollywood." Curt would remark later that Nudelman seemed to have had little conscience of his own.

As was customary, Curt was asked to be available to sign autographs after his event at which time he could also sell copies of his recently published memoirs or other ephemera. To this end he brought with him a box of philatelic curios.

When the U.S. Post Office issued the Classic Movie Monster series of stamps in 1997, Curt had made a commemorative four-color folio celebrating the writers who created the primal Universal monsters: Mary Shelley, Bram Stoker, Gaston Leroux, John Balderston and himself. These had been sold to the citizenry of Three Rivers at a gala "Wolf Man Day" held on the First Day of Issue. Inserted into the folio was a mint plate block sheet of 20 stamps depicting Frankenstein, Dracula, the Phantom, the Mummy and the Wolf Man. Also included were First Day Covers cancelled at the Three Rivers "Wolf Man Station," the movie's famous pentagram symbol incorporated into the postmark. Bonus! The "Wolf Man" cover was autographed by Curt as was the folio.

Curt had a quantity of these left over which he brought with him expecting that the Cinecon audience would seize on them as a $20 collector's item. Hell, the stamps alone were worth six and a half dollars as raw postage.

Cinecon has a traditional memorabilia auction, the proceeds of which help fund the convention. He had kept the poster-sized Wolf Man display used in Three Rivers. "Here," said Curt, handing the Wolf Man poster to Nudelman. Uncapping a Sharpie pen, the author of "Even a man who is pure in heart..." boldly autographed the portrait of his brainchild.

"Take my Wolf Man for your auction." Nudelman gratefully accepted the poster. He also took charge of the folios to spare his elderly guest the indignity of schlepping them about.

The Cinecon crowd proved less than keen to drop 20 bucks on monster stamps, especially as Curt was signing their memorabilia for free. Most of the stamp folios remained unsold and there was a full box left on the table at the end of Curt's meet-and-greet. When it came time for Curt to leave on Sunday, Nudelman could not produce the folios. "Just send them to me in Three Rivers," Curt told him. "You have the address."

Subsequently Curt and I kept in touch every few weeks by phone. In the spring he called with news. The Writers Guild West had selected him to receive a Lifetime Achievement Award at their annual awards banquet on March 5. Would I return to Three Rivers and conduct him to his new honors in Los Angeles?

By happy accident, concurrent with the awards ceremony, Martin Koerber's restoration of *Menschen am Sonntag*, the remarkable 1930 *avant garde* film Curt had conceived, was programmed as part of the Los Angeles Country Museum film series "Berlin Between the Wars" and Curt was invited to introduce it.

People on Sunday, as it is known in English, is one of the seminal works not only of German cinema but of world cinema. It anticipated Italian neorealism by nearly two decades. Based on a literary treatment by Curt, it examines the simple pleasures of young working class Berliners on their day off. The roll call of principals attached to it is remarkable: directed by brother Robert, with participation by Billy Wilder, Fred Zinnemann, Edgar G. Ulmer and Eugen Schüfftan.

Wolfgang Rudolph, the courtly German Consul in Los Angeles, arranged dinner for Curt at a wonderful French restaurant in Beverly Hills, the now-vanished Brasserie des Artistes on Wilshire Boulevard. The menu was resplendent with Gallic delicacies. Curt and I compared culinary notes. Would we have the *Poulet Dijon*, chicken in wine and mustard? The time-honored snails in garlic butter, *Escargots Meuniere*? He pointed to the menu and tapped it with his finger. "Would you like to share *this*?" he asked.

I have never been fond of organs in my diet. As a child, I would refuse to leave my bedroom in protest when that bright tell-tale odor signaled that my mother was frying up liver for supper. And while my grandfather may have hailed from Scotland, the thought of haggis still turns my complexion verdant.

Curt thought a full order was more than he could handle, and I didn't wish to disappoint his cultured

appetite on a special occasion. Here was a gourmand who had feasted in Germany, Switzerland and France (and England, where he found the food abominable). So I agreed: We would split the entrée. It was a night of adventure and I was game for anything. We would have the *cassoulet de veau*.

Chef Jean-Pierre outdid himself. Prepared in butter and wine and shallots, the *cassoulet* was delicious. "This is very good," I remarked to Curt. "Is this one of your favorite dishes?" This highly civilized European man, who had wined and dined around the world for nearly a century, looked at me in surprise.

"No. I have never eaten brains before. They are very good."

And thus, both of us novices in matters of the culinary mind, I shared a plate of calves' brains with the author of *Donovan's Brain*. It was my first brain, though not Curt's, if literary precedent is worth anything. Little did I know that Donovan would make a subsequent, less agreeable appearance that evening.

Our bellies were sated with encephalic essence of Donovan as we arrived at the County Museum at seven o'clock. In the car Curt had complained about Robert's high-handed disregard for his contributions to *Menschen am Sonntag*. To his dying day Robert denied that Curt had written a treatment (typed on that very typewriter Robert had given to Curt in 1929), instead giving credit for a screenplay to a neophyte newspaper reporter. "There was no screenplay," insisted Curt. "We made up the scenes with actors as we went along based on the ideas I had written down. Robert did not want two Siodmaks' names prominent on the movie so he gave screen credit to that *Zeitungsreporter* and put my name in tiny print under Billy Wilder."

The slight stung twice as badly because Curt had in part financed the movie to help Robert get his start, kicking in nearly half of the budget from his literary earnings. Robert had no problem taking Curt's money and his credit.

Once in the Bing Auditorium, Curt was taken in tow by the tireless Ian Birnie, director of the Film Department, and seated down front on the aisle from where he could make a graceful ascent to the stage. The audience began to arrive, among them a potbellied man wearing a beige polyester suit, circa 1978, and a pencil moustache, circa 1938. It was the unmistakable figure of Forrest J (no period) Ackerman, the Famous Monster. He made a beeline down the aisle and stopped at Curt's bald head, smiling like a greasy jack-o'-lantern.

Ackerman was one of the colorful fringe characters of the Los Angeles demimonde, the self-anointed alpha and omega of sci-fi fandom. The primeval fanboy had become famous as the editor of the children's magazine *Famous Monsters of Filmland* which featured stories and photos of him and his famous doings in Hollywood, attending monster movie premieres and meetings of "The Count Dracula Society" or, armed with Electrolux, vacuuming his famous living room.

He fancied himself a literary agent, though somehow he never got around to the inconvenient legal requirement of obtaining an agent's license. He claimed to be Ray Bradbury's agent, which must have surprised Ray Bradbury's agent, Don Congdon.

For decades whenever "Mr. Monster" appeared in public, he would parade up and down, waving his Dracula ring and cradling under his arm some book or magazine featuring him on the cover. Had he put on cap and bells, or a sandwich board with flashing lights, he could not have been more ostentatious. This evening he was toting an oversized paperback book from which the blood-red word ACKERMAN blazed like a beacon above a ghastly electric green brain, bisected by a lightning arc.

Like patrons at a dumb show pantomime, Herr Rudolph and I watched in horror as, from across the auditorium, Ackerman brandished the book at Curt. A loud outpouring of Teutonic invective befouled the Bing and hung in the auditorium like a profane cloud of *Umweltverschmutzung*. Ackerman stood there with a stupid smile frozen on his face as Curt upbraided him. We could not make out the words but the force of their delivery was astonishing.

Later we would learn the reason for the *sturm und drang*: Ackerman had taken it upon himself to republish *Donovan's Brain* under the all-caps banner **FORREST J ACKERMAN PRESENTS** in a lavishly large font and positioned above the author's name. Curt knew nothing about this and had never authorized it. Also in the series was *This Island Earth* by Raymond F. Jones, a deceased Latter Day Saint who was likely having too much fun to protest since presumably, as promised by Mormon doctrine, he was busy ruling his own personal Metaluna in the Hereafter. His longtime agent in the here-and-now, the Scott Meredith Literary Agency, likely would object. Curt's wrath could have been worse had he known that Ackerman had also pilfered a new edition of the *Donovan* sequel, *Hauser's Memory*.

So there it was, the double whammy. Like brother Robert, friend Forry had no problem taking what was not his. Robert had taken Curt's money and put his name in teeny-weenie letters under Wilder. Now Forry took Curt's money and placed his own name above Curt's.

Curt's anger threw a pall over an evening that should

have been a triumph. The dignified Martin Koerber of the Filmmuseum Berlin-Deutsche Kinemathek, the man who had carefully reassembled *Menschen am Sonntag*, was introduced. Curt was brought on stage to be interviewed, still seething after the exchange with Ackerman. No sooner had poor Mr. Koerber opened his mouth than Siodmak shut it for him, not permitting Martin to utter another word. He was in no mood for more puppet masters and lectured extemporaneously for a half-hour about the production of the film.

He and *Menschen am Sonntag* were both well received. On the way back to the hotel he remarked with satisfaction about being the last man standing: "Robert is gone but so what? I am here tonight." He rationalized Ackerman's impudence as the desperate act of an old friend in need. "*Ach*, he lives in that big house and he can barely afford it. I guess he needs the money more than I do."

Well, hardly. I had seen the alarming photos in the *Los Angeles Times* of an anguished Ackerman literally crying poverty as he sold his Los Feliz house (for $1.3 million, as it turned out). But living in Three Rivers, Curt would be unaware that Ackerman's ceaseless poor-mouthing didn't square with his jet-set, bachelor pad lifestyle, allowing that one's bachelor pad was an 18-room mansion crammed with pulp magazines, crumbling rubber monster toys and naif art of zaftig women in fetish costumes. Anything of real value had been looted years before by con artists.

Visitors touring "the Ackermansion" (it can only be described as *Cabman Gray Meets Grey Gardens*) were escorted at journey's end to the egress and encouraged to linger near a sideboard where a judiciously seeded, deep-dish "donation bowl" overflowed with coins. Artfully crumpled dollar bills topped the bowl as casually as fried onions are strewn on a green bean casserole. A tearful sign pleaded with the visitor to give generously to the upkeep of this "museum."

Mercifully, Curt would never learn that his friend-who-cried-poverty (while pocketing Curt's royalties and affixing his own name on Curt's books) would effortlessly donate $153,000 to the American Cinematheque as a tax dodge, conditional on affixing his name on 153 seats in the Egyptian Theater along with 153 of his famous monsters and friends. Weirdly, one of the seats is named for Henrietta, but there is no seat for Curt.

Curt found it in his heart to excuse Ackerman, but he didn't excuse Robert Nudelman.

"Nudelman!" he exclaimed to me, disgusted. "You know what that means? *Noodle Maker*. That damn Noodle Maker still has my stamps and won't give them

Curt and Henrietta Siodmak.

back. I have called him again and again but he will not return my call. Maybe you can get my stamps back." I promised I would try.

Curt was visibly excited to attend the Writers Guild dinner the following evening at the Beverly Hilton. Herr Rudolph again accompanied us and it gratified Curt that a representative of the German government was there to pay him homage.

He had long ago embraced America with both arms. "It is the only country that did not tell me 'Get out,'" he said. He knew that nationalism, jingoism and religious fanaticism were the eternal authors of global misery. But his heritage was Jewish and German and his identity was inexorably bound to both worlds. He had nothing but horror in his soul for the conduct of the Nazis. He was sickened by the ongoing failure of the German people to admit their responsibility for the annihilation of six million Jews and the destruction of Weimar *kultur*.

The Writers Guild presentation sickened him, too. It unfolded like a surreal minstrel show. No white fool in blackface, our Mr. Bones was a desultory African-American stand-up comic who likely had no idea who the bald-headed old coot *was,* seated down there at the

stage apron. Hyperactive, vulgar and breathtakingly unfunny, the brother from another banquet turned his gaze on the guest of honor and shouted into his mike, "*Mistuh* See-*odd*-mack! Ah jus' *loves* yo' movies! Dat *Love Slaves o' da Amazons,* man, ah used to *masturbate* to dat *all da damn time!*"

The German Consul turned the color of borscht. Curt, looking as if he had just been shot in the head point blank, averted his gaze in embarrassment; not just embarrassed, but tangible anger.

Beverly Garland came to the rescue. The plucky star of *Curucu, Beast of the Amazon,* who had proved her grit by surviving the Amazon, the Neanderthal Man and Roger Corman, strode on stage and picked up the shattered pieces of Curt's tribute. "Curu-so-oo-oo-oo!" she warbled, turning the title of their B-picture into plainsong chant that would have done a hog caller proud. Lovingly she described the tribulations of their weeks in the Brazilian jungle a half century before, and Curt's intransigence in completing the job against overwhelming odds. Her genuine affection for him came through and dispelled the rancid flavor of Mr. Bones.

Curucu must have been an odd excursion for all concerned. Beverly would tell interviewers that she had to rebuke a lonely Curt's amorous attentions, while to

---

me Curt confided that Beverly went "sex crazy" in the jungle and pursued him. Doubtless the truth lies somewhere in between. What happens in Curucu stays in Curucu. Curt once asked me my age. When I told him, he looked thoughtful for a moment before leaning in to offer a nonagenarian's advice: "Get all the sex you can," he whispered. "It's not much good after 50."

I last saw Curt seven weeks later. He invited my wife Liz and me to Three Rivers for Easter Sunday. Curt was a thoroughly secular Jew. He dismissed the superstitious underpinnings of all organized religions while, paradoxically, entertaining the possibility of mystical phenomena. Easter was observed for the pleasure of his gentile bride, Henrietta. In the spirit of a traditional German Frühlingsfest, we joined Curt, Henrietta, their son Geoffrey and their close friends, the science fiction writer Ib Melchior and his wife, the architect Cleo Baldon.

Siodmak signs autographs for fans at the 1993 *Famous Monsters* convention in Crystal City, Virginia. Wife Henrietta is on the left.

Persistent telephoning had paid off and I had managed to pry the remnants of Curt's stamp folios from the Noodle Maker's sticky fingers. I returned them to Curt that morning. He looked at the pathetic contents of the nearly empty box, obviously looted since the close of Cinecon. "Noodle Maker!" he muttered. But it no longer mattered.

Cleo and Ib were in the living room with Curt. Liz and I were sitting at the dining table with Henrietta when Cleo's voice broke in a sharp cry from the living room. Liz and I drew near to learn the reason for the outburst.

"I have cancer," Curt announced matter-of-factly, as blandly as if saying he had toast for breakfast. "Lung cancer." He shrugged. Ever the rationalist, Curt tried to understand how he had come to such a predicament. Reaching back 80 years, he found an answer that made sense to him. "It was the trains. The asbestos from the train brakes." As a student of 18, Curt had been a stoker and engineer on trains in Stuttgart just after World War I. His perspicacity demanded a pseudo-scientific rationale, even if it meant bridging eight decades to find an explanation for his fate, however illogical.

Through the spring and early summer I kept in touch with him on a weekly basis. Talking became increasingly difficult and tiring for him and by late summer I stopped calling.

September 2, 2000, was a Saturday. I had known Curt exactly one year. I woke at dawn. It was one of those early autumn mornings when the death of summer is in the air. Overnight, autumn had arrived, heralded by an ineffable change in the atmosphere. Curt was urgently paramount in my mind. By 7:30 I felt compelled to call Three Rivers. The Siodmaks' housekeeper answered and gently told me that Curt had died just before dawn, there in the house in his own bed. He had refused morphine until the very end, wishing to keep his brain clear.

I met Cleo Melchior again at a Woodbury University writers' conference in 2003. We reminisced about that bittersweet Easter Sunday at Blossom Ranch. Henrietta had outlived Curt by eight months. "Henrietta had the most beautiful death," said Cleo mistily. Henrietta died as gracefully as she had lived, in her beautiful home in Three Rivers surrounded by flowers and candles and family and friends, with Caruso, her Meistersinger, trilling a plaintive Todeslied.

TEN THINGS I LOVE ABOUT LON CHANEY JR.

By Frank J. Dello Stritto

I grew up in the 1950s and often saw Lon Chaney on television, usually in Western series. I particularly remember his appearance in "The Jose Morales Story," an episode of *Wagon Train*. Chaney and fellow guest star Lee Marvin play an Alamo defender and attacker, who meet 30 years later, and must form a alliance to fight off an attack of hostile tribes. They sacrifice themselves to save a family of homesteaders, but not before Chaney nails a great scene as he tells with both bitterness and pride how he alone escaped the Alamo. I have always remembered that moment, and was surprised to learn a few years later that *Wagon Train* got it right where Walt Disney got it wrong: One Alamo defender did cross Colonel Travis' line in the sand, and escape to tell his tale.

Through the 1950s and into the 1960s, I discovered Chaney's movies. My favorite Lon Chaney movie memories are below. They are in chronological order, and tell a tale of an actor who should not be overlooked.

Of Mice and Men (1939): In 1939, Chaney's Lennie created a sensation. The dimwitted giant's sad end remains one of the most poignant moments in film history. In the 1960s, *Of Mice and Men* aired once a year on WPIX Channel 11 in New York, and the station always gave it a big build-up. I really wanted to see it, but year after year my parents refused (like most families, we had only one television). I never understood why, for they were always so indulgent of what I wanted to watch. I finally saw it in 1977 at a revival theater, and understood. I left the theater in tears, mainly due to Chaney. Characters like Lennie did not get Oscar nominations in 1939. The mentally challenged would have to wait 40 years. Peter Sellers in *Being There*, Dustin Hoffman in *Rain Man* and Tom Hanks in *Forrest Gump* all deserve the recognition they received. But it all started with Chaney in *Of Mice and Men*. His performance compares well with theirs, and in my opinion is the best among them.

One Million B.C. (1940): Hal Roach leased his film library to television years earlier than most producers. I remember seeing his Little Rascals and Laurel & Hardy movies at a tender age, and also my first dinosaur movie, 1940's *One Million B.C.* The dinosaurs are pretty cheesy (though Oscar-nominated): a man-in-a-suit passes for a very short Tyrannosaurus, a pig-in-costume for a very small triceratops. Lizards with paste-on fins and horns play the giant monsters. At age five, a year before I saw *King Kong*, I thought them fantastic, and I also remember well Lon Chaney as Akhoba, leader of the Rock People. He is the original alpha male: One hand holds a thick staff, the other reins in barely domesticated wolves. Our tiny television screen could barely contain his broad chest. In a cave scene early in the film, Akhoba and his son Tumak (Victor Mature) fight for a hunk of meat. I remember my terror when Tumak strikes his father. I knew that the blow would not faze such a goliath, and that punishment would follow swiftly. Tumak is beaten almost to death. Later in the movie, Akhoba is crippled in a fight with a wild bull. Chaney is not nearly as effective as a pathetic wreck; but the actor never projected more sheer physical presence than in the first half of *One Million B.C.*

Man Made Monster (1941): "Dynamo" Dan McCormick is another role split in two. Once mad doctor Lionel Atwill begins using him as a guinea pig in his electrical experiments, Dan becomes weak and lethargic, and Chaney's character is not very interesting. Before then, Chaney would never be more lovable. He fills the screen with an infectious charm and boyish playfulness. When he talks so animatedly about his carnival act, "strictly yokel stuff," the viewer yearns to see him in action. Alas, that never happens, for Atwill is soon sticking electrodes in him. Chaney never really had the opportunity to play an engaging character again, or show that side of his talent.

The Wolf Man (1941): Lawrence Talbot is horror's great blue-collar protagonist. Curt Siodmak's script rips Dr. Jekyll from his mansion and laboratory, and transforms him into Everyman. Lawrence spends a good amount in *The Wolf Man* in his father's mansion, but he does not

Chaney with Burgess Meredith and Betty Field in *Of Mice and Men*, his premier screen achievement.

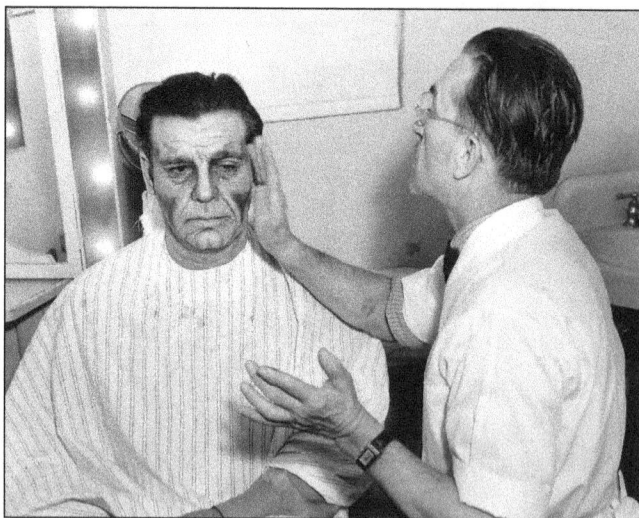

Universal's makeup master Jack Pierce goes to work on Chaney in this backstage shot from *Man Made Monster*.

belong there. In fact, he does not belong *any*where: adrift between America and Britain, aristocracy and commoner, boy and man, and finally between man and beast (and in the sequels, between life and death). Bela the gypsy transforms to a full wolf as the moon rises; but not Lawrence, caught halfway between as a hellish man-beast. Chaney is perfect as a man forced to live in a world where he simply does not fit in, for whom loneliness and alienation are the only fate. Intentionally or not, Lawrence Talbot mirrors an aspect of Chaney's own life. After a decade of little success as an actor, he "returned to his father's mansion"—gravitated towards the types of roles and grotesque makeups associated with his father. But neither the senior Chaney nor the other horror kings, past (Karloff, Lugosi) or future (Lee, Cushing, Price), could have equaled Chaney's Lawrence Talbot, or captured the internal struggle between what a man knows he is and what life and fate compel him to be.

* * *

Creighton Chaney reluctantly became "Lon Chaney Jr." in 1935 and, starting with *The Wolf Man*, he dropped the Jr. forever from his name. Under any name, had Chaney turned his back on acting after *The Wolf Man*, he might be remembered as a performer of no little versatility. From a pathetic giant to a prehistoric alpha male to a rousing carny hustler to a tormented son, Chaney acquitted himself quite well. *The Wolf Man* launched him as a star, but Universal channeled him into roles ill-suited to his talent. As an actor, Chaney's range was narrow, but in his niche he could invoke great power and empathy. Except for his gigs as Lawrence Talbot, he found that niche rarely in his Universal years.

His six roles in the Inner Sanctum series are as bland as the films themselves. Had he played Frankenstein's Monster as Lennie, or Count Dracula as Akhoka, movie historians might have more to write about; but the performances are at best adequate. No actor could do much in mummy makeup, but somehow Chaney found at least one golden moment in Kharis' wrappings.

* * *

The Mummy's Tomb (1942): The four Kharis movies (Chaney played the mummy in three) depict the saga of the Mummy's love for Princess Ananka. Kharis' overseers are a series of high priests of a secret cult; and a key element in some of the movies is the priest's forbidden desire for a woman. In *The Mummy's Ghost*, the object of the affection is the reincarnation of Ananka herself, but otherwise she is only someone who catches the priest's wandering eye. Kharis reacts violently on learning the priests' carnal intents, except in *The Mummy's Tomb*. He is confused, uncertain of what to do, conflicted by orders from his master that he knows undermine the very purpose of his unending existence. In Kharis makeup, facial expressions are impossible; but Chaney achieves an exquisite pantomime via body language, subtle movements of his head and torso. He is helped by a fine texture of shadows and light. Until that moment, a viewer might doubt that Kharis could think or feel at all. It is Chaney's finest moment as Kharis. Kharis never has such doubts again. In *The Mummy's Ghost* and *The Mummy's Curse*, he kills the men who break their vows and defy the ancient gods.

House of Frankenstein (1944): Chaney's Lawrence Talbot performances rank among his career high points. Perhaps he is too whiny in *Frankenstein Meets the Wolf Man*, too dour in *House of Dracula*. He's at his best in *House of Frankenstein*. His seething impatience with Dr. Niemann's foot-dragging is the film's most powerful element; and Chaney's scenes with Karloff rank with his finest. Chaney's performance is helped immeasurably by J. Carrol Naish as hunchback Daniel. Though the two characters never exchange dialogue, their love triangle with the gypsy girl Ilonka is the best thing about the movie. Talbot's anger and frustration are always in the forefront, but Chaney achieves one of his most touching moments with Ilonka. He only wants to be left in peace; but the flirtatious girl pesters him. "What's your name?" she asks. "Do they call you Larry?" Talbot looks deep within himself, perhaps remembering times when he heard that name from the father who would slay the Wolf Man, and die of grief when he realized that he had killed his own son. "They used to," is his sad reply.

Here Come the Co-Eds (1945): Lou Costello is strapped to an operating table, spinning wildly as a menacing Lon Chaney hovers over him. The ending of *Abbott and Costello Meet Frankenstein*? Yes, but the same thing happened three years earlier, midway through this 1945 comedy. During Chaney's five years as a Universal contract star, his ability to play a hulking brute was exploited only in a few Westerns, but never better than as a foil to Abbott and Costello. At a girls' college, "Strangler" Johnson is their short-tempered, shady boss. As a masked wrestler, he tangles with Costello's character in a mismatch reminiscent of Alfalfa's bout with Butch. The gem of the movie occurs earlier, when Costello swallows a pair of dice. An x-ray shows a four and a two. "Six," says Abbott. "Betcha I can make that point!" He and Chaney toss around the little man, and the next x-ray shows two threes. Double-or-nothing, but Johnson wants "a better shake than that for my dough." He straps Costello to the table and spins him until he coughs up the dice. "Box cars!" Johnson is the winner; Costello earns a slap in the face from Abbott; and Chaney gets the best comic scene of his career. And not as a bystander or straight man to the comics. The three men play off each other wonderfully.

Abbott and Costello Meet Frankenstein (1948): Chaney's fine interplay with Abbott & Costello continued in his last outing as Lawrence Talbot. Until the finale with the Wolf Man pursuing Dracula, all his scenes are with the comedians. He is almost a third member of the team. Their dialogue scenes are fine, but the pantomime is outstanding. Twice in the movie, the Wolf Man stalks Wilbur (Costello), once in a hotel room, later in the woods. Wilbur is oblivious to the threat, and the comic value of the scenes depends on the two actors being in very close proximity, with the Wolf Man never quite overcoming Wilbur's dumb luck. Many movies try and fail in that delicate balance, but Chaney and Costello pull it off. In the hotel room, the Wolf Man seems confused that his prey could be so stupid, and waits just a moment too long to spring. In the woods, the Wolf Man is foiled by a branch that

Chaney and pro wrestler Ted Christy lock up in a candid shot from Abbott and Costello's *Here Come the Co-eds* (1945).

snaps back into his face as Wilbur passes, and a vine that Wilbur pushes aside to unknowingly trip the predator. Finally the two are side by side, but Chaney and Costello manage their stances so well that Wilbur's escape hardly seems far-fetched. In that moment, watch Chaney's left hand and wrist. The paw is threatening, ready to lunge, but leaves Wilbur the opening to flee. A superb interaction between the two men.

The Defiant Ones (1958): The end of Chaney's Universal contract and the eclipse of horror film popularity in the mid-1940s freed the actor from the confining roles allotted during his star years. He found work mainly in supporting roles: small parts in major productions, larger ones in low-budget films. The big-budget picture roles offered him little screen time, but often suited him quite well: the burned-out sheriff in *High Noon*, the drunken father in *Not as a Stranger*, the Confederate renegade in *Springfield Rifle*, the old gangster in *I Died a Thousand Times*, the lifer on the lam in *Big House, U.S.A.* and his

The Alligator People featured "Lon Chaney as the hook-armed, hate-maddened Cajun" (trailer narration), here showing Beverly Garland some Southern unhospitality.

gem, Big Sam in *The Defiant Ones*. Tony Curtis and Sidney Poitier deserved their Oscar nominations, but both are overshadowed in Chaney's pivotal scene. The Southern townspeople want to lynch the two chain gang escapees; Big Sam saves them with a forceful, moving rant on decency and law. Chaney had not shown such on-screen presence since *One Million B.C.* Later he helps the caged men escape; and on his wrists are seen the scars left from manacles. Big Sam himself was once a convict on the chain gang. The three men exchange knowing looks. Chaney would not have a more moving moment for the rest of his career.

The Alligator People (1959): In the early 1950s, horror was out of vogue, but the low-budget independents kept milking what was left of the genre, and looked for name stars to give their wares some cachet. Beyond his jungle police commissioner role in *Bride of the Gorilla*, he played moronic brutes in *The Black Castle* and *The Black Sleep*, a killer brought back from the dead in *Indestructible Man* and a greedy entrepreneur in *The Cyclops*. Chaney's problems with alcohol limited the dialogue that he could (or cared to) handle. Like his

roles in more prestigious films, his horror parts tended to give him one meaty scene, and then push him into the background. The exception is *The Alligator People*, with Chaney stealing the show as a ragin' Cajun wagin' war on gators for biting off his hand. Less a poor man's Captain Hook than a po' boy's Ahab, Chaney hardly lets up through the movie, cussing as much as censors of the day allowed, and killing time by killing gators, either with his gun or his truck. *The Alligator People* is a rather dreary film, greatly helped, but not entirely saved by the over-the-top dramatics of Chaney and leading lady Beverly Garland. They bring life to a movie that needs it, and their scenes together—including an attempt by Chaney's unwashed, unshaven, disheveled character to share something more intimate than a hatred of gators with Garland—deserve a better film.

And Chaney deserved more roles suited to him, to bring out a talent that too often lie buried. But two sensations in less than three years (*Of Mice and Men* and *The Wolf Man*) gave him a stardom that, as an actor, he might have fared better without.

INTERVIEWS: WILLIAM PHIPPS, TOM NEAL JR. AND HERMAN COHEN

By Tom Weaver

William Phipps

It was as if there were two Franchot Tones. I remember walking into the Encore Restaurant on La Cienega, which was *the* spot at one time, and sitting at a table were Franchot and Barbara Payton, having a drink. As I walked over to say hello, Franchot did a wonderful thing: When I approached the table, *he stood up*. He acknowledged my presence by standing up, which was so great. When someone does that as you approach them, it sets the tone of gentility, it puts you on your best behavior, you realize that the person is genteel, is civilized, that it's going to be a good and pleasant time.

But he was an alcoholic. Whenever Burgess Meredith [director and co-star of *The Man on the Eiffel Tower*] was out here from New York, he'd stay wherever he could stay for free; he was a mooch, a leech. He once stayed at an apartment of Joan Fontaine's that she seldom used, he once stayed with Elsa Lanchester after [her husband] Charles Laughton died, and so on. On one particular occasion he stayed at the Chateau Marmont, on the top floor, Lerner and Loewe's apartment. Over the years I spent a lot of time with Burgess because he "pursued" me. (In retrospect, I think he "pursued" me because he wanted to use me to get girls. I have never lacked female companionship!) So I'm hanging out with Burgess one afternoon when Franchot showed up, drunk, bellowing, "Where are the broads? Where are the *broads? Where in the hell are the broads*?" I guess he figured that if Burgess had Lerner and Loewe's penthouse at *the*

> In 2015, there probably aren't a lot of people still around who knew Barbara Payton, Franchot Tone *and* Tom Neal. One of them is actor William Phipps. He worked with Tone in France in 1948 in the movie *The Man on the Eiffel Tower*; later met Payton through Tone; and appeared in a play with Tom Neal. In this interview, he shares his impressions of all three.

famous Chateau Marmont, and Bill Phipps was there, the two of them, then they're gonna be swimming in broads [*laughs*]!

I think Franchot was attracted to "bad girls." I don't know about Joan Crawford, to whom he was married in the 1930s, but later he married Jean Wallace, who was also in *The Man on the Eiffel Tower* with Charles Laughton, Franchot and Burgess. By the time we did *Eiffel Tower*, Franchot and Jean Wallace were divorced but Franchot, who was one of the producers, hired her anyway. Laughton said about her, "She's got the face of an angel and the soul of a devil. But Franchot keeps going back to the same type over and over again." At one point during the making of that picture, Franchot gave Jean Wallace a black eye, and she couldn't work for a few weeks. I also remember that one day when the company was out shooting and I was not working and Jean was not working, for some reason or other she asked me to come up to her apartment at the Champs-Élysées Hotel at such-and-such a time. Well, I went up to her room per her invitation and she was stark naked! Not *half*-naked. Not in a slip. She was *naked*. Not a stitch [*laughs*]! No matter how much I was tempted, I didn't stay very long—I got out of there as quickly as I could. I did not take the bait. It would've been the wrong thing to do—for many, many reasons! She would have really had me in trouble. That's probably what she was trying to *do*—stir up some drama. She would have then gone right to Franchot.

Getting back to that night at the Encore Restaurant, when Franchot stood up as I approached: He invited me to sit down at the table where he was sitting with Barbara Payton, and I did join them. I think that both of them enjoyed having an audience! That was my first meeting with Barbara Payton. My first impression of her was that she was kind of silly, but she was drinking so you can't go by that. Barbara was very likable, but… she had that addiction. I think she was not only on alcohol, but lots of other things too, but I don't know for sure. I'm sure Franchot was attractive to women but he had the drinking thing, and that would put a lot of people off, especially a normal girl. A crazy, fucked-up broad like Barbara Payton would *love* that kind of thing [*laughs*]! Or Jean Wallace—they were both lushes, and, "Let's get it *on!*"

I know less about Tom Neal than I do about the others. I didn't *want* to know him! We worked together. It was at the Sombrero Playhouse in Arizona, the play was *Sailor Beware* with Mickey Rooney, Jane Nigh and

Ninety-three-years-young man-about-Malibu William Phipps in a February 2015 pose with gal-pal Maria-Flora Smoller.

Tom Neal. At one point in the play, as part of the action, he restrains me, he grabs my arms and shoulders and holds me. Every performance he used to do it *much*, much too roughly, as if to say, "Look how *strong* I am," "Look what I can *do*," "If you're not careful, I'll break your *back!*"—that was the implication. That used to piss me off. He was psycho, and I recognized that. Neal restraining me—it was only a few seconds' action on stage and then it was over, so I used to just ignore it and walk away from it. I wouldn't say anything to him, I wouldn't even say hello or goodbye, I'd never talk to him. 'Cause I realized that he was a powderkeg.

Then there was that "fight" that Tom Neal and Franchot had. Franchot was probably drunk, and Tom Neal was a muscular bodybuilder type fella, so Franchot didn't stand a chance. People called it a fight but it *wasn't* a fight! It was no more a fight than a man stepping on a bug is a "fight."

As I say, Franchot was an alcoholic, so even though he was a very charming man and a person of obvious good breeding, civilized, genteel…when he was drinking, he had that other side to him. For instance, that day at the Chateau Marmont when he showed up drunk and raving, "Where in the hell are the *broads*?!"—that same day, I paid him a compliment, I'd seen *Advise & Consent* [1962] at the Directors Guild Theater and I thought he was terrific as the president and I told him so. And he said [*drunkenly, belligerently*], "You're God damn fuckin' *right* I was good!"

This next story was told to me by Charles Laughton, who was also in *Advise & Consent*, and it took place while they were filming *Advise & Consent*, either in a restaurant or maybe in Franchot's dressing room. On that picture, they were having a problem with Franchot: He was drinking throughout the thing, and it was touch and go about his working. So one day he had some scenes coming up, and he and Laughton were sitting together at a table. Franchot was getting close to being hammered, and he had a martini sitting in front of him. Laughton coaxed him and cajoled him and persuaded him *not* to drink it—to wait until after they got the shots that were coming up. It took Laughton about 15 minutes to convince Franchot not to have that martini. So Franchot left the martini sitting on the table, got up and went out and finished his filming for the day. I said to Laughton, "What happened to the martini?" and Laughton said, with a straight face, "I drank it!" [*Laughs*] My jaw hit the floor. Incidentally, I was around Laughton a lot when he drank and, boy, *could he drink!* Oh my *God*. But I never saw him drunk. Although he obviously *was*, at times. He was always in control.

The last time I saw Barbara Payton must have been shortly before she died. I was a regular at the Coach & Horses on Sunset Boulevard, a restaurant-bar—I lived just a few blocks from there, in Nichols Canyon in Hollywood. I was in there in the afternoon and sitting at the other end of the bar was this…this *hag* [*laughs*]! This *crone*! With a tooth missing and no makeup and the hair looking like Medusa, scraggly hair, like she hadn't combed or washed it in a month. Somebody said to me, "See that dame over there? That's Barbara Payton." I was indignant, I said, "I know Barbara Payton, that's not Barbara Payton. Are you *crazy*?" Well, I went to the men's room or something, and when she saw me she said [*exuberantly*], "Hi, Bill!" It *was* Barbara Payton!

So we talked. She had had a few drinks but she wasn't drunk yet…but she was on her way. I had to go to Santa Monica that day and I can't remember why…maybe I was going to the unemployment office. Anyway, she rode with me, and every once in a while she'd say to me, "Bill, let's make a movie!" And I'm thinking, "My God, *look* at her. She can play a homeless wino…but there's not much call for that!" Then once we got to Santa Monica we went to a restaurant, and I think I said something that implied that she should eat something, I can't remember exactly what it was, but when I suggested that she have something to eat, she got indignant, she got on the defensive. But it passed very quickly.

There are millions of people who are like Franchot and Barbara but they're not famous, and these millions of un-famous people handle things—their character flaws, their *demons*—the best they can. Franchot and Barbara, being famous, had to handle them publicly. And, sadly, they both died before their time. Barbara died at 39 and Franchot died at 63—to *me* now, I'm 93, that's young! In my talking about Franchot and Barbara, I'm not being critical, I'm just observing here. I *liked* Franchot and I *liked* Barbara Payton and I want to end on that note, that they were likable and fun and good to *be* around.

Tom Neal Jr.

I'm old enough and mature enough to realize my dad had his faults. Don't get me wrong, I loved my dad dearly, but he was human like everybody else. I went through a period in my *own* life, in my late 20s and early 30s, where I was kind of an "angry young man" type; I tended to look for slights everywhere, and it wasn't difficult to piss me off. But I don't think that way any more and, like my dad, I've mellowed a lot over the years. That's what life's all about.

Fate stuck out a foot to trip Al Roberts, the tragic protagonist of *Detour* (1945)…and then did the same to the actor who played the role, Tom Neal. Even his son Tom Neal Jr., born in 1957, had more than his share of hard luck in his early life. His mom died when he was a baby, stepmom Gail Kloke was no bargain…and then in April 1965, just two weeks after Neal Jr.'s eighth birthday, his dad shot and killed her. By December, Tom Neal had been tried and sentenced to one to 15 years in prison.
Father and son got to really know each other following Neal's 1971 release but then Fate again put the finger on Neal, who died of heart failure in August 1972. In this interview, Neal Jr. recalls some of the things his dad told him about the ups and downs in his life and career.

When my dad died in 1972, I was 15. I wasn't a *real* young child—I mean, I wasn't an *adult* yet but I was old enough to know what was going on. He'd just recently gotten out of prison, and he and I had a lot of time to talk about different things. He did mention Barbara Payton, he said that she seemed to have the sex drive of a man, that she could have sex at the drop of a hat. That kind of leads me to believe she had certain psychological issues.

He talked a little about Vicki Lane, his second wife, and also about Payton. You know, certain sexual proclivities—I won't get into the blow-by-blow thing [*laughs*], it's kind of prurient in nature! But he said that they were both a little bit on the wild side—I guess I can sum it up that way. I got the impression, from the way my dad talked about Payton, that she was the type who would pit men against one another. I've known women similar to her. If an actress nowadays did the kinds of things she did, nobody would bat an eye, but back then it was rogue behavior for a woman, especially one in the limelight. To me it just seemed like she was kind of mentally and emotionally screwed up. With a lot of these women, the way that manifests itself is through nymphomania.

Payton *was* pretty loose with her affections and she got involved with a *lot* of guys. Back in those days, there was the Hollywood casting couch, and actresses had to play the game with the producers and directors and the studio heads. Heck, I can understand that, and I don't hold that against them 'cause that's the way Hollywood operated back then. (And it probably operates that way somewhat today. Not just with girls, but with guys too!) Payton knew the game and she played it. Maybe early in her life, when she was a young girl, some man took advantage of her, and she figured, "Well, if men are going to use *me*, I'm gonna use *them*." A lot of women have that attitude: If they've been hurt or burned, it's like, "Hey, all bets are off now, asshole!" Unfortunately they sometimes take it out on innocent men who *want* to do the right thing. You can't judge all people by one person.

Despite all the crap she went through, whether it was self-perpetrated or not, I find her a

Tom Jr. followed in his father's film noir footsteps by starring (with Lea Lavish, pictured) in writer-producer-director Wade Williams' 1992 remake of *Detour*. Interiors were shot in Kansas City, Missouri, exteriors in the Mojave Desert.

sympathetic character, I feel sorry for her. I don't think she was evil or anything, I think she was just…*messed up*! My dad spoke fondly of her, he said she was a wild one, but he never badmouthed any of his ex-girlfriends or ex-wives. He talked about a couple of instances where he got into fights with them. For instance, Ann Savage, who he did *Detour* with. He was dating her for a while and he said she could really fly off the handle and get angry in a heartbeat. He told me about one time when they were driving somewhere and they got in an argument in the car, and she ripped off the rear view mirror and threw it at him [*laughs*]. It was like, "*Damn,* woman!" And I'm sure my dad could say things to piss women off. Hell, he said things that pissed *me* off, but he was bigger than me and a lot tougher, so I didn't say anything!

About the fight with Franchot Tone, my dad said it was unfortunate that it happened but…woulda coulda shoulda. Franchot Tone and my dad, they were kind of opposites, not just physicality but mentality. Tone came from a pretty good background, and…Well, my *dad* did too, surprisingly. My dad's father was a banker and they lived pretty well, even during the Depression. My dad had two sisters and when they all turned 16 they all got

their own cars and everything. That was unheard of back then; in those days, a lot of *families* didn't own a car. So my dad's dad had some money. But my dad kind of did his own thing and he was kind of the black sheep of the family.

He started acting, on the stage, on Broadway, and eventually in movies. He was even at MGM for a while. He was on his way up, but he pissed off the wrong people. Maybe it was his temper, maybe the fact that he was a little narcissistic and egotistical like a lot of young guys are. He was good-looking and the women liked him and it kind of went to his head and he didn't handle it well. Anyway, he made some wrong moves and that kind of sealed his fate right there [Neal went from MGM to smaller studios, even Poverty Row]. The studio bosses were dictators, and you toed the line or they could find somebody else. Nobody was indispensable.

In those days, my dad was a fun guy, but he had his moments when he could be a jerk, or egotistical. But he was Joe Life of the Party, he was that type, and I can see how those three—he and Barbara Payton and Franchot Tone—may have come into each other's orbit. Barbara Payton…talk about a sad story. At the time when she and my dad met, she was a lot bigger than *he* was. She was the next darling of Hollywood until she, too, made some wrong moves. Theirs was one of those unholy symbiotic relationships: You don't know who ruined who, was it my dad who brought *her* down or was it her that brought *him* down? 'Cause misery loves company. I've often thought that one of the biggest lies in the world is "Opposites attract." I think *like* attracts *like*, basically. Barbara Payton and my dad were at the same point mentally and emotionally, and that's probably why they came into each other's lives. They were both very attractive people, and I can definitely see the sexual attraction there, but there's a lot more to it than that, it went a lot deeper, I think there was some kind of a mental co-dependency. A mental-emotional co-dependency where they kind of used each other as a crutch. And blamed each other for their problems and yet they couldn't live life with*out* one another or something…? *I* don't know, I'm second-guessing my dad to some degree. He told me these things when I was a lot younger and I'm trying to bring up all the files in my mind and evaluate them now as an older adult male.

I guess Payton and my dad had their issues to deal with like anybody else, but it's difficult when you're in the limelight where everybody can see every little thing you do and hear every little fart you let. It's no wonder these people [Hollywood stars] end up like they do! Nowadays you hear about these celebrities doing crazy stuff and going off the rails and, well, I can kind of understand it because I know my dad's story. Because they're not dealing with reality like the average person has to deal with, especially if they've have a lot of money. My dad never had a lot of money. I mean, he was *around* people with money, he was *born* into money, but he never seemed to have much himself. He was married five times and his second wife came from a *huge* amount of money and they lived very well, a house in Bel Air and all. But that, compounded with all the Hollywood publicity and the silliness…it doesn't exactly lead to a normal-type life.

In the late '50s or early '60s, after his acting career had ended, my dad and some other guys put together an electronic components company. Also, he had a degree in landscape architecture and he started a landscaping business. There was a lot of building going on in Palm Springs at that time, a lot of new homes, and people wanted really nice gardens and attractive displays, and he had a nursery and everything. He made good money.

He wasn't rich by any means, but he did well, lived well. He'd left the Hollywood thing behind at that point and started a whole new life and he was happy with it.[23]

My mom died in 1958 when I was an infant, and then he married again [Gail Kloke]. Franchot Tone did show up at my dad's trial, if you can believe *that*! By that point I guess they'd reconciled or my dad had apologized to him, and Franchot Tone found it in his heart to be sympathetic towards my dad and to come as a supporter. I'm not saying he was a witness or anything like that, he obviously was out of the scene at that point. My dad didn't have anything against Franchot Tone, he said he was a nice guy and a classy guy, but they had their famous fight because my dad lost his temper, I guess. I don't know who threw the first punch. My dad said that Payton *also* came to the trial—again, not as a witness in the box, just as a supporter.

My dad, in his later years, became a Christian Scientist and changed his whole attitude. He wasn't the a-hole bad boy jerk any more, he'd kind of mellowed out. We go through different phases in our lives; as I mentioned earlier, in my 20s and early 30s, I was a whole different person than I am *now*. I think most human beings are that way, especially men. They need a few kicks in the ass before they wake up to reality on certain issues. And life will do that to you. But, anyway, my dad was a lot mellower and kinder and nicer. He didn't regret his time in Hollywood, but it wasn't like he looked back on it fondly. He met people that he really liked and loved and cared about, but he said it was basically a racket. He also blamed himself, he said, "I made a lot of mistakes, I did things I shouldn't have done and I was hotheaded." He looked back at it as stepping stones and lesson-learning time, and took a more philosophical-metaphysical-spiritual view of it.

My dad really *was* a good man. He was a good guy and a smart guy *who did stupid things*. And he lived to regret them. But eventually he even gave up the regrets. It was like, well, it's water under the bridge. He had a definite belief in God and that's how he lived his later life. As I mentioned earlier, I think we all go through a lot of those types of changes. Women go through different types of mental and emotional changes, and men do too. With guys, I think a lot of it is ego. But life can knock you upside the head, and hopefully you learn from it. If you don't, it gets more painful. What was that line that John Wayne had? "Life's hard. It's even harder when you're stupid."

Herman Cohen

TW: How did you get your job with Jack Broder's Realart Pictures?

Herman Cohen: After I got out of the Marine Corps in 1949, I was working for Columbia, in their publicity department. What was I making? Fifty bucks a week? Anyway, Jack Broder and his family owned theaters in Detroit. I'm also from Detroit. But I had never met the man. And I talked to a couple of people who said, "Oh, Jack Broder's looking for an executive assistant." At that time, Jack was president of Realart Films—did you ever hear of Realart?

TW: They were re-releasing Universal's old monster pictures at the time.

Cohen: Not just the monster pictures. Jack Broder had put up a tremendous amount of money, millions, for all of Universal's old pictures. But what a mistake he made: He bought 'em for theatrical only, not knowing at that time about TV, video, DVD, you name it. Oh, God, the millions more he would have made! Universal at that time was in trouble financially, so they sold him the reissue rights to all their Abbott and Costellos, *all* their pictures. And now that Jack was making a lot of money with this, everybody started asking him, "Why don't *you* make films? Why don't you go into production and make second features?" At that time, there were still double features in the drive-ins and what have you. "You could make money with second features if the price was right." So Jack Broder decided to put together a unit called Jack Broder Productions to make some second features.

TW: And that's when you came into the picture.

Cohen: That's right. I was interviewed by him—I think I had a *couple* of interviews with him. I had to meet his wife Beatrice and his kids, too, for *them* to say yes or no. (They had six kids.) Anyway, he hired me. And that's how I started working for Jack Broder.

TW: He hired you because he was about to start making pictures, and he was looking for a...

Cohen: He needed a schlepper—he needed somebody to stick the broom up their ass and clean his office [*laughs*]. We started with *Two Dollar Bettor* and *The Basketball Fix*.[24]

TW: What prompted Broder to make a horror picture, *Bride of the Gorilla*? Was it the fact that the Universals had done well for him?

Cohen: That's right. Siodmak...which Siodmak was it? Curt? Yes, *Curt* Siodmak had this story, *Bride of the Gorilla*—well, it wasn't called *Bride of the Gorilla* at first. But anyway, he had a horror story which needed a lot of work. So we *all* worked on it. And we hired [as director] Curt, who had been in this country a long time but, if you talked to him, you'd think he arrived yesterday! And that's when we did *Bride of the Gorilla*. We had a pretty good cast, because I was able to sign Lon Chaney...Raymond Burr, who was tremendous. I used him, even when I went in production myself.

TW: You hired Lon Chaney based on the fact that he was popular from the Universal horror pictures.

Cohen: Right.

TW: Did anyone notice, or care, that Siodmak's screenplay was very much like Lon Chaney's *The Wolf Man*, which Siodmak also wrote? It's South America and a gorilla instead of Wales and a werewolf.

Cohen: Nobody [at Realart] ever saw *The Wolf Man*, including me. Well, you look at the horror pictures, they all stole from each other. But I never saw *The Wolf Man*.

TW: Lon Chaney—depending on the movie, and depending on who I'm talking to, he could be either a wild man or a pussycat. Which one did you wind up with?

Cohen: For some reason, maybe because I was so young at that time, he got to like me. He was my responsibility. And he was a pussycat. He didn't like the other actors, though, and he didn't like Siodmak—he couldn't understand him! Lon would come to me and say, "What the hell's this man *talking* about?" [*Laughs*] So I would have to interpret! I was the only one who could understand Curt Siodmak's English, so they all came to *me*: "What did he say? What did Curt say?"

TW: Did Chaney like Barbara Payton at least?

Cohen: Ummm...not really. No. When he was through shooting, he walked off and he went into his dressing room and started drinking—he was drinking in those days. He just did his job. I don't think he was too

> The last of my several interviews with producer Herman Cohen concerned Lon Chaney Jr. and the three Jack Broder productions in which Chaney appeared; on all three, *Bride of the Gorilla*, *The Bushwhackers* and *Battles of Chief Pontiac*, Cohen was screen-credited as "Assistant to Producer." This interview originally ran in *Cult Movies* #38 in 2003.

happy *doing* it because everyone would compare him to his father. But…he needed the money, and he did the job. And *we* wanted his name.

TW: And even with him taking his nips in the dressing room, he was still always ready for the cameras when needed?

Cohen: He never held us up. He was very professional in front of the camera.

TW: You also had a very professional guy behind the camera, Charles Van Enger.

Cohen: Oh, he was wonderful, that oldtimer, he was great. We used him on a lot of pictures at that time. Charley Van Enger did a lot of big pictures years before, and he taught me a great deal also. See, I was *learning*—that's why I took the job with Jack Broder. 'Cause I'd be doing *every*thing. And instead of giving me money, Jack would give me titles: He made me a vice-president of Realart, a vice-president of Jack Broder Productions and what have you.

TW: You made *Bride of the Gorilla* at the time when Barbara Payton was romantically linked with both Franchot Tone and Tom Neal.

Cohen: Franchot Tone was a very wealthy man and he had been quite a star at one time. In fact, he had been married to Joan Crawford—did you remember that? So he was dating Barbara. And Barbara was *also* swinging with this half-assed actor named Tom Neal. We told the captain at the Goldwyn gate that, if Tom Neal was coming, call the stage immediately, and *especially* if Franchot was there—she had to get rid of him!

TW: Tone and Tom Neal didn't know about each other?

Cohen: They could have known about each other, *that* I don't know, but they never met *at* the studio. They came close, but they didn't meet. The big fistfight they had was after our picture was made.

TW: So both visited the set individually?
Cohen: Oh, yeah.

Payton "thought she was gonna be another Joan Crawford," said Herman Cohen (pictured), "and she ends up doing *Bride of the Gorilla!*" The closest Payton got to being another Joan Crawford: They both married (and split from) Franchot Tone.

TW: Did you like Barbara Payton?
Cohen: Yes, I liked her. Look, like all whores that I've ever met, she had a heart of gold. She was just a fun person. She liked to laugh…and she was a little crazy. I think she was doing drugs…she certainly was drinking. But not on the set. And as much as she was pissed off at Warners, 'cause she *knew* they were gonna dump her, and that therefore *Bride of the Gorilla* was on her way to being dumped, she never let it interfere with her work. I've got some pictures…very intimate pictures of her with me…I was a young guy, she was a beautiful girl at that time. Barbara Payton was a lovely person. She was a whore who got lucky. And deep down, she was a lovely person, she was very sweet. It was horrible how she died, downtown, as a whore, selling herself for five, ten bucks. That just made me ill when I heard about that. I actually liked her.

TW: Despite your youth, did Jack Broder have a lot of confidence in you once a picture got rolling?

Cohen: I doubt it [*laughs*]! But Jack Broder didn't *know* anything about production. And I was *learning*. I always hired the top production supervisors and assistant directors, people who really knew their stuff. And when things would come up in a meeting and they'd ask me to make a decision (I was making the decisions on the film), I'd say, "We'll discuss it tomorrow morning." And that night, I would dash to UCLA, to the Cinema Library, to read up on what the fuck they were *talking* about [*laughs*]! That's a true story! I'd read up, *or* I'd call up a couple friends, a couple film editors I knew from Columbia, and ask *them*. The next morning, suddenly I became *very* bright!

TW: These early Realart pictures—was Broder on the set a lot, or did he leave everything to you guys?

Cohen: He would only go there to take pictures with his kids. And watch a few important scenes. He was more interested in the schedule, if we were behind. He was always threatening, "Herman! If you're late, I pool the switch! I pool the switch!"

TW: On *Bride of the Gorilla*, you were the "Assistant to Producer"—

Cohen: But I was actually running the show for Jack.

TW: Curt Siodmak told me that one guy that Chaney reeeally didn't get along with was Raymond Burr. Do you have any memory of that?

Cohen [*scoffing*]: We didn't have the *time* for them not to get along with each other. We made the whole picture in ten days and we came in under budget. So there was no time to fight, not at all. But, on this picture, there were no friends among the actors.

TW: But *you* got along with everybody.

Cohen: I learned very young that you have to be a diplomat. Therefore I was kissing *every*body's ass. 'Cause I knew that if I kiss their butts, they're gonna be on the stage, they'll know their lines. I was even reading lines with Barbara and reading lines with Lon. With Raymond I didn't *have* to, 'cause Raymond knew *all* his lines. Oh, he was so professional. And a wonderful guy.

TW: And you used him in at least one other picture…

Cohen: *Several* pictures—I used him again in *The Brass Legend* [1956] and in *Crime of Passion* [1957]. Raymond was a hell of an actor. Great actor, great voice, and I *knew* he was gonna become something. God,

Cohen and Carol Varga, who plays Dina's maid Larina in *Bride*. The character wasn't in Siodmak's first draft; perhaps it was created to add yet more hotcha to the proceedings.

when I gave him the part of the inspector of the LAPD in *Crime of Passion*, he was terrific. And he was terrific in *Bride of the Gorilla*. It wasn't a bad picture if I remember, *Bride of the Gorilla*, considering we did it in ten days.

TW: I thought Chaney was excellent in *The Bushwhackers*, playing an elderly, arthritic villain—and looking rather like the old sheriff he played in *High Noon* [1952].

Cohen: What did you think of the cast I put together for *The Bushwhackers*? Names like Lawrence Tierney, Wayne Morris (he'd just left Warner Brothers), Dorothy Malone, John Ireland…for a cheap picture, it had a hell of a cast. And we signed a young guy who had never directed before, named Rod Amateau. A hell of a talent. Rod and a buddy of his [Tom Gries], the guy he was rooming with, wrote the script. They were very close friends at that time. For *The Bushwhackers,* we rented the Western Street from Warners, and we also used the Western Street at Columbia a couple days. We shot in and around town, we didn't go on location any further than the Western Streets.

TW: Why did Broder want to get into Westerns? Because it was just "the thing to do" at that time?

Cohen: That's right. One of the first pictures we did was *Two Dollar Bettor* [a 1951 movie about a compulsive racetrack gambler], and the only reason for that is that Jack Broder loved to go to the races [*laughs*], that's why we did it. We did *Bride of the Gorilla* because we thought, "Hey, let's do a horror picture. They always make money." At that time, Westerns also all made money. That's when these two young guys Rod Amateau and Tom Gries

Herman Cohen on the saloon set of the Jack Broder Western *The Bushwhackers,* shot about a month after *Bride of the Gorilla* wrapped. Cohen considered it the best of the pictures he made for Broder.

brought in their [*Bushwhackers*] script, and Jack liked the script. Jack's ten-year-old son Bobby used to read it to him! Bobby Broder's a top agent now, by the way.

TW: And he's in *The Bushwhackers*, according to the credits.

Cohen: I think a *couple* of Jack's kids were put in *The Bushwhackers.* Bobby was the oldest son. Jack would come in some mornings, when there was something that he had to make a decision about, and say to me, "Bobby told me last night that..." blah blah blah, "and here's what I've decided." Well, I had already *called* little Bobby the day before and said to him, "Look, tell your dad..."

TW: Oh, that's brilliant!

Cohen: I used to take Bobby for ice cream sundaes and stuff, to get him on our side! I knew that he would tell his dad what to do, and his dad would do it. He was 11 or 12, maybe, at that time.

TW: How was Chaney on *The Bushwhackers* and *Battles of Chief Pontiac?* Did he seem to like those pictures better?

Cohen: He liked Rod Amateau on *The Bushwhackers*, he had a lot of respect for him, and he liked the cast. However, Lon never spent time with any of the cast. When he finished his work, he went his own way. He

was never close to John Ireland. Of course, John Ireland was hot, trying to "make" Dorothy Malone all the time. Oh, I gotta tell you a funny story about this. At that time, there was no rating system, so we had to submit everything to the MPAA. The head of the Production Code at that time was a wwwonderful Englishman named Geoffrey Shurlock. We sent him over rushes of *The Bushwhackers*, and I got a call from Geoffrey, can I please come to see him. I came to see him and he said, "Look, I gotta show you something in the screening room."

We went in the screening room, and there's John Ireland having this love scene with Dorothy Malone—and he had a hard-on [*laughs*]! John Ireland, he had a reputation in town of having one of the biggest schlongs outside of Milton Berle, and there he had his hard-on. Well, *we'd* all looked at the rushes, but nobody looked at his fucking cock! But Shurlock brought it to my attention, Geoffrey said, "We can't let that scene pass." So our film editor had to cut the scene up, he had to use other takes and what have you, boom boom boom. And I went to talk to John Ireland. John was....he was kind of strange. Nice guy...but very weird, strange guy... didn't have many friends. He was married to Joanne Dru, who was gorgeous. I was at their house for dinner many times. I told him about the meeting with Geoffrey Shurlock, and he said, "Yeah...I'm kind queer about

Cohen went on to become the daddy of teenage horror flicks, among them 1957's *Blood of Dracula* with (left to right) Shirley De Lancey, Heather Ames, Lynn Alden, Gail Ganley and Barbara Wilson. In 1960 Cohen told *Variety* that he was now "typed" as a horror movie producer and "it's awfully hard to change when you're making money."

that…" I said, "What do you mean?" He said, "Well, before I have a love scene, I always go in my dressing room and I…start jerking off." He *told* me this! I said, "John…! You've *got* to stop *doing* it—I'm not gonna be your psychiatrist!" [*Laughs*] Here I am, I'm a pisser at the time, and I'm telling him, "John, you can't *do* it! We won't be able to release the movie!"

This particular interview right now is supposed to be about Lon Chaney, right? So what am I telling you all these other bubbameisters for?

TW: On *Battles of Chief Pontiac*, who made the decision to shoot in South Dakota?

Cohen: While we were trying to determine where to shoot, we found out from talking to location people that MGM had just built a fort outside of Rapid City, South Dakota, for a movie. I called the Chamber of Commerce and found out that the fort was still standing. It needed some work but it was still there, right by the lake. I went there several times to check the locations before I made the deals.

TW: On this picture, you were the associate producer, and the producer was Irving Starr.

Cohen: Irving Starr was a card-playing buddy of Jack Broder, they used to go to the track together and what have you. And Irving Starr was down on his luck—he'd been a producer at Columbia until he had a fight with Harry Cohn and he was thrown out of Columbia. That just killed him. He was out of a job, needed money— and Jack Broder was always helping his friends. So he hired Irving Starr to produce *Battles of Chief Pontiac*, and Irving Starr had nothing to *do* with it. In fact, he never even came to the location. But he was a nice guy, I have nothing bad to say about Irving Starr. He said, "Herman…*you* make the picture."

I flew up to South Dakota, oh, three or four times, to check the locations, to talk to the head of the Office of Indian Affairs—we also needed Indians for the picture, right? I met a couple of the chiefs, chiefs of the different segments of the Sioux tribe, because I had to make a deal with them. That was quite fascinating for me. (There wasn't a picture I made that I didn't *learn* something—my entire life in this business has been a learning process.) To make the deal, I had to go to a peace meeting, and I had to smoke a peace pipe, me and my assistant director Richard Dixon—oh, he was a wonderful guy, I used him on half a dozen pictures. What a sweetie he was. Anyway, here we are in this huge teepee, the chief's teepee, sitting on fur pelts and what have you, talking about how many young braves we needed, and who could ride horses, and this and that and what have you. And they pass the peace pipe along. Then the chief said, "Me want $5000 a day." Well, *Battles of Chief Pontiac* was a cheap budget picture! MGM had *ruined* these guys by paying 'em a lot of money. So I got pissed off. I got up, and I wipe my lips from the pipe, and I said, "For $5000 a day, *I'll* be the chief!" [*Laughs*] I turned to Dick and I said, "Dickie. Come on. Let's get the hell out of here." And we started walking away. Well, as we walked away, the tribal council came out of the teepee, running after us, bowing to me: "If you don't make a deal, we get a new chief!" They all wanted to be in the film!

I walked away. Got my car and left. (I thought I was gonna get an arrow in my back as I was leaving!) Next morning, oh God, it's like six-thirty, seven o'clock, I hear, "*Woo* woo woo woo, *woo* woo woo woo, *woo* woo woo woo," tom-toms going and what have you, outside of the Alex Johnson Hotel. The phone rings and it's Dickie, my assistant, and he says, "Herm, look out the window, look out the window!" I say, "What? What?" He says, "The chief and his tribe are here to make peace with you!" See, the Sioux tribe had all kinds of different tribes-within-the-tribe, and these guys I had met with didn't want me to go some place else, they wanted to make peace with me. They came up to the hotel and they brought me a magnificent pair of cowboy boots—I don't know where they stole 'em or how they got my size, I never did find out. And I did make peace with 'em. I can't remember what I paid the chief who I put in charge—I think it was five *hundred* a day, not five *thousand* a day.

TW: And the chief who asked for the $5000 a day—was he "out" at that point?

Cohen: No, no—he was the main dancer in front of the hotel! We kept him as the chief, and he got $500 a day or something like that. He was like the wrangler, he was the one who got the [Indians] we needed. Each day Dick Dixon would tell him, "Tomorrow we need 12 braves" or "We need six women" or "We need five kids"—and he would get 'em.

For the Indian village in the movie, we got the land, and then the Indians all came with their teepees—they brought their teepees and everything from where they *were*. They put the village together, and that's where they lived. In the morning, food had to be delivered to them. We made a deal with a bakery in Rapid City and they each got a loaf of white bread…they got a hunk of buffalo meat…and a quart of milk. That was their breakfast. However, one morning, I got a call that the Indians were packing their teepees, they were leaving. "Leaving?" "Yes. The bread truck didn't show up!" So I woke up Dick Dixon and we dashed to the bakery—they were late in baking the white bread, and they didn't have a driver for the truck. So I ended up driving the bread out to the location, in the truck, with Dick, to stop them from leaving!

TW: Lex Barker, the star of *Chief Pontiac*?

Cohen: Lex was quite a ladies' man, and a nice guy. He just came off doing Tarzan, so he was used to cheap films. This was one of his first films with clothes, playing this scout. Lex was a nice guy and he knew exactly what he had to do. But he was a lousy actor [*laughs*]! The leading lady, Helen Westcott, was a very good actress.

TW: Where did you get the actors and extras who played all the English soldiers, and the German Hessians?

Cohen: I went up there scouting locations and they had an Air Force base, Rapid City Air Force Base. I knew I needed extras—we couldn't bring 'em from Hollywood, this was a budget picture! So I called the commanding officer, who was Brigadier General Richard Ellsworth, and went to meet him. We became instant friends. Gen. Ellsworth said, "You can have whatever you want." For instance, water was at a premium, so he sent out the Air Force water trucks for my whole company. And, of course, that's where I got the Army for the Brits as well as the Hessians. Ellsworth and his wonderful wife and two daughters, we all became good friends and we'd have dinner in their home on the base. He told me not to touch his daughters—and not to let Lex Barker get near 'em [*laughs*]! Then there's something I shouldn't tell you but I will: On weekends, if I had to get to L.A., he'd have an Air Force jet take me back! With Dick Dixon, and with Ellsworth's wife, who wanted to go shopping in Beverly Hills, and Lex Barker—whoever wanted to get back to L.A. for the weekend. This could never be done by a president, but if you were the commanding general of a base, you were the king. You didn't requisition anything, you just did what you wanted to do [*laughs*]! Especially if you were in a base like in Rapid City, South Dakota! He was so happy that I would hire his people, 'cause they

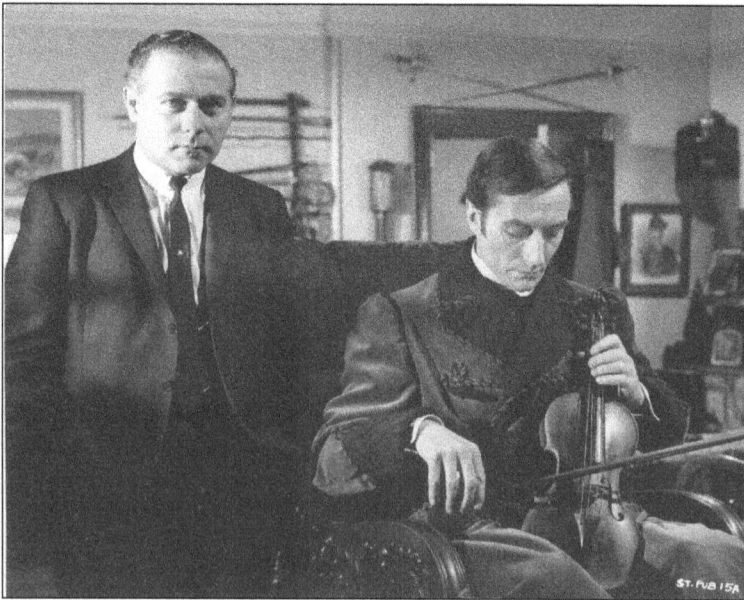

Cohen's later horror movies were made in England. Above: *A Study in Terror* (1965) with John Neville as Sherlock Holmes is well-regarded. Right: His Joan Crawford starrers *Berserk* (1967) and *Trog* (1970)...not so much!

were so *bored*—there was *nothing* fuckin' to do there. And we hired several hundred of his people. To determine which of his guys we were going to give speaking parts to, we had interviews at the Service Club on the base. I remember this one Saturday morning, I was going there with my staff to interview whoever would show up. Since it was the weekend, we doubted that anyone would be there. Well, as we drove close to the Service Club, there were guys standing around the *block*! They all wanted to get in the film. After all, Rapid City, South Dakota, there was nothing to do there, except go to Mount Rushmore. And how many times can you see it?

A short time later [March 1953], Gen. Ellsworth was on board a plane that hit a mountain in the Azores, and that's when he was killed. They renamed the base after *him*, the Ellsworth Air Force Base.

TW: I know Lon Chaney was a great outdoorsman. How did he enjoy going to South Dakota and making *Chief Pontiac*?

Cohen: He spent all his time with the Indians, he was with the Indians all the time. He was playing Chief Pontiac and he wanted to "get the feel of the Indians and their lives"—he didn't want to live in a suite at the Hotel Alex Johnson in town, where *we* all were. So we built a big teepee for him, and he lived out there with the Indians. And he put himself in his role. He took *Chief Pontiac* seriously. And he did *not* drink during *Pontiac*, by the way.

TW: Once you start making the movie, what were the Indians like to work with?

Cohen: Terrible. 'Cause they would drink like crazy every night. There were two or three of 'em killed during the course of the shooting—killed at the Indian village, their deaths had nothing to do with us. We hired Indian deputy sheriffs to [maintain order] at the village, because the Indian men would get drunk at night and fight and this and that. We'd been told by the government Indian Office that we better have security, because of the alcoholic problem with the Indians. We also needed deputy sheriffs to keep the Indians *there*—otherwise, somebody we established in the movie *today*, tomorrow he's gone! Another thing I recall: The young teenagers who we used as braves, they were quite Americanized, and they resented being called Indians! When someone would say, "You five Indians over there..."—they didn't like that at *all*. They felt they were Americans, and that we were looking down on them.

TW: The Indians were terrible to work with—but Chaney liked them?

Cohen: Oh, yeah, he liked them. Lon was into history, the history of the Indians, and he knew the history of Fort Detroit. By the way, that's one of the reasons why Jack Broder liked the script: He was *from* Detroit, and this was [set at] Fort Detroit. And some of the story was true. The involvement of the German Hessian troops was true. Spreading smallpox on blankets to kill the Indians, that's true too. And of course there really *was* a Chief Pontiac. That's where the Pontiac cars came from—do you remember Pontiac cars? If you look at that Indian head [on Pontiac cars], it looks just like Lon Chaney! [*Laughs*] No, seriously!

One day, we suddenly saw a couple white guys, in suits, on the location. "Who *are* those guys?" "I dunno… they look like they could be union organizers…" So I said, "Dick…go find out who the hell they are." Sure enough, they were union guys who had flown up from L.A.—somebody had squealed that, instead of bringing people in from L.A., we were using Indian laborers, to pick up the horse shit and everything. And they threatened to close down the set. So I told the Indians to get rid of 'em! Well, the Indians pushed 'em out of the way, "Get the fuck out of here!" and what have you! And they left! But when I came back to L.A., I was called in front of the Film Council and we were fined for using Indian laborers. They came all the way to South Dakota—on *our* cheap picture!

TW: Was there any nightlife in South Dakota?

Cohen: There was nothing to do at night except have a drink in the bar or something and go to sleep. We had to get up four-thirty, five o'clock in the morning.

TW: Was there anybody there who claimed to be descended from Chief Pontiac?

Cohen: You're forgetting, this was the Sioux, the Sioux in South Dakota. Chief Pontiac's tribe was out of Detroit. The tribe we hired was a different tribe.

TW: And your director, Felix Feist?

Cohen: He was a very good director who'd just done a hell of a picture [*The Big Trees*, 1952] with Kirk Douglas. But he had the rep of being a difficult director, and therefore, he couldn't get a job. He probably resented that he had to do a picture like *Battles of Chief Pontiac*. He wasn't difficult with *us*, but…he was *too good for the film*, let's put it that way. Here we're making a shitkicker in ten days, and on location besides, with all the problems of location, and we had a pretty classy director. He was tough to push and handle, Felix was. But a hell of an intelligent guy.

Everybody I worked with was either down on their luck, or couldn't get a job—but had terrific credits! Who was the director of photography on *Pontiac*? Charles Van Enger again? Oh, I loved that old guy.

TW: And, again, Chaney was good in the picture, wasn't he?

Cohen: Lon loved the part. He thought he *was* Chief Pontiac! In his speeches that he gave to his people before they went to war, he had tears in his eyes. Here is this two-bit movie we're making, and here's Lon Chaney with tears in his eyes doing his scenes. He thought he *was* the fuckin' Indian chief! He ate their food, by the way—the loaf of bread, the hunk of buffalo meat and the quart of milk.

TW: Did you ever see him again after these three movies?

Cohen: No. But, you know, that's the business.

TW: And when you think back on Lon Chaney—what lasting memories?

Cohen: He was a nice guy. He had problems. His father was a big silent star…and he was living off his dad's name. He was a *good* actor. I mean, he did *Of Mice and Men*, and he thought he was going to be a big star after that. We had a couple conversations, when he would be drinking and talking about Hollywood and everything else. He was unhappy because of his career—his career but *no place* outside of Universal [his Universal horror films] and a couple others. He was a *damn good* actor, but nobody gave him the credit. So he wasn't a very happy man.

TW: Did you hang out with him much?

Cohen: Not much, no. Don't forget, I was [still quite young], I wasn't gonna hang around Lon Chaney. And Lon Chaney wasn't gonna hang around *us*. And he never did. For instance, on *The Bushwhackers* we all went out together for dinner one night, John Ireland, Dorothy Malone, Myrna Dell, Wayne Morris, Lawrence Tierney…but Lon wasn't one of the group at all. Lon was *never* with the actors. He just wasn't interested in being with the actors or the crew. He did his job, and that was it. That's the way he was. And when we were in Rapid City, he was with the Indians all the time. He just loved the area. We had a tough time even getting him into town, for production meetings and what have you. He *loved* it out there in the Indian village. He was an outdoorsman. He was *always* an outdoorsman. He went fishing, and he went hunting, and he went here and there. He became friends with some of the Indians. He could have been fucking some of the squaws, I don't know [*laughs*], but he was *always* with the Indians!

Lon Chaney *should* have been, and *could* have been, a hell of a top actor. He could have been a big star. But

A late-in-life shot of Herman with his dog Sally (left) and their friend Kelly.

because of his father, and because of what he had to live up to, everybody wanted him for horror pictures. That's why he loved the part of Chief Pontiac, it was something different. That's why, the minute I offered him the job,

he took it. And he was a *nice* man. A big, *big* bruiser—and a nice, gentle guy. I always find that, the bigger the guy is, the nicer they are. It's the little short scrappy one that wants to start trouble! Lon, he was just a nice guy.

EVOLUTION OF A HORROR STAR
The Lon Chaney Jr. Timeline
By Greg Mank with Tom Weaver

Saturday, February 10, 1906: Creighton Tull Chaney is born near Oklahoma City. He claims he was born dead and that his father, Lon Frank Chaney, a traveling actor, dunked him into Belle Isle Lake to shock life into him.[25] His mother is Frances (Cleva) Creighton Chaney, an actress. The future star of *The Wolf Man* is born on the date of a full moon. Spending part of his childhood with his dad's deaf-mute parents, the boy learns sign language.

1920: The 1920 Census shows Lon Chaney, "Actor," living at 228 North Edgemont in Los Angeles. Residing with him: 32-year old wife Hazel (Lon and Cleva have bitterly divorced), 14-year old son Creighton, Chaney's uncle Roy Willard, his brother-in-law Charles and sister-in-law Maud. Chaney has scored in *The Miracle Man* (1919) as "The Frog," and will appear in six 1920 features, including a dual role in Universal's *Outside the Law*, directed by Tod Browning. Curt Siodmak, scenarist of *The Wolf Man* (1941) and other Chaney Jr. films, will relate that Chaney tells him that, when he was a boy, his father brutally beat him with a strap. It's impossible to know if that really happened; but one wonders why Chaney and/or Siodmak would make up such a story.

Mid- to late 1920s: Silent movie superstar Lon Chaney, known as "The Man of a Thousand Faces" (because he did his own makeups), was at the peak of his popularity in the 1920s. And yet the star of such macabre melodramas as *The Hunchback of Notre Dame* (1923) and *The Phantom of the Opera* (1925) harbored fears that it would end abruptly. And because of this attitude toward the movie business, he wanted his son Creighton to put from his mind all thoughts of pursuing such a career. The kids of other stars may have had big

allowances and flashy lifestyles, but Creighton finished out of the vo-dee-oh-*dough*: His after-school and summer hours were spent laboring in slaughterhouses, digging ditches, delivering ice, etc.

1930: The 1930 Census lists 24-year-old Creighton Chaney living at 735 North Laurel Avenue in Hollywood. Residing with him: his 24-year old wife, Dorothy, 20-month-old son Lon and baby Ronald. His occupation is listed as "Advertising Manager, Water Heaters" (Chaney's father-in-law owns the business). Lon Chaney, still Hollywood's Man of a Thousand Faces, is now under contract to MGM and one of the biggest stars in the world.

Tuesday, August 26, 1930: *The Los Angeles Examiner* reports: "Lon Chaney, famous character actor of the films, died at 12:55 a.m. today at St. Vincent's Hospital." Cause of death, according to his death certificate: a pulmonary hemorrhage, due to bronchial cancer. His age: 47.

Thursday, August 28, 1930: The Lon Chaney funeral takes place at the "Little Chapel" of Cunningham and O'Conner, 1031 South Grand Avenue. Interment follows at Forest Lawn's Great Mausoleum, beside his father. (Still no marker in 2015.) Chaney leaves an estate of $550,000, the bulk going to his "dear beloved wife" Hazel. Creighton receives an unspecified life insurance payment, shared with two uncles and an aunt. Creighton's mother Cleva Creighton Bush, then living in Pasadena, receives one dollar. Chaney's son's feelings for him will swing back and forth for the next 43 years, from hero worship to bitter resentment.

Tuesday, January 26, 1932: *Los Angeles Herald* headline: **Lon Chaney's Son Ready to Launch Career**

in Films. He's "Creighton Chaney," RKO-Radio is the studio, and the article reveals: "The contract calls for a starting salary of $250 a week, including an agreement for five years, with options, and will pay as high as $3,000 a week, if he makes good, officials stated."

Friday, February 12, 1932: *Los Angeles Examiner*: A columnist (probably Louella Parsons) writes, "I am very glad that Radio Pictures will not advertise Creighton Chaney as Lon Chaney Jr. Creighton Chaney has a long way to go before he can emulate his distinguished father... There was talk that his name be changed to Lon Chaney Jr., but, I understand, Metro-Goldwyn-Mayer registered a violent protest, inasmuch as Lon Chaney's pictures are being shown in the provinces and elsewhere... At any rate, it's far better to keep his own personality and win his own spurs."

Wednesday, May 4, 1932: *Los Angeles Examiner* headline: **Mower Nips Lon Chaney II**. The article reveals that four-year-old Lon Chaney almost lost his left thumb after deciding to investigate a lawnmower while the gardener was resting. (Slow news day in L.A.!)

June 1932: The actor will receive top billing for the first time in *The Last Frontier*, a 12-chapter serial now shooting in Kernville, in the southern Sierra Nevada. Decades later, its co-director Spencer Gordon Bennet will tell serial expert Alan Barbour that Chaney was drunk during most of the filming.

Tuesday, January 24, 1933: *Los Angeles Examiner*: "Gwili Andre, Creighton Chaney and Julie Haydon, three young players who joined Radio with much ballyhoo, are not having their contracts renewed... Creighton Chaney did not measure up to expectations..." (Julie Haydon will later claim to have provided Fay Wray's "scream" in *King Kong*.)

Monday, November 6, 1933: *Los Angeles Herald Express*: "Creighton Chaney, actor and son of the late Lon Chaney, today was given a suspended sentence on a speeding charge when he explained he was racing to the bedside of his dying stepmother, Mrs. Hazel Chaney, at the time he was cited for speeding... Mrs. Chaney died shortly afterward."

Thursday, May 17, 1934: *Los Angeles Examiner*: "Lon Chaney's son, Creighton, has at last found himself. He wasn't such a hot shot in the movies, but he has been a success in one of the five plays MGM put on at the Little Theatre in Beverly Hills. Maybe now he will do better in pictures."

Saturday, November 17, 1934: Monogram releases *Girl O' My Dreams,* a college kid comedy with songs, in which co-star Creighton Chaney plays the same kind of callow college boy as castmates Eddie Nugent, Arthur Lake(!) and Sterling Holloway(!!). Chaney is shotput- and discus-throwing field-and-track team member Don Cooper, and in one scene he wears a monocle in one eye and reclines atop a piano crooning "Thou Art My Baby." The screenwriter, George Waggner, will later direct Chaney in *The Wolf Man.* Waggner also writes the lyrics to "Thou Art My Baby"; Edward Ward, who will work with Waggner at Universal (and eventually be fired by him due to his drinking), composes the music.

Saturday, January 5, 1935: *Los Angeles Examiner*: "Hollywood's 'Man of a Thousand Faces' will return to the screen, in name at least, it was learned yesterday, with announcement by Creighton Chaney, 28-year-old son of the late Lon Chaney, that he would assume his father's name for screen purposes. So, hereafter, his screen credits will read, 'Lon Chaney, Jr.'"

Saturday, March 16, 1935: It's the twentieth anniversary of Universal City and tonight, 2200 celebrants crowd onto Universal's Phantom Stage (built for Lon's *The Phantom of the Opera*) to honor studio president Carl Laemmle. There's dancing, 12 acts of vaudeville and special appearances by such local luminaries as the man who designed Universal City, its builder, its first mayor, first chief of police, etc. Also on hand are a number of "second-generationers": Carl Laemmle Jr., Wallace Reid Jr., Noah Beery Jr., Allan (son of Jean) Hersholt...and Lon Chaney Jr. At one point in the evening, as a poem is read in memory of gone-but-not-forgotten Universal greats, Lon Jr. places flowers on the stage.

By taking the screen name Lon Chaney Jr. (and, later, just Lon Chaney), the actor tosses a unique monkey wrench into his dad's legacy. In subsequent generations, film fans and historians needing to differentiate between father and son, whether in conversation or in print, will simplify things for themselves by redubbing the silent-era Lon Chaney "Lon Chaney Sr."—a name that was never his in real life, and never seen on-screen. Try to think of another famous movie star...or another famous *anybody*...now usually remembered by a name that wasn't his and that he never used!

Late June 1935: Chaney finally achieves stardom (stardom times 24, in fact) when Commodore Pictures, an Eastern concern, schedules him to star in eight action movies a year for the next three years. He begins with *The Shadow of Silk Lennox*, which commences production in late June.

August 1935: The same year that Karloff and Lugosi play twin brothers (in *The Black Room* and *Murder by Television*, respectively), Jr. portrays two characters (but not brothers) in *Scream in the Night*, his second for Commodore Pictures, which begins shooting in August. It's a good showcase for Chaney as he plays a young detective, a scarred, bearded baddie *and*, in a way, a third role, the detective made-up and posing as the baddie. Sometimes he acts opposite himself courtesy of some not-bad split screen work. According to a contemporary article, Chaney had his own makeup box (formerly a box for fishing tackle) and made himself up for this role. His baddie looks suspiciously like his dad's Singapore Joe in *The Road to Mandalay* (1926).

Tuesday, March 3, 1936: It's Day #1 of production on *Undersea Kingdom*, Republic's second serial, set 10,000 feet below sea level in the domed continent of Atlantis, which is unaccountably sunlit. It's Chaney's first science fiction credit. Ray (Crash) Corrigan plays heroic U.S. Naval Academy Lt. Crash Corrigan, who comes to Atlantis from "the upper world" (that's us) in a rocket submarine with other expedition members. Monte Blue is Unga Khan, a Ming the Merciless-like villain, and eleventh-billed Chaney is Hakur, captain of Unga Khan's imperial guard. Hakur and his men all wear black so that even the dimmest kid audience member knows they're the bad guys.

Saturday, June 6, 1936: *Los Angeles Examiner* headline: **Chaney Café Case Again Is in Spotlight**. Chaney explains he gave money to one Gertrude M. Davey to obtain a liquor license for her place of business at 7625 Melrose Avenue. Liquor license was not renewed due to café's proximity to Fairfax High School. Chaney claims he had no more to do with Ms. Davey, who apparently named her establishment "The Lon Chaney Jr. Café."

Friday, June 26, 1936: *Los Angeles Examiner* headline: **Lon Chaney's Son Sued by Mate**. Article states Lon and Dorothy H. Chaney separated on May 7, 1936, after ten years of marriage. She charges Chaney with "excessive drinking, staying out nights without explanation, and

with being sullen and sarcastic." Dorothy seeks custody of seven-year-old Lon Ralph Chaney and six-year-old Ronald Creighton Chaney. A month later, Judge Parker Wood grants a divorce, approving a property settlement in which Dorothy will receive certain real estate and personal property, and 20 percent of Lon's earnings over $3600 per year. She also gets custody of the two boys.

Friday, October 30, 1936: Paramount releases *Rose Bowl*, a college football yarn, with Chaney uncredited as a Sierra football player. Charles T. Barton, who directs the film (and will later direct Chaney in *Abbott and Costello Meet Frankenstein*), will remember that, even at this time, the 30-year-old Chaney had a serious drinking problem: "Oh God, *awful*. By later afternoon, he didn't know where he was."

Monday, January 11, 1937: Chaney's seven-year contract commences at 20th Century-Fox. The terms:
- Year One: 10 out of 13 weeks, $125 per week; 10 out of 13 weeks, $150 per week; 20/26 weeks, $200 per week
- Year Two: 40/52 weeks, $275
- Year Three: 40/52 wks., $350
- Year Four: 40/52 wks., $450
- Year Five: 40/52 wks., $600
- Year Six, 40/52 wks., $850
- Year Seven: 40/52 wks., $1200

Darryl F. Zanuck picks up the first option only if Chaney agrees to stay at $125 per week. It will continue this way for two years. Meanwhile, Chaney plays mostly lowly bits at Fox.

Tuesday, January 11, 1938: *Los Angeles Examiner* headline: **Lon Chaney Jr. Wed 3 Months**. Article reveals that Chaney wed Patsy Beck on October 1, 1937, in Colton, California. The only others who knew were actor Robert Kent and his actress wife Astrid Allwyn; they accompanied the elopers to Colton, "whence the Chaneys embarked on a trailer honeymoon." Chaney says, "Proves it's possible to keep a secret in Hollywood after all."

Thursday, August 18, 1938: *Variety* reports that Fox's *Jesse James* cast—Henry Fonda, Nancy Kelly, Henry Hull, Brian Donlevy, John Carradine, etc.—leaves today by special train to Pineville, Missouri, for location shooting. Tyrone Power and director Henry King left for the site by plane the previous day. In Pineville, Chaney falls off his horse and, badly bruised, tells King, "I'm through for the day." King, who blames the fall on

Chaney with his second wife Patsy Beck, whom he married in 1937. They would remain married, throughout some stormy times, until his 1973 death.

Chaney's drinking, responds, "You're through in the picture!" and sends him back to Hollywood. Chaney will appear at the very bottom of the on-screen cast list as "One of James Gang."

Monday, December 12, 1938: A note with this date in his Fox file reports that Chaney, on loan to Paramount for Cecil B. DeMille's *Union Pacific*, completed his role on December 11, 1938, at 2:34 a.m. Chaney played Dollarhide, a bearded gambler looming in background shots behind villain Brian Donlevy. He has no dialogue, at least in the release version.

Tuesday, December 20, 1938: *Los Angeles Examiner* headline: **Chaney Jr. Faces Ex-Wife in Court**. The article describes him as looking like "a character out of the old Wild West" (he still has his *Union Pacific* beard) and notes that Dorothy has cited him for alimony contempt. Chaney admits he's not "in such good shape" financially, and adds, "I gave her everything when we separated. An automobile, six rooms of furniture, a house and a $36,000 promissory note which pays her $195 a month. I thought that was enough support for them." Judge Leslie E. Still clears Chaney of the contempt charge but orders him to pay $50 more per month in child support.

Wednesday, January 11, 1939: Fox drops Chaney, exactly two years after his contract began.

Thursday, April 6, 1939: Chaney opens as Lennie in the play *Of Mice and Men*, based on the John Steinbeck novel, at Hollywood's El Capitan Theatre. Wallace Ford and Isabel Jewell co-star as, respectively, George and Curley's Wife; Ford, who played in the Broadway production, personally coaches Chaney to emulate Broderick Crawford, who'd played Lennie in New York. The *Variety* reviewer writes:

> One of the finest acted dramatic performances of recent years... Typical first night turnout of picture people rose to their feet at the final curtain and gave the cast a reception rare in local theater annals...

> Particularly outstanding was the portrayal of Lennie, the idiotic giant, by Lon Chaney, Jr., whose performance was rated equal to that of Broderick Crawford, who created the role. Wallace Ford plays the part of George...with fine professional polish. Isabel Jewell is capital as the lonesome wife... *Of Mice and Men* should be a pushover for those who like their drama in strong doses.

Of Mice and Men runs April 6 to April 22 in Hollywood; then April 24 to May 13 in San Francisco at the Geary Theatre; then back to the El Capitan for one week.

Saturday, June 10, 1939: Fox starts shooting *Frontier Marshal*, starring Randolph Scott. John Carradine is the chief villain and Chaney has a reasonably good heavy role at the studio that had dumped him five months earlier.

Monday, August 14, 1939: *Variety* reports the start of production on the film *Of Mice and Men*, produced by Hal Roach for United Artists release. Chaney had personally visited director Lewis Milestone at his office and asked for a test as Lennie. Milestone claimed he'd already cast the role in his mind (he reportedly wanted Guinn "Big Boy" Williams). Nevertheless, Milestone tested Chaney and awarded him the part. Burgess Meredith plays George, and Betty Field Curley's Wife (called Mae in the film). Location shooting is on the Agoura Ranch.

Monday, November 6, 1939: Hal Roach begins directing *One Million B.C.* on location in Nevada. The producer (allegedly): D.W Griffith. The three stars: Victor Mature, Carole Landis and Chaney as Akhoba. Chaney develops his own makeup, but union rules

Isabel Jewell backstage with Chaney at Hollywood's El Capitan Theatre during the run of *Of Mice and Men*.

prevent him using it. George E. Phair in his *Variety* "Retakes" column notes, "Prehistoric man, as portrayed in *One Million B.C.*, looked like Lon Chaney Jr. on a cold day in a nudist camp."

Friday, December 22, 1939: *Of Mice and Men* has a gala premiere at the Four-Star Theatre in Los Angeles. Hal Roach and his wife host an opening night party at their Beverly Hills estate, transformed to resemble a ranch. Among the 225 invited guests: Clark Gable, Carole Lombard, Errol Flynn, Marlene Dietrich, Tyrone Power, Bette Davis, James Cagney, Fay Wray, Spencer Tracy, Norma Shearer, Walt Disney, Deanna Durbin, Lionel Atwill and Lon Chaney Jr.

Sunday, January 7, 1940: CBS Radio's *Pursuit of Happiness* presents a scene from *Of Mice and Men* with Meredith, Field and Chaney, who flies to New York for the broadcast.

Tuesday, February 20, 1940: Chaney signs a term contract with Hal Roach Studios.

Saturday, February 24, 1940: *Variety* reports that Chaney will join Ed Sullivan's touring stage show, also to feature Jean Parker, Carole Landis, Marjorie Weaver, Phyllis Brooks, Douglas McPhail...and Bela Lugosi. It would be his first stint with Lugosi, but Chaney drops out (as do Parker, Landis and Brooks). Arthur Treacher becomes the emcee.

Tuesday, March 26, 1940: *One Million B.C.* previews at the Fox California Theatre in San Diego.

Wednesday, April 3, 1940: Chaney reports for Cecil B. DeMille's *North West Mounted Police*, as Shorty.

Monday, May 6, 1940: *Variety* announces that Chaney will star in Roach Studios' *The Unholy Horde*, about Louis XIV's reign.

1940: The National Census lists Lon Chaney Jr. and his wife Patricia living at 12750 Hortense Street in North Hollywood. His two sons are not listed as living with their father and stepmother. It will be Chaney's home throughout and beyond the World War II years.

Monday, October 7, 1940: Universal begins shooting its "Million Dollar Super Serial" *Riders of Death Valley* in Red Rock Canyon (where in 1932 Universal filmed exteriors for *The Mummy*). Chaney, apparently free of his Roach contract, joins the cast. On October 9, the *Variety* column "Hollywood Inside" tells a strange story:

> Lon Chaney Jr. draws down two checks for his role in Universal's *Riders of Death Valley*. First is for his regular salary, the second a weekly $25. The unusual circumstance involves a long story. Part of it concerns the late Lon Sr. When latter left U years ago because studio refused to give him a $35 increase on an option lift from $75 weekly, the elder Chaney vowed, so the story goes, that when he next worked for U it would pay him ten times that salary, plus the $35. Then came *The Miracle Man* [1919] and when Chaney next drew a U bid, he made his promise stick. Chaney Jr. was similarly under U contract five years ago, and was nipped by a $25 option lift. Now back, traditional difference was recalled, and carrying on, studio will ante the $25 weekly.

Watching this Million Dollar Super Serial in 2015, one can't help but wonder where $850,000 of that million went.

Wednesday, December 11, 1940: Chaney, in makeup for *Man Made Monster*, in which Lionel Atwill transforms him into an electrical freak, joins

In September-October 1941, just prior to starring in *The Wolf Man*, Chaney was the baddie in Universal's outdoor adventure *North to the Klondike*. Here he's visited on the set by his father's brother George, an antique dealer from Appleton, California. According to the snipe on the back of this still, George Chaney "hadn't seen a movie set since the untimely death of his famous brother more than ten years ago." (Photo courtesy John Antosiewicz)

a ceremony on the stage built for *The Phantom of the Opera*, dedicating a plaque to his father's memory. (The plaque long ago went missing; the soundstage itself was razed in 2014.)

Tuesday, Christmas Eve, 1940: *Variety* reports that Chaney will play his father's role in a remake of *Tell It to the Marines*. He doesn't, but he is at MGM New Year's Eve, playing the small role of "Spike" in *Billy the Kid*. It's his first time working on the lot where his father became famous; he's assigned to Dad's old dressing room.

Thursday, February 6, 1941: *The New York Times* writes that Chaney, Bela Lugosi and Erich von Stroheim are all under consideration to star in the Chicago company of *Arsenic and Old Lace*, the Broadway sensation that had opened January 10, starring Boris Karloff. Von Stroheim will win the Karloff role.

Monday, March 24, 1941: *Variety* reviews *Man Made Monster*:

When Universal perpetrates horrific drama on the public it does so with an experienced hand,

and *Man Made Monster* is no exception... [P]icture packs enough suspense and goose pimples in its footage to satiate the most bloodthirsty ticket buyer... Chaney Jr. seems to be following in his father's footsteps as far as delineating screen monsters goes and gives an excellent account of himself.

Wednesday, October 15, 1941: *Variety*: "With the press on the sidelines, Broderick Crawford and Lon Chaney Jr. yesterday staged the climax of their fistic battle in Universal's *North to the Klondike* in a frontier saloon. It was part of a brawl which is designed to compare with the major fights in pictures since the classic in *The Spoilers*." Meanwhile, Chaney and Crawford have been getting drunk, beating each other up, and trashing the dressing room bungalow they share at Universal.[26] The studio, after warnings, reassigns the bungalow to Evelyn Ankers and Anne Gwynne. Chaney takes out his anger on Ankers, the film's leading lady, who will primarily remember him as a drunken lout.

Monday, October 27, 1941: *The Wolf Man* begins shooting at Universal, produced and directed by George Waggner under the title of *Destiny*. Chaney stars as Lawrence Talbot; Evelyn Ankers recites scenarist Curt Siodmak's "Even a man who is pure in heart..." poem. The cast boasts Claude Rains, Warren William, Ralph Bellamy, Maria Ouspenskaya, Patric Knowles and Bela Lugosi (who, as Bela the gypsy, gnaws Chaney to stardom). Chaney again delights in persecuting Ankers; he also complains about Jack P. Pierce and his arduous makeup applications. The actor gets along nicely with Moose, a German Shepherd who plays the original werewolf in *The Wolf Man*. Moose becomes Chaney's constant companion.

Monday, November 17, 1941: *Variety* writes that Universal has engaged Chico de Verdi, violinist, and his Hungarian gypsy orchestra to play in the carnival episode of *The Wolf Man*, which will require 100 extras for two days. In this episode, Chaney, as Talbot, fights a

600-pound bear. Between scenes, the bear gets loose and chases Evelyn Ankers up into the catwalks. Universal will cut the bear out of the picture.

Monday, December 15, 1941: Eight days after Pearl Harbor, Universal starts shooting *The Ghost of Frankenstein*. With Karloff still in Broadway's *Arsenic and Old Lace*, Chaney plays the Monster. He bitches that Evelyn Ankers is too heavy for him to lug around and demands a strap be provided to tie her to him and reduce the weight strain; hence Universal's "Evelyn Ankers Strap," which mortifies its namesake. Chaney's Monster comes off as a mute, back-from-the-grave Lennie. Off-screen, he charms little Janet Ann Gallow, and eventually wants to adopt her. "I truly loved this man," Janet remembers decades later.

Friday, December 15, 1941: For publication, Chaney writes a diary-style account of this day's *Ghost of Frank* activities. He's up at 3 a.m., he's in Jack Pierce's makeup chair at 4 a.m. and on the set by 8. Under Pierce's sponge rubber makeup, Chaney feels like his forehead is on fire; when the makeup is removed with acetone, it's a "lovely mass of blisters." Skin specialist Dr. Woods figures out that the actor is allergic to sponge rubber, so from now on there will be a layer of oil silk between his skin and the rubber. "Wish Dad had kept a diary. Remember that he suffered agonies while making some of those pictures, and we never heard about it at home. …Funny that they called him the man with a thousand faces. Can only remember one—the one with the smile. If he could take it like that, guess I can, too. Hope so, anyway."

Saturday, December 20, 1941: *The Wolf Man* has its Broadway opening at the Rialto Theatre.

Friday, January 23, 1942: *The Wolf Man* and *The Mad Doctor of Market Street* open at the Vogue Theatre on Hollywood Boulevard. In person on opening night: Bela Lugosi, Evelyn Ankers and Warren William from the former film, and Lionel Atwill, Claire Dodd and Nat Pendleton from the latter.

Thursday, March 26, 1942: In a Universal PR stunt onstage at the Hollywood Pantages Theatre, where *The Ghost of Frankenstein* is playing, Atwill, Lugosi and Ankers present Chaney a plaque, hailing him as "The New Master Character Creator." The ceremony also takes place that night at the RKO Hillstreet Theatre, also playing *The Ghost of Frankenstein*. Atwill and Lugosi

probably resent the hype for Chaney, and Ankers can't stand him, but all are team players.

Tuesday, March 31, 1942: Chaney starts a new contract at Universal.

Wednesday, June 3, 1942: *The Mummy's Tomb* begins shooting at Universal. Chaney stars as Kharis. He hates the makeup and the role, claiming it gives him little chance to act.

Sunday, October 18, 1942: Chaney, who began work on Universal's *Frankenstein Meets the Wolf Man* this past week (as the Wolf Man, of course), joins the Leading Men vs. Comedians Football Game. He appears climactically in full Frankenstein Monster makeup and costume, chasing everybody off the field. Betty Grable and Rita Hayworth are team captains. Final score: Leading Men 94, Comedians 79.

Thursday, November 5, 1942: A bad day for *Frankenstein Meets the Wolf Man*: Lugosi, as the Monster, faints during a scene on the lab operating table, and Chaney and Maria Ouspenskaya are in a coach when it overturns. Lugosi goes home to recuperate; Chaney suffers cuts; Ouspenskaya breaks an ankle (and won't return to the picture).

Monday, November 9, 1942: *Variety* announces that Chaney will inherit his father's role in Universal's lavish Technicolor remake of *Phantom of the Opera*. Chaney is thrilled.

Thursday, January 7, 1943: *Variety* reports that Claude Rains will star in the title role in Universal's *Phantom of the Opera*. Chaney is angry. His consolation prize: *Son of Dracula*, which starts shooting today. According to Curt Siodmak, who co-authored the *Son of Dracula* script, Chaney, during the shoot, smashed a vase over the bald head of director Robert Siodmak, Curt's brother.

Monday, March 1, 1943: *Variety* writes that Chaney is among the celebrities on tour raising money for the Red Cross $125,000,000 appeal.

Sunday, April 4, 1943: Chaney guest stars on radio's *Inner Sanctum*, broadcast from New York.

Monday, April 19, 1943: Universal starts shooting *Cobra Woman*, Technicolor kitsch starring Maria Montez

Radio "Quiz Kid" Joel Kupperman, appearing in Universal's *Chip Off the Old Block* (1944), meets Chaney, star of the simultaneously shooting *The Mummy's Ghost*.

as good and evil twin sisters. Chaney gets special billing as Hava, a heroic mute. During filming on the back lot, his beloved dog Moose becomes road kill. Additionally, Chaney dislikes the imperious Montez—so much so that, according to Curt Siodmak, Chaney throws a bag of excrement at Montez's studio bungalow door.

Wednesday, May 19, 1943: Universal begins *Frontier Badmen*, which special-bills Chaney as "Chango, the Mad Killer."

Monday, August 23, 1943: *The Mummy's Ghost* begins shooting at Universal, starring Chaney as Kharis and John Carradine as the evil high priest. Director Reginald LeBorg tries to shoot as much as possible before lunch, due to Chaney's rambunctious boozing. Leading lady Ramsay Ames, late in life, refuses to discuss Chaney.

Monday, October 18, 1943: *Calling Dr. Death*, first of Universal's *Inner Sanctum* series, goes before the cameras. The *Inner Sanctums* will characteristically present Chaney as brilliant and a babe magnet. The "babe" in *Calling Dr. Death*: Patricia Morison. Her

memory of Chaney: a professional who was courteous to her and never appeared to be drunk.

Monday, January 17, 1944: *Variety* reports that Chaney and Ann Savage (who will play the rabid *femme fatale* Vera in PRC's 1945 *Detour*) are touring Southern states to sell bonds for the Fourth War Loan Campaign. Meanwhile, scuttlebutt claims Patsy Chaney is learning Judo to protect herself from her husband's drunken fits.

Tuesday, April 4, 1944: Universal begins shooting *The Devil's Brood*, released as *House of Frankenstein*. Karloff is topcast as the film's Mad Doctor, Chaney second-billed as the Wolf Man. Also featured in this Monster Rally: John Carradine as Dracula, Glenn Strange as Frankenstein's Monster, and J. Carrol Naish as Karloff's hunchbacked sidekick. Elena Verdugo plays the gypsy girl, killed by the Wolf Man while shooting him with a silver bullet.

Wednesday, July 26, 1944: *The Mummy's Curse* begins shooting at Universal. Virginia Christine, as the reincarnated Ananka, remembers Chaney as intoxicated throughout the entire shoot. Robbins Coons of the Associated Press covers the movie, ruefully reporting, "Lon Chaney was an actor once, at least he was an actor in *Of Mice and Men*. He was almost as good as his late father... But down by the old back lot swamp, where the sun beats hot, Lon is just a mummy's boy. He's all wound up in dirty rags with a long-underwear foundation. He has a dirty-rag face, too, like a thoroughly embalmed actor. In fact, he looks like anybody else of his size and build all wrapped up, and what is embalmed for the moment is actually his career." Chaney says, "I've bet that some day one of these [Mummy] pictures will lose money, and then I won't have to do any more. So far, though..." With that, according to Coons, the actor shrugs in despair.

Wednesday, August 16, 1944: Chaney announces that he and Patsy plan to adopt an eight-year-old boy, Burrell Howard Devine. The boy's stepfather and mother work on Chaney's ranch (which he's named "Lennie's Ranch") in Stockton, California, where Burrell has been living with his parents and five other children in a one-room home. "I fell in love with the kid!" says Chaney, who significantly adds, "The lousiest thing in the world is to grow up without love." Years after Chaney's death, Patsy recalls that the adoption fell through after Burrell's mother caused trouble.

Friday, December 22, 1944: *House of Frankenstein* and *The Mummy's Curse*, a Chaney double feature, open as the Christmas show at Hollywood's Hawaii Theatre.

Thursday, September 20, 1945: Universal begins *House of Dracula*, another Monster Rally, with Chaney top-billed as Larry Talbot (in lots of footage) and the Wolf Man (less than a minute and a half). One day on a cave set, Glenn Strange as the Monster is trembling with cold as he lies in "quicksand." Chaney gives him a drink from his flask; he also pulls off his Monster headpiece, ending Strange's work day (Jack Pierce has gone home). The Universal front office is outraged.

Tuesday, October 23, 1945: At Forest Lawn's Wee Kirk o' the Heather, the funeral takes place for Flora Beck, Patsy Chaney's mother, who died October 19. At the same time, Lon Chaney II, Chaney's 17-year old son, is suffering a broken leg from a school football game.

Monday, December 24, 1945: Chaney and Patsy renew their vows as he surprises her with a party and a five-carat diamond ring.

Monday, March 11, 1946: *Variety* notes that four Universal stars have left the lot in the past week: Martha O'Driscoll, David Bruce, Robert Paige and Chaney. The studio had declined to pick up the option on all but Paige, who'd refused a role, and terminated his contract by mutual consent. The studio soon becomes Universal-International.

Thursday, February 5, 1948: Universal-International begins shooting *The Brain of Frankenstein*, soon retitled *Abbott and Costello Meet Frankenstein*. Chaney plays the Wolf Man, Lugosi plays Dracula, Glenn Strange the Monster. Bud Westmore has replaced Jack Pierce at Universal City and Chaney's makeup ordeal is considerably less severe. During shooting, Strange fractures his ankle in the laboratory chase scene while throwing the villainess through a skylight; Chaney takes over for him briefly in the Monster makeup and costume. The film, released in the summer of 1948, will become one of the great hits in the studio's history.

Thursday, April 22, 1948: Tonight, Chaney argues violently with wife Patsy, bursts out of the house at 12750 Hortense Street in the San Fernando Valley,

Chaney had a good gig at Universal, a star at a mini-major studio, but drinking eventually turned his life and career upside down.

The road company of *Born Yesterday* in 1948: Jean Parker (her hair dyed red for her role as Billee Dawn), Chaney, Richard Barbee and Scott McKay.

returns and, according to reports, gasps, "I just swallowed 40 sleeping tablets." He lurches back outside, collapsing in the bed of his truck. Rushed to Van Nuys Emergency Hospital, transferred to St. Joseph's

Hospital in Burbank, he's near death and lies in a coma for 48 hours. Son Ron claims his father and stepmother have been waging "many arguments." Patsy denies this, and a family spokesperson virtually blames it all on Chaney Sr. and the Wolf Man: "Chaney was very near collapse from overwork, due to the ordeals of roles in which he tried to follow the grueling characterizations originated by his father. Recently he has been working as a wolf-man in a series of shots which required him to stand in trying positions, motionless, for eight to ten hours a day to permit trick photography effects... It was a tremendous ordeal for the actor, and he has been extremely exhausted lately." Chaney recovers and reconciles with Patsy.

Wednesday, June 2, 1948: Chaney guest stars on Abbott and Costello's radio show.

Monday, September 27, 1948: Chaney and Jean Parker open in Baltimore Ford's Theatre in the touring company of *Born Yesterday*, playing the parts Paul Douglas and Judy Holliday created on Broadway. In an interview published in this day's *Baltimore Sun*, Chaney says, "I get paid to be dumb, ugly and mean, and I don't like to be mean." He also claims his Wolf Man role required an 18-hour makeup application: "I can't move a muscle, can't even move my eyes. There isn't anybody in Hollywood who will do it. They've tried the best stunt men in the business and they quit at noon." During the interview, a woman asks Chaney for an autograph and says, "I'll never forget your father." Chaney's response: "I'm delighted. I hope you never will."

Decades later, Chaney's *Born Yesterday* co-star Parker tells an interviewer, "Every Wednesday [Lon] would do the play in sign language for the deaf. That was an interesting side of him. Such a worthy person. You should be writing about him!"

Tuesday, September 28, 1948: *Baltimore Sun* critic Donald Kirkley runs his review of *Born Yesterday*, writing that Parker and Chaney "are as good or better as the actors who have been doing the same roles on Broadway." He praises Chaney: "His interpretation of Brock is by far the best thing he has ever done... It is a florid, robust, brash performance... Mr. Chaney plays the vulgarian for all he is worth and makes him a vivid and believable figure."

Tuesday, May 10, 1949: A ghost from Chaney's past makes news: his mother. The former Cleva Chaney, now known as Mrs. Frances Cleveland Bush, is arrested at a Pasadena beauty parlor on an intoxication charge. She claims to be a hostess in a café in Pasadena and forfeits a $50 bond by failing to answer the charge in municipal court.

1949: Irving Brecher, creator-producer of the radio comedy show *The Life of Riley*, prepares to bring his long-running series to TV, but its star William Bendix turns down the TV role because of movie commitments. Now in search of a new Chester A. Riley, Brecher has Chaney play the role in a test film. The film is run for various people, including the sponsor and TV executives, and enthusiasm runs high. *But*—and what a revoltin' development *this* is—when push comes to shove, Brecher goes with stage and nitery comic Jackie Gleason as the series star.

Sunday, March 11, 1951: In New York, Chaney appears as Frankenstein's Monster on TV's *The Colgate Comedy Hour* starring Abbott and Costello.

Late 1951: Lon Jr., again following in Dad's footsteps, becomes part of a vaudeville show. In December 1951, *Variety* reviewer Lowe caught it at the Capitol in Washington:

> Hollywoodite Lon Chaney makes a pitch for attention via a sentimental spiel along nostalgic lines about the glory that was vaude. Does it on the ground that he wants to revive the "lost act," the old dramatic skit that was part of the routine when Chaney Sr. trod the boards. Assisting him in a trite bit of trivia called "A Garden of Roses" is newcomer Charles Bang, whose handsome blondness makes a good foil for the Chaney brand of ruggedness. Despite some off-stage flubs with the props, which brought laughs at the tragic climax, payees seemed to like.
>
> Reaction here would indicate that Chaney has the germ of a sound idea, if only he took the trouble to develop his material as befits his talents and the confidence the galleries obviously have in him.

Friday, January 18, 1952: Chaney plays the Monster, bald and scarred, in "Frankenstein" on TV's *Tales of Tomorrow*, emanating live from an ABC studio in New York. While being made up by Vincent J-R Kehoe, Chaney turns a lot of full bottles into empty ones. When a kid actor asks what he's drinking, the lit-up Lon responds, "Oh, that's spirit gum. You see, the makeup is so heavy that I have to drink it to make the stuff stick on my face from the inside out!" Chaney gets so drunk that he thinks the live telecast is the dress rehearsal, so he doesn't smash the breakaway props.

Years later, on TV's *The Pat Boone Show*, Chaney says he applied his own *Tales of Tomorrow* monster makeup.

Wednesday, January 30, 1952: Viola Swisher in her column "Just for *Variety*": "Hear tell FCC again irked by Arthur Godfrey's use of double entendre and smoking car jokes on the air. Which reminds me of the Lon Chaney Jr. faux pas on a recent show when a door didn't close promptly. Chaney growled, 'Shut the so-and-so door.'"

While *Hawkeye and the Last of the Mohicans* was in production in Canada, star John Hart married actress Beryl Braithwaite, and Chaney was the best man; Chaney and Beryl's 14-year-old sister Shari signed the marriage certificate! Left to right, Hart's mom Enid, Chaney, newlyweds Beryl and Hart, and sister Shari.

Monday, June 30, 1952: Erskine Johnson mentions in his column that an indie producer is interested in making a film bio on Lon Chaney Sr. and has been talking to Jr. about it. On the set of *Springfield Rifle* (1952) Johnson talks to Chaney about it, and the actor says there'd be no family objections to putting his dad's story on the screen. "Paul Muni in his heyday would have been perfect," says the son of the Man of a Thousand Faces. "I wouldn't insist on playing it myself, I couldn't do it unless they'd let me act like my old man did instead of directing me."

In other news from the *Springfield Rifle* set, Lon stashes his jug of whiskey with the honey wagon driver, but another actor keeps getting into it. "If you ask Lon for a drink, he'll give it to you," actor Ewing Mitchell tells interviewers Jim and Tom Goldrup years later, "but you don't snitch it." Mitchell goes on to say that Lon asked him how to keep the other actor from getting into his jug, and Mitchell replied, "That's simple. Let the bottle get about this full and then piss in it. The color is the same." According to Mitchell, Lon did so, and after that the other actor never touched it again.

Wednesday, July 30, 1952: United Artists releases *High Noon*, produced by Stanley Kramer, directed by Fred Zinnemann. The film wins four Oscars, including a Best Actor statue for Gary Cooper. Chaney, as arthritic former sheriff Martin Howe, is part of a distinguished cast including Grace Kelly, Thomas Mitchell, Lloyd Bridges, Katy Jurado and Otto Kruger.

Tuesday, June 15, 1954: Chaney joins Bela Lugosi and Vampira on *The Red Skelton Show*. He plays George, Lugosi's half-wolf half-brother.

Thursday, November 11, 1954: Production begins on *Indestructible Man* with Lon in the title role. He gets top billing for the first *and only* time in the 1950s.

July 1955: Chaney impresses as Robert Mitchum's drunken father in *Not as a Stranger*, released this month, produced and directed by Stanley Kramer.

Thursday, February 9, 1956: Bel-Air Productions begins shooting *The Black Sleep*, starring Basil Rathbone, Akim Tamiroff, Lon Chaney, John Carradine ("Kill the infidels!") and Bela Lugosi, at the former PRC studio on Santa Monica Boulevard. Reginald LeBorg directs; Chaney plays mute, lumbering Mungo, one of Rathbone's experiments-gone-wrong. As eyewitnessed by Lugosi's teenage friend Richard Sheffield, Chaney between scenes boisterously grabs the 73-year-old Lugosi (in a frail state after his drug addiction treatment, and still suffering from alcoholism), picks him up like a sack of potatoes, and throws him over his shoulder. In a scene in which he chokes actress Patricia Blake, Chaney chokes her for real. Bela's wife Hope, who visited the set, remembers Chaney as roaring drunk: "I wonder if he was able to stand up! He had *big* problems!"

Sunday, April 8, 1956: Chaney guest stars on TV's *Telephone Time* in "The Golden Junkman." He plays a Greek immigrant whose educated sons are later ashamed of him because he owns 20 junkyards. Chaney and his wife Patsy will consider it his finest TV work.

Thursday, June 7, 1956: Chaney joins John Carradine, Bela Lugosi and Tor Johnson on a *Black Sleep* publicity tour appearance at the Heathman Hotel in Portland. Chuck Moses, who supervised the tour, remembered that Lugosi was so ill and devastated by alcohol that he couldn't answer the press' questions, so they planned a "very dramatic act": Lugosi would fake a collapse, and Chaney (remembered by Moses as "a prince of a guy") would carry him out of the room. Lugosi collapses for real and Chaney, as planned, lugs him off. That night, Lugosi collapses again, this time while leaving the stage of Portland's Paramount Theatre. Moses sends him home to Hollywood, where Bela Lugosi dies on August 16.

Thursday, June 7, 1956: Chaney will receive from Universal a percentage plus $50,000 for his portion of *Man of a Thousand Faces,* the soon-to-be-filmed biopic of his father, according to Army Archerd's "Just for *Variety*" column. According to an October "Just for *Variety*" column, Universal is considering letting Jr. play his own uncle (i.e., Lon Chaney Sr.'s brother) in the James Cagney-starring movie.

Late July 1956: In Pickering, Ontario, a hamlet about 40 miles outside Toronto, shooting begins on the TV series *Hawkeye and the Last of the Mohicans* with John Hart as frontiersman Hawkeye and Chaney as his Indian blood brother Chingachgook. Since it's Canada's first-ever commercial telefilm series, there's a shortage of equipment, studio space and technicians. *Variety* likens the situation to the era when the first films were made in Hollywood. About three-quarters of every episode will be shot outdoors because the studio can only handle two sets. The Canadian members of the crew have never before worked on a TV film series. According to *Variety,* "Chaney, to get himself some comfort while on location (while weather holds, location shooting goes five days a week), designed and built a trailer for himself, with bunks, galley, etc."

November-December 1956: *Man of a Thousand Faces* with James Cagney is shot at Universal. Dennis

Rush plays Creighton (Lon Jr.) at age four, Rickie Sorensen at eight, Robert Lyden as 13 and Roger Smith at 21. In his book *Cagney by Cagney,* published decades later and after the passing of Lon Jr., Cagney recalls *Man of a Thousand Faces* and mentions that there were several stories about the Chaneys "that for one reason or another we felt constrained from using. Now that the son, Lon Chaney Jr., has gone, it is possible to tell at least this fascinating and truly pathetic anecdote." He continued:

> It seems clear that [Cleva] deserted the family, leaving Lon and Creighton alone. But the boy very doggedly persisted in trying to find his mother.
>
> She had an unusal and distinctive name—Cleva. Creighton went to great lengths to find her and finally got a lead to her whereabouts. He made his way to a remote ranch somewhere out on the desert, full of anticipation that his long search was at last near its end. He knocked, and a woman came to the door.
>
> "Yes?"
>
> "Hello. My name is Creighton Chaney, and I'm looking for Mrs. Cleva Fletcher."
>
> "What's the name?"
>
> "Cleva—Cleva Fletcher."
>
> "Oh, I'm sorry," she said. "No one here by that name."
>
> Then, directed to the woman, came a voice from inside the house: "Who is it, Cleva?"
>
> This infinitely sad story we were unable to use. The agonizing pathos of it—a desperately needed mother talking to a son she wanted no part of—that story seemed both crueler and larger than life itself.

Several months after the filming of *Man of a Thousand Faces,* *The Cyclops* is released by Allied Artists, with Chaney Jr. over the top in a supporting role. Co-star Gloria Talbott will remember that, during shooting in Bronson Canyon, Chaney's "mama"—presumably the notorious Cleva—would visit, bringing him lunch and an air mattress on which "he laid out in the sun and went to sleep." Talbott's other memory of Chaney: "a darling, darling man—but drunk as a skunk!"

Saturday, November 30, 1957: Baltimore's *Shock! Theatre,* on Channel 11 at 11:15 p.m., presents *Frankenstein Meets the Wolf Man. Shock!,* a package of

52 Universal films leased to TV by Screen Gems, has become a sensation across the country.

Saturday, September 27, 1958: United Artists releases *The Defiant Ones*, starring Tony Curtis and Sidney Poitier, produced and directed by Stanley Kramer. Chaney plays ex-convict Big Sam. The film receives two Oscars (Best Writing, Best Black & White Cinematography) and an additional seven nominations. Chaney should have received a Best Supporting Actor nomination.

Wednesday, July 15, 1959: *Variety* reports that Chaney "hit a new record" in Mexico City, completing all his scenes in Fernando de Fuenetes' production of *The House of Terror* in two days. Chaney appears in the film as a mummy, a werewolf and "a normal human." Three cameras shot Chaney from every angle at the San Angel Inn Studios, which, as *Variety* writes, "never saw such a bustle of nervous activity and speed."

Tuesday, October 20, 1959: *Variety* writes that Chaney (and wife Patsy) will leave for Stockholm this coming weekend, to narrate and host the TV series *13 Demon Street*, produced at Svensk Industri Studios. The show's writer: Curt Siodmak.

Monday, October 2, 1961: Chaney reunites with Betty Field for the first time since 1939's *Of Mice and Men* for the *Route 66* TV episode "The Mud Nest," that starts shooting today in Baltimore, Maryland.

Friday, October 26, 1962: Chaney joins Boris Karloff and Peter Lorre as guest stars on *Route 66*'s "Lizard's Leg and Owlet's Wing" episode. Karloff dresses up as Frankenstein's Monster, Lorre dons a cape and top hat, and Chaney boisterously appears in makeup and costume as Quasimodo, the Mummy and the Wolf Man.

Wednesday, August 28, 1963: American-International releases *The Haunted Palace*, based on a Lovecraft story and a Poe poem and directed by Roger Corman. Chaney co-stars with Vincent Price and Debra Paget. Price will remember, "He was very ill at the time. I had admired him enormously and wanted to meet him. He was not really very happy. I didn't really get to know him. I spent a lot of time with him, trying to talk to him and make him cheer up, but I couldn't do it."

Monday, November 18, 1963: *Variety* reports that Chaney has launched "a spirited attack" against Jay Ward and his *Fractured Flickers* TV series, which adds comical

Chaney as warlock Simon Orne in AIP's spooky *The Haunted Palace*.

dialogue to silent movies. Ward had refashioned the 1923 *The Hunchback of Notre Dame* so that Chaney Sr.'s Quasimodo appeared to be a football game cheerleader. Chaney Jr. calls the satire "unjust, unfair and completely uncalled for," accusing Ward of bad taste because "he is using respected people who are now dead and can't fight back." Chaney also reveals that his mother Cleva is still alive, and although the family has no legal claim on Chaney Sr.'s movies, the question is one of a "moral" principle.

Sunday, April 12, 1964: In New York's *Sunday Daily News*, Henry Lee's two-page article "There's No Ghoul Like an Old Ghoul" encapsulates the history of the horror film from Universal's *Dracula* and *Frankenstein* on up. After describing Chaney Sr.'s Phantom of the Opera as a monster who nowadays "couldn't scare a 4-H club," Lee adds that no one today (1964) would remember Sr.'s name "except for one thing. He had the historic honor of fathering Lon Chaney Jr." Lee then writes about Jr. (whom he presumably interviewed), mentioning that Jr. "mourns quietly that there was no such thing as residuals when he was monstering for [Universal]," and quotes him as saying that after the recent death of Peter Lorre, "there are only myself and Boris Karloff left of all the genuine horror actors."

Wednesday, May 13, 1964: Paramount releases *Law of the Lawless*, a potboiler Western in which Chaney, as a baddie named Tiny, menaces saloon singer Yvonne De Carlo. It's the first of eight low-budget oaters Chaney makes for producer A.C. Lyles, who stocks his films with grizzled rumpots.

Monday, October 24, 1966: Chaney guest stars on TV's *The Monkees* as a gangster named Lenny—another

In 1969, a one-minute TV commercial for the new Pontiac, produced at a reported cost of a quarter million for talent and production alone, featured (left to right) Chaney, J. Carrol Naish, Robert Strauss, Leo Gorcey and, not pictured, Broderick Crawford, Mike Mazurki and Elisha Cook Jr. (Photo courtesy Leonard Maltin.)

"homage" to his Lennie of *Of Mice and Men*. His gangster partner, played by Len Lesser, is named George.

Saturday, February 11, 1967: TV's *Pistols'n'Petticoats* presents Chaney in his fifth and final appearance as Chief Eagle Shadow. It will also be his final prime time TV acting job. The telecast comes three weeks after the death of the show's star, Ann Sheridan, who'd succumbed to cancer on January 21, 1967.

August 1967: Actor R.G. Armstrong bows out of his role as a frontier sheriff in MGM's *Day of the Evil Gun* because of a conflicting commitment and Chaney steps in. Well, staggers in. When he arrives in Durango, Mexico, where the Glenn Ford Western is shooting, he's very inebriated and obviously not ready for work, according to the book *Glenn Ford: A Life* by Glenn's son Peter Ford. Director Jerry Thorpe asks Peter, 22, to run Chaney's dialogue with him. "I spent many hours with him in his room, but it was a lost cause. Jerry sorely wanted to give this once-fine actor a special moment on-screen, but Lon was unable to pull himself out of his delirium. The once fearsome 'Wolf Man' broke down crying in my arms when he was sent home without

having done a single scene." Paul Fix is hired to play the sheriff and does so, receiving fifth billing.

Sunday, December 24, 1967: *Spider Baby, or the Maddest Story Ever Told* is released. The Jack Hill-directed film was shot several years before and held up due to a bankruptcy problem. It's set in a crumbling old house and Chaney plays (very well) Bruno, a chauffeur who cares for his dead employer's trio of murderous, cannibalistic offspring (Beverly Washburn, Jill Banner and Sid Haig). Chaney sang the "Spider Baby Theme" over the credits, bellowing with laughter as he belted out such lyrics as, "Frankenstein, Dracula and even the Mummy/Are sure to end up in *some*body's tummy!"

Friday, November 8, 1968: Tonight's *Gomer Pyle— USMC* episode "All You Need Is One Good Break" begins with Gomer (Jim Nabors), Sgt. Carter (Frank Sutton), Duke Slater (Ronnie Schell) *et al.* preparing to go to Hollywood to appear in the Marine movie *Leathernecks of the Air*. Gomer's bringing along his autograph book, already signed by such luminaries as Minnie Pearl, Tex Ritter and Linton Johnson. (No, not the president, Linton with a t. An ice skate sharpener who passed through Gomer's home town.)

GOMER: Do you know whose autograph I hope to get more than anybody else's? Lon Chaney Jr.

SLATER: Lon Chaney Jr.?

GOMER: Mm-hmm. He's my favorite actor. I've seen *all* of his pictures: *The Wolf Man*, *The Ape Man*, *The Return of the Wolf Man*, *The Return of the Ape Man*… [*laugh track*]

Later, at the studio commissary, Gomer meets a pretty stunt girl (Judy Brown) who offers to show him around town. "Hey, you know what else I'd like to do? Do you suppose we could drive by the house where Lon Chaney Jr. was born?" [*laugh track*]

Tuesday, April 1, 1969: April Fool's Day takes on new proportions as shooting starts on director Al Adamson's *The Blood Seekers*, an indie horror film starring Chaney and J. Carrol Naish. It eventually morphs into *Dracula vs. Frankenstein*. Chaney, bloated, suffering from throat cancer, vomiting between scenes, wracked by gout, arthritis, beri-beri and cataracts, plays a mute monstrosity named Groton; Naish, with a glass eye (that doesn't move with his other eye as he reads the cue cards) and ill-fitting dentures, is Dr. Frankenstein. Chaney and Naish share a dressing room, where Chaney can be heard rasping to Naish, "Well, I guess we're gonna die pretty soon." Naish's reply: "Oh, shut up, Lon!"

Friday, August 1, 1969: Production begins on Al Adamson's *A Time to Run* (later retitled *The Female Bunch*), featuring Chaney as an alcoholic hired hand on the ruthless gals' desert ranch. It was shot on the Spahn Movie Ranch near Chatsworth. Living there at the time: the Charles Manson "family." The murders of Sharon Tate, Jay Sebring, Wojciech Frykowski, Abigail Folger

Calling Dr. Death-House of Frankenstein-Strange Confession co-stars Chaney and J. Carrol Naish, together one last time in *Dracula vs. Frankenstein*.

and Steven Parent take place on August 9. Pasqualino LaBianca and his wife Rosemary are slain on the 10th.

Wednesday, October 8, 1969: Chaney guests on Johnny Carson's *Tonight Show*. He discusses his father's career and his own, with considerable hyperbole. He blames his hoarse voice (the result of throat cancer) on having growled like the Wolf Man for the trick-or-treaters who'd come to his San Juan Capistrano house the previous Halloween. At Mount St. Mary's College in Emmitsburg, Maryland, student Greg Mank sees the show with several classmates—one of whom, having never heard of Chaney and amazed by his tall tales, asks, "Do you think this guy is full of bullshit?"

Several years earlier, an El Paso newspaper writer thought Lon was full of b.s. In 1964, when Lon arrived in that city to make personal appearances at a pre-Halloween party at Western Playland amusement park, his manager Mark Hanna said that Chaney had so far made 467 films (140 would have been more like it) while Chaney claimed to have been in show business for almost 60 years. "[This] means," the writer interjected, "he was wowin'' em in the front rows from his cradle."

Monday, April 19, 1971: *Variety* reports that the newly formed Kinema Co. is preparing its first two movies, both to be directed by writer-actor-director Duke Kelly: *Ride the Hot Wind* and the Chaney-John Carradine-starring *Night of the Werewolf*. The former gets made, the latter, alas, does not.

Thursday, July 12, 1973: At 4:30 p.m., Lon Chaney Jr., 67, dies of a sudden heart attack at his home, 207 Calle de Ansa, in San Clemente. According to his wishes, the family donates his body to the University of Southern California School of Medicine as an anatomical specimen; the school is eager to study the body due to Chaney's greatly enlarged liver. Reportedly the school displays his liver and lungs to show the dangers of alcoholism and cigarettes.

Wednesday, October 25, 1995: Lon Chaney Jr. joins the long list of notables whose lives were examined on the A&E TV series *Biography*. The 60-minute Halloween (actually October 25) episode "Lon Chaney—Son of a Thousand Faces," written by David J. Skal, incorporates comments from his co-stars Patricia Morison (*Calling Dr. Death*), Elena Verdugo (*House of Frankenstein*, *The Frozen Ghost*) and Beverly Garland (*The Alligator People*), fans Ronald V. Borst, Bob Kokai, *et al.*, many terrific photos, parts of some of his best scenes from *Of Mice and Men* and lots of clips from p.d. trailers of Lon's Universal monster movies. Richard Kiley narrates.

Tuesday, September 30, 1997: At Universal City, Boris Karloff's daughter Sara, Bela Lugosi's son Bela Jr. and Lon Chaney Jr.'s grandson Ron are present at the unveiling of the U.S. Postal Service's 32¢ stamps honoring the classic horror stars. There's a stamp for Chaney Sr. (as the Phantom of the Opera), Chaney Jr. (as the Wolf Man), Lugosi (as Dracula) and two for Karloff (as Frankenstein's Monster and the Mummy).

February 2005 …is the date on the issue of *National Geographic* which features an article on the Salton Sea that includes reminiscences from Bob Miller, "a tall, mustachioed cowboy who'd look perfectly at home in a Marlboro ad." Miller remembers the days when stars came to the Salton Sea to race speedboats, water ski, etc. "As a boy [Miller] and his dad would take Lon Chaney, Jr., Hollywood's 'master monster,' fishing. 'He liked to sit on the front of the pontoon boat and drag his feet in the water,' says Miller. 'He had the biggest, gnarliest toes I've ever seen.'"

Early 2010: Universal releases *The Wolfman* with Benicio del Toro and Anthony Hopkins, a remake of Chaney Jr.'s most famous film. Audiences stay away in droves.

November 2011: Ron Meyer, longtime head of Universal, appears at the Savannah (Georgia) Film Festival and admits, "We make a lot of shitty movies. Every one of them breaks my heart. …One of the worst movies we ever made was *Wolfman*. *Wolfman* and *Babe 2* are two of the shittiest movies we put out." A 2014 *Los Angeles Times* article lists *The Wolfman* among the most expensive flops of all time.

Endnotes

1 The script called for this scene to give us another subjective look at the succarath, in a mirror in Dina's room.

2 A cloak-and-*what*?? I never heard the term before, and Googling "cloak-and-suitor" didn't much help. A cloak-and-suiter turns out to be "a manufacturer or seller of clothing" (Random House Dictionary), which wouldn't seem to describe the Broders. When I put the question to the denizens of the Classic Horror Film Board, Monster Kid Dan Lewis directed me to the book *Hollywood and Anti-Semitism: A Cultural History Up to World War II* which says the term signifies "the Jewish parvenu." *Baaack* to the dictionary, Merriam-Webster this time, to learn that "parvenu" is "a person from usually a low social position who has recently or suddenly become wealthy, powerful, or successful but who is not accepted by other wealthy, powerful, and successful people."

3 I think the *Black Cat* half of this combo turned out to be the 1941 *The Black Cat*.

4 "Caveat emptor!" on that last tidbit of information: The *Filmfax* piece gives the surface impression of being well-researched, but it completely misreports how Realart got started, and not once does it mention its president Paul Broder. Starting with the article title, Paul's brother Jack Broder gets all the credit for Realart and is called its president, when in fact he was initially "only" its vice-president.

5 In Hollywood in the days before unions, "the mob" was very much a presence, according to Orson Welles, quoted in the book *My Lunches with Orson*. And "the mob" was mainly the Purple Gang, and they controlled the Teamsters, said Welles. "When L.B. [MGM's Louis B. Mayer] needed extra money, he got it from the Purple Gang. When he wanted strong-arm work, he'd call the Purple Gang, who'd send their tough guys into town." [Interviewer Henry Jaglom: "Louis B. Mayer had people hit?"] "Beat up. I wouldn't put it past him to have people killed. He liked to think of himself as a founding father and capo of the Mafia."

6 Maybe Robert feared that some reviewers would mistakenly think *he*, Robert, directed *Bride of the Gorilla*—and in at least one case, that's what happened! In a blistering *Oakland Tribune* critique of *Bride* (December 7, 1951), Wood Soanes said it was written and directed by Robert Siodmak, "who was obviously suffering from indigestion…"

7 Right from the get-go, the trades called the movie *Bride of the Gorilla*, Siodmak's title *The Face in the Water* apparently having been discarded more or less instantly. The often (always?) sarcastic Siodmak wrote in his autobiography that Realart put the new title on it "to prove its artistic sense." Herman Cohen took credit for the movie's new name, telling me that Jack Broder "wanted an exploitation title, and I came up with *Bride of the Gorilla*."

8 *The Los Angeles Times* couldn't win for losing in their few attempts to cover *Bride of the Gorilla*. Get a load of their November 16, 1951, review: "Anybody expecting Lon to be made up, like the late Papa Chaney, in ape's skin, will be disappointed. Lon is merely a man…who goes jungle and talks to wild animals when fed an herb by a cursing old native woman. Chaney stands out in a good male cast, his eyes having a peculiarly magnetic glitter which adds strength to his ability as an actor."

9 The only other feature shooting there at the time was the Goldwyn production *I Want You*, a drama with Dana Andrews, Dorothy McGuire and Farley Granger. Barbara Payton had been on the Goldwyn lot several months earlier, making *Drums in the Deep South*.

10 *Bride of the Gorilla* was *not* Gisela's one Hollywood movie; she appeared in more than a dozen. In the anecdote above, Siodmak gives her husband's name as Franz Piffl but other sources list him as John Piffle. Piffle may have been an extra, as Siodmak states, but he also did a bit of acting; his movie appearances were almost always, or perhaps always-always, uncredited. Surely you remember him (not!) as the proprietor of the café where Irena and the Cat Woman have their eerie encounter in *Cat People* (1942) and as the flower vendor who won't give Clo-Clo a free flower in *The Leopard Man* (1943).

11 One wonders if Cantankerous Curt would have had an understanding and forgiving attitude if *he* hadn't directed *Bride* and someone *else* had shot the succarath footage ruinous to his movie's central idea.

12 "On every one of his trips to South Vietnam, he goes equipped with comedy material to entertain the troops—but he has never used it," *The Hollywood Reporter* revealed. "Upon arrival at a military post, he asks the men whether they would like him to entertain—or just sit with them and talk about things in the United States. Invariably, the servicemen just want to talk to him about home."

13 Lyon unsurprisingly doesn't mention *Bride of the Gorilla* in his autobiography *Twists of Fate—An Oscar Winner's International Career* but does write about Raymond Burr, whom he directed in several *Perry Mason*s. Lyon lauds Burr as "one of the really bright actors of our time."

14 Reviewing *Bride of the Gorilla* online, DVD Savant Glenn Erickson called Van Gelder Manor "one of those plantation settings that only occur in Hollywood, a lavish house…in the midst of a manicured, tame jungle of rented greens. Is it the Dutch East Indies? [Taro] has a black deputy named Nado…so is this Africa? Old-crone witch Al Long is of indeterminate origin, but uses magic that resembles voodoo. Sexpot chambermaid Larina (Carol Varga) is definitely Latin. Confusing matters further, the trio of plantation workers we see dress and talk like Hollywood versions of Colombian coffee bean pickers.

15 Actor Richard Erdman, who lived in the same apartment building at Payton at this time, realized there'd been trouble when from his window he saw police cars. Up until that point he hadn't talked much with his notorious neighbor, but in the aftermath to this incident they began occasionally chatting—and soon Erdman climbed aboard Barbara Payton's romantic merry-go-round! According to film historian Alan K. Rode, who talked with Erdman for me in February 2015, their now-and-then fling lasted about six months. Erdman said he found

her to be sweet and very smart and he liked her a lot.

16 This seems only fair: Payton certainly *had* double-**crossed her T** (Tom), so he **dotted her i.**

17 How funny to consider the possibility that *Lady in the Iron Mask* producer Walter Wanger may have been the one to kick Payton to the curb for her unbecoming public behavior (being part of a love triangle that led to bloodshed): On a December evening three months later, Wanger, enflamed by the thought that his actress wife Joan Bennett and MCA television exec Jennings Lang were lovers, shot Lang in a service station parking lot (with Bennett Payton-ishly present to witness the violence!). The veteran producer, charged with assault with a deadly weapon with intent to kill, entered a double plea, not guilty, and not guilty by reason of insanity.

18 They did not go unnoticed or unmentioned by the media *or* by Tone. By the spring of the following year, the romantic embers of marriage were stone cold and Tone had slipped the bonds of unholy matrimony.

19 Movieland columnist Edith Gwynn wrote on December 18, 1951, "*Bride of the Gorilla* (starring Barbara Payton) a dismal flop in Chicago. Proving it doesn't ALWAYS pay!" Did it really flop in Chicago, or was Edith Gwynn a wannabe Louella Parsons, practicing her black journalistic arts on a celeb (Payton) of whom she disapproved? The latter, I suspect. In a *Variety* article datelined Chicago, December 11, it was reported that *Bride* had made a "Sock $18,000" at Minsky's Rialto during its opening week. According to a *Variety* story datelined the 18th (the same day as Gwynn's snipe), *Bride* had done okay in its second week—better than other movies then in their second week in Chicago theaters (*Fixed Bayonets!*, *The Man with the Cloak*, *The Unknown Man*)—despite a general pre-Christmas moviegoing lull, a heavy snowstorm and subzero weather.

20 You'd think that Wood Soanes, author of this review, had thoroughly vented his spleen on the subject of *Bride of the Gorilla*, but a week later he was back on the attack in the *Oakland Tribune* article "Producers Held to Blame for Lax Movie Morality," a treatise on misbehaving actors: "We have an example on the screen of the Fox-Oakland this week in Barbara Payton, who not only isn't a star but who shows little promise of ever becoming one. If Hollywood were really interested in cleaning house it would have dropped *Bride of the Gorilla* on the refuse heap. It didn't cost peanuts to make and if the major studio heads were in earnest [about cracking down on celebutards], they could well afford to give independent producer Jack Broder a check for his production expenses and a reasonable profit on his investment to forget the picture."
  Louella Parsons began her *Modern Screen* article "Hollywood's Most Tragic People" by disqualifying two contenders from consideration because she did not consider them "responsibilities of Hollywood." The first was Lawrence Tierney, "an emotionally ill boy [who] would be his own worst enemy in any walk of life, anywhere." The second was "the blonde Payton woman [who] would be a trouble-making femme fatale even in a pickle factory."

21 Well, maybe Larina *is* supposed to be Al Long's daughter: At one point, Al Long says to her, "Talk to me, my child." But

Hats off to the Realart decisionmaker who had the bright idea of letting *The Basketball Fix* make its Midwest debut in Peoria, Illinois—the home of scandal-rocked Bradley University. It was also the birthplace of star Marshall Thompson.

oldsters call young people "my child" in movies all the time. Surely no viewer ever wondered if native belle Larina (20-ish hubba hubba Carol Varga) was the daughter of Al Long (Gisela Werbisek, born ugly and built to last, and in real life almost old enough to be Carol's great-grandmother).

22 I wonder if this is the same Leo Guild who ghostwrote Barbara Payton's autobiography *I Am Not Ashamed*. A 1965 *Variety* story revealed that the case was still untried.

23 At a glance, which is all I gave it, actor-writer John Gilmore's book *Severed: The True Story of the Black Dahlia Murder* appears to be a mostly fictionalized heap of rubbish posing as a meticulously researched anatomy of a real-life crime, in this case the unsolved 1947 killing of Los Angeleno Elizabeth "The Black Dahlia" Short. (Laudatory back-cover blurbs from notorious fabulists Kenneth Anger, Charles Higham and Gary Indiana are all you need to see to know that you needn't see any more.) So take this for what it's worth, which is zilch: Gilmore says that in 1963, when he claims to have been writing

screenplays, "tough-guy actor Tom Neal wanted to produce and star in a movie based on the [Black Dahlia] case. …The deal with Tom offered cash up front and a big carrot on the other end when he raised the financing 'to get the cocksucker on a roll,' as he put it. …The project collapsed almost two years later, when he was convicted of murdering his own wife…"

24 In 2001, *Two Dollar Bettor* and *The Basketball Fix* made their home video debuts via Something Weird Video, and I reviewed them for the magazine *The Phantom of the Movies' VideoScope*. My review is reprinted below:

These two recent Something Weird releases combine sports backgrounds and crime stories. The obligatory "crime does not pay" message of both movies comes through loud and clear.

The pick of this two-movie litter is *Two Dollar Bettor*, based on a novel *The Far Turn* by Howard Emmett Rogers and adapted for the screen by Rogers—who goes mysteriously unbilled in the opening credits. John Litel plays a widowed bank comptroller with two daughters (Barbara Logan, Barbara Bestar), a genial nature, a Santa Claus complex—and a newfound interest in betting on horse races. Unfortunately for Litel, his beginner's luck quickly runs out; hooked on the Sport of Kings, he graduates from the $2 window to the $100 window, and also progresses from wagering money from his wallet to wagering wads of cash pilfered from his bank's basement safe. As Litel continues to bet on long shots in hopes of a big payoff that will put him back on his financial feet, Marie Windsor, the local bookies' go-between, lends a sympathetic ear and even seems to muster up some romantic interest in him. But this *is* Marie Windsor, after all: In reality, she and her beau, con man Steve Brodie, are plotting to dupe Litel into bringing them 20,000 more dollars out of that oft-visited basement safe, and then leave Litel holding the proverbial (and empty) bag.

Two Dollar Bettor is setbound and, perhaps needless to say, never gets within 100 furlongs of an actual rack track (all horse racing scenes are stock footage). Other minuses include unfunny comic relief from Carl "Alfalfa" Switzer as a local football hero(!) and much screen time devoted to some of the squarest kids ever seen in a 1950s movie; the local teens' idea of a hot time is a square dance in the Litel parlor, with somebody's grandmother pounding out "Golden Slippers" on the piano. But the story of the plight of poor Litel, compulsively extending his disastrous losing streak in the days before Gamblers Anonymous, is believable and sobering, mostly due to Litel's expert performance. Everything that *can* go wrong for him *does*—including the unexpected announcement of an early bank audit—and there's a smidgen of actual suspense in the closing reels. Without wishing to give away the ending, mention must also be made of a climactic confrontation *very* much like a scene in Stanley Kubrick's *The Killing* (1956)—the similarity made even more apparent by the presence of Windsor in both. Funnily enough, Litel is seen in nearly every scene of the movie but is third-billed, while Brodie doesn't show up until 55 minutes into this 72-minute film but gets the top slot. Perhaps the true message of this movie is simply that—Litel just can't win!

In *The Basketball Fix*, a crooked gambler and his henchmen put pressure on a star player (Marshall Thompson)—a premise which, on its surface, seems to promise more excitement than *Two Dollar Bettor*'s cautionary tale of an old coot who doesn't know you can't beat the ponies. But Thompson is so miscast as the basketball ace, and the story features so many weak elements, that it comes out as the lesser of the two. John Ireland is top-billed as a sports columnist who sees great promise in high school hoop star Thompson. Ireland helps Thompson get a scholarship to a local college where he soon becomes his basketball team's MVP. Thompson has a ten-year-old brother to support and a new girl (Vanessa Brown) to impress, a disastrous combination when a slick gambler (William Bishop) is hanging around the margins of the story, offering him big bucks to miss a shot here and there. He finally succumbs, accepting money to help insure that his team wins games by less points. But credulity is now strained by scenes in which police begin tailing Thompson because they sense that this extraordinary player, who *still* outscores everyone else on his team and has led it to the state championship, might actually not be giving it his *very* best efforts!

Perhaps a greater understanding of college basketball would lead to a greater appreciation for *The Basketball Fix*. But a movie about an amiable soul who is considering exchanging his life of poverty for a promise to win by a few less points hardly quickens the pulse; who gets hurt by "point shavers," other than John Litel types who are illegally betting on the games? The "dramatic ante" eventually gets a much-needed boost when Thompson tries to break away from Bishop, but these livelier scenes (a beating, threats against Brown) are too little too late. The story is told in Ireland-narrated flashbacks and shot in striking noir style by the estimable Stanley Cortez, who spent his unusual cinematographic career ping-ponging between hall of famers like *The Magnificent Ambersons* and bargain-basement B flicks.

25 Wellll, that's the way he told the story…sometimes. Other times it was an old pioneer doctor who did the dunking as a nerve-wracked Lon Frank Chaney stood beside him.

26 Interviewed by Jack Gourlay in *Filmfax*, Crawford pooh-poohed the notion that his brawls with Chaney were over the top. "We kidded a lot, and kicked each other with cowboy boots on," recalled Brod. "We got some exercise, but we never hit each other in the face or anything."

Showman's Manual
SHOCKING!
...ALONE in the JUNGLE!
A BLONDE BEAUTY and a SAVAGE BEAST!
JACK BRODER Productions presents
Bride of the GORILLA
Starring
PRIMITIVE! PASSIONATE! Nothing like it ever before!
BARBARA PAYTON
LON CHANEY
RAYMOND BURR · TOM CONWAY
Written and Directed by CURT SIODMAK
A JACK BRODER PRODUCTION
MAT No. 402
ADVERTISING ★ PUBLICITY ★ EXPLOITATION

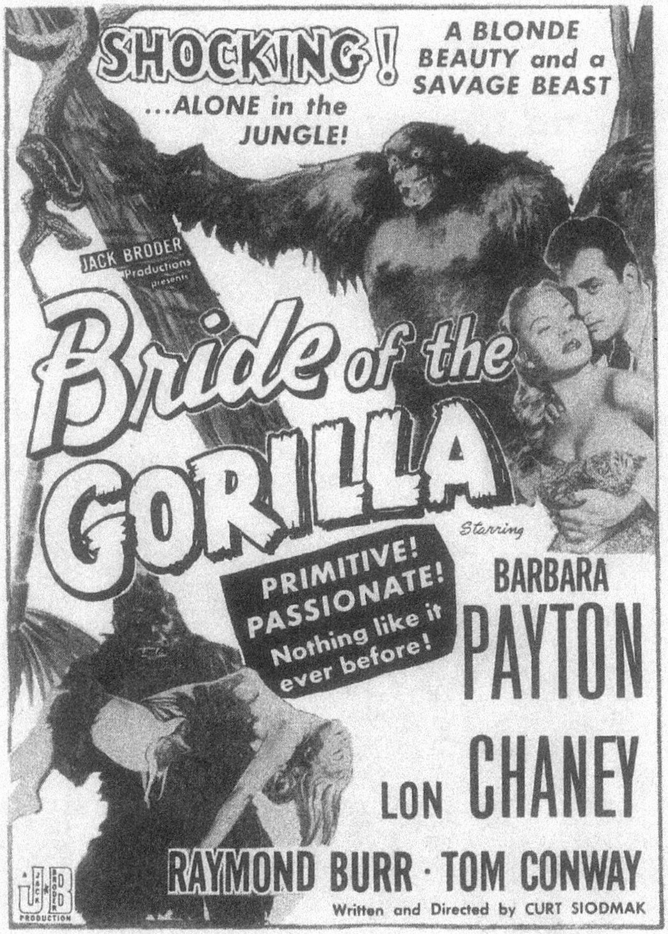

Ad Mat No. 303

Ad Mat No. 201

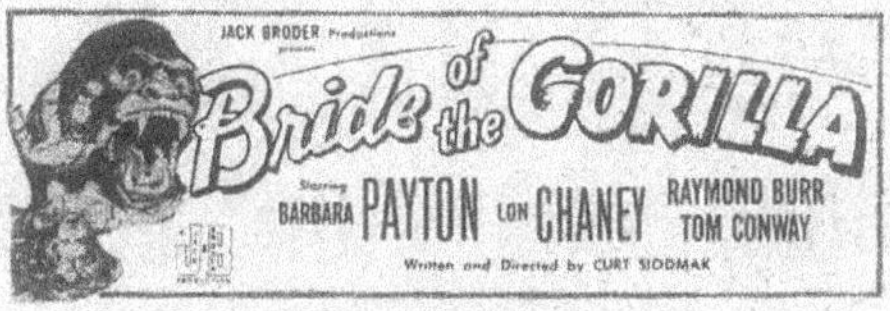

Ad Mat No. 203

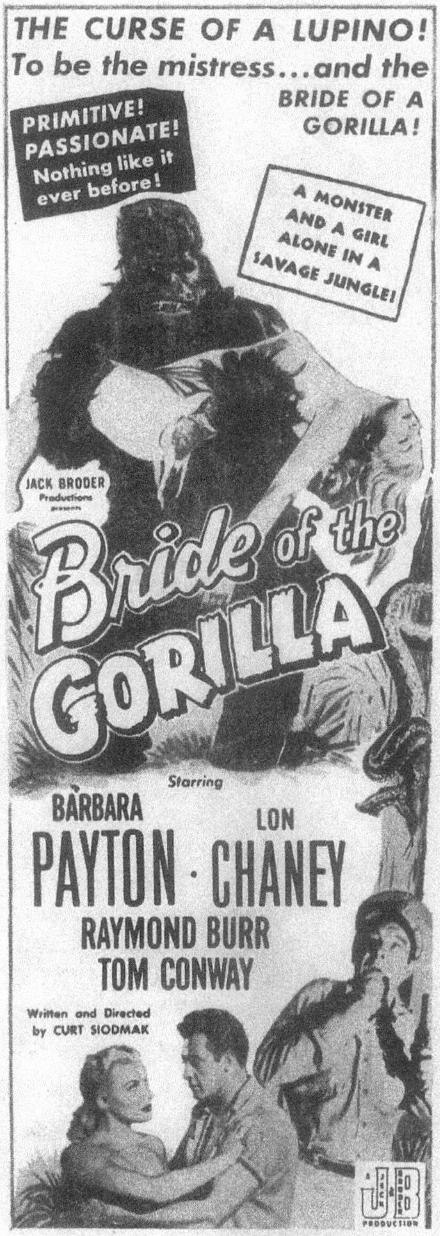

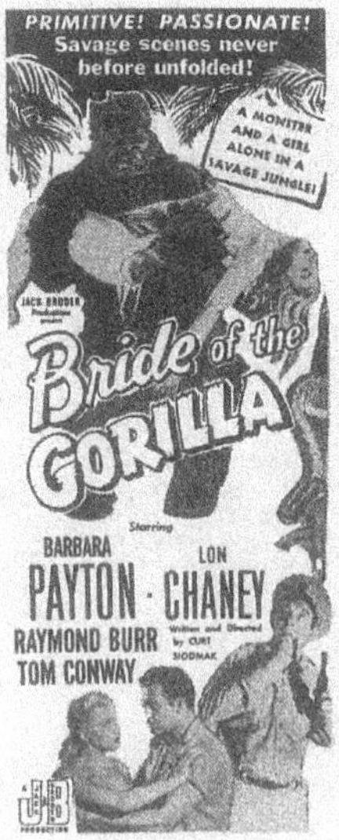

Ad Mat No. 105

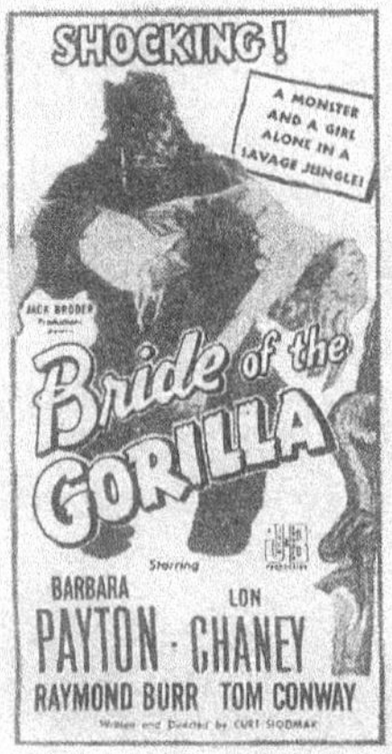

Ad Mat No. 104

Ad Mat No. 205

Ad Mat No. 102

Ad Mat No. 304

Ad Mat No. 204

Ad Mat No. 401

Ad Mat No. 101

Ad Mat No. 103

Ad Mat No. 202

Ad Mat No. 106

Ad Mat No. 302

Ad Mat No. 501

SPECIAL ADVERTISING STILLS

Six 8 x 10 Photos of the Key Art used in this Pressbook Ad Campaign. Excellent material for making Lobbies, Blow-ups and Special Ads. Available at your National Screen Service Branch.

PUBLICITY

Probing a Killing

2 Col. Scene Mat No. 2A

A strange death in the jungle has occurred and the police are investigating the killing in this tense scene from the exciting new adventure film, "Bride of the Gorilla," which opens .... at the .... Theatre, and co-stars (l. to r.) Raymond Burr, Tom Conway, beauteous Barbara Payton and Lon Charney. A Jack Broder Production, the film is a Realart Pictures release.

'Bride of the Gorilla' Is An Exiting New Adventure Film

(Prepared Review)

Excitement, suspense and thrills galore filled the screen of the .... Theatre when the new Jack Broder Production, "Bride of the Gorilla," began its local engagement there yesterday, through Realart Pictures release.

Filmed against the background of a steaming, mysterious and frightening Spanish American jungle land, "Bride of the Gorilla" tells the strange story of beautiful young dancer who marries a middle-aged rubber plantation owner. Although her marriage brings her a sense of security she has never known before in her professional life, she soon tires of the tedium of looking out into the silent and forbidding jungle and she finds new interests in the admiration of her husband's handsome plantation manager.

Sensing that his wife is unhappy, the husband inadvertently involves his manager in a wild fist fight. The result is that the husband is knocked down and while he is in a prone position, he is bitten by a venemous snake an' dies almost instantly.

Subsequently, the young widow and the manager are married. But the spell has been cast. And the instrument to carry out the ancient curse of the jungle turns out to be an old native woman who was the dead man's faithful servant for many years. Her diabolical plan works all too well. For soon the jungle curse has descended in full terror and fury on the dead man's household. The manner in which the plot is finally resolved and the stalking gorilla is brought to bay furnish one of the season's most thrilling and spine-tingling screen climatic highlights.

Co-starring in the film's top roles are a quartet of outstanding Hollywood players. Lovely blonde Barbara Payton plays the top role of the disenchanted dancer who marries to live in a strange world among strange people and things. In the role of police commissioner, Lon Chaney again displays the great acting talent which is his heritage from his famous father. Raymond Burr portrays a properly disturbed and envious plantation manager. And suave and handsome Tom Conway brings an air of authenticity to his portrayal of a jungle land doctor.

Written and directed by Curt Siodmak, "Bride of the Gorilla" features a cast of notable supporting players headed by Paul Cavanaugh in the part of the ill-fated plantation owner.

"Bride of the Gorilla" is definitely one of those thrilling screen adventure experiences no one can afford to miss. Certainly it rates tops with this reviewer for chilis, excitement and entertainment.

Famous

1 Col. Scene Mat No. 1C

Husky actor Lon Chaney, Jr., who followed in the path of his illustrious father, has already established himself as a famous star in his own right. Currently he plays a top role in Jack Broder's thrilling and exciting adventure melodrama, "Bride of the Gorilla," opening .... at the .... Theatre, through Realart Pictures release.

Petite Film Actress Is Also Judo Expert

Petite brunette Carol Varga, who plays her most important featured role to date in the thrilling Jack Broder Production, "Bride of the Gorilla," currently showing at the .... Theatre, through Realart Pictures release, can claim the distinction of being an almost immediate screen success.

Born in Honolulu 23 years ago, Carol came to the U. S. for the first time in 1948. She immediately applied for a screen test at Universal Pictures and was promptly signed and appeared in four productions in 1950.

A talent scout brought her to the attention of Producer Jack Broder; again her charmed luck held out. He also promptly signed her for the important role of the native girl in "Bride of the Gorilla," which co-stars Barbara Payton, Lon Chaney, Raymond Burr and Tom Conway.

Athletically inclined, Carol's favorite sports are tennis, swimming and horseback riding. Her friends, who have challenged her, will also tell you that she is a remarkable "judo" artist.

Chaney Goes 'Straight' For Role In 'Gorilla'

According to screen star Lon Chaney, there can be "disadvantages, too, in being the son of a famous movie star.

Lon, who currently stars in the Jack Broder Production, "Bride of the Gorilla," opening .... at the .... Theatre through Realart Pictures release, naturally has nothing but admiration for the work of his famous dad who was one of the greatest film stars of all time and whose monster-like makeups earned him the title of "the man with a thousand faces."

"Everybody," said Chaney during a recent interview, "expected the son, with no acting experience, to know what his father had learned in thirty hard years on the stage and screen. I'd always had a sort of secret desire to act, but while my father was alive I preferred to stick to mechanical engineering."

"When I did finally become an actor," continued Lon, "I was expected to play the kind of roles he made famous. So I did. And believe me, it wasn't easy to wear those masks and body harnesses, in trying to carry out the tradition set by my dad."

"However, in this picture, 'Bride of the Gorilla,' I have a different type of role in playing the Police Commissioner, and it really felt wonderful not to have to report to the studio three hours before shooting time to have a monster-like makeup put on me."

With more than 150 pictures already racked up to his credit, Lon frankly says that he likes his straight portrayal in "Bride of the Gorilla" as one of the best of his acting career. He shares co-starring credit in the picture with blonde and beautiful Barbara Payton, Raymond Burr and Tom Conway. Curt Siodmak both wrote and directed the film.

'Bride of the Gorilla' Stars Noted Film Scion Lon Chaney

Lon Chaney is writing the sequel to the page of motion picture history his illustrious father did not live long enough to finish.

The son of the famed character actor, Lon Chaney, Jr., was literally born between curtain calls and reared in an atmosphere steeped in theatrics. His parents were with a stock company touring the midwest at the time of his birth. Lon, Jr., made his first dramatic native entrance into the world in Oklahoma City. He naturally regards it as his native town.

Chaney did not want to become an actor, nor did his father want him to. His interest was mechanical engineering and his education was pursued with an engineering career in mind. He attended grammar and high school in Hollywood. Only the death of the elder Chaney, in 1930, at the pinnacle of his screen fame, while his epochal performance in the "Hunchback of Notre Dame" was fresh in the minds of moviegoers, was the factor which diverted the son from his planned route in life to the histrionic path blazed by his father.

He did not take advantage of his father's name or contract. Unannounced and unsung, and with no advance notice, he began as an extra player. Bit parts followed and finally he won contracts with several major studios.

His progress from then on has been swift and steadily upwards. Then he realized that he was slowly becoming "typed" in heavy roles. And, in order to broaden his scope, he forsook film work to play "Lennie" in the Pacific Coast stage run of John Steinbeck's "Of Mice and Men," in 1939. He later won the same role in the Broadway stage play and in the screen version, and in every instance he was a tremendous success.

In his latest co-starring role in Jack Broder's thriller production, "Bride of the Gorilla," which opens .... at the .... Theatre, Chaney has still another new type of role to interpret. He enacts the part of a native Spanish American police commissioner. Co-starring opposite him in the film are lovely, blonde Barbara Payton, Raymond Burr and Tom Conway. Released by Realart Pictures, "Bride of the Gorilla" has a noted featured cast of supporting players headed by Paul Cavanagh.

Film Stars Real People; They Cook and Eat, Too

Almost everybody likes to eat, especially if they're tasting something new for the first time, and actors are no exception. This was evidenced during the shooting of the new Jack Broder production, "Bride of the Gorilla," which is now playing at the .... Theatre, through Realart Pictures release.

Lon Chaney, who stars in the film, had his house trailer on the set as a dressing room. Every afternoon, Lon, who loves to cook, would prepare a lunch for the entire crew, with the able assistance of another excellent cook, his blonde and beautiful co-star in the picture, Barbara Payton.

The entire production crew had a grand time during the filming, looking forward to what new dishes Lon and Barbara would prepare each day. Soon a concensus showed that the crew's favorite dish from Lon was his special recipe for preparing chicken livers, fried in a special sauce which he will not reveal to anyone. And their favorite from Barbara was the way she prepares southern fried chicken. A culinary talent, she says, she inherited from her mother whose cooking has won many prizes.

In their latest screen assignments in "Bride of the Gorilla," which has been hailed as a "tremendously thrilling melodrama," Lon and Barbara share co-starring honors with rugged Raymond Burr and suave Tom Conway.

Raymond Burr Co-Starred In Thrilling New Movie

Handsome, rugged Raymond Burr, currently enacting the leading "heavy" role in the suspenseful Jack Broder Production, "Bride of the Gorilla" now showing at the .... Theatre, through Realart Pictures release, has a varied background of experience to fit him for a successful screen career.

Born at New Westminster, British Columbia, on May 21, 1917, he is the son of William Johnston Burr, a merchant, and Minerva Smith Burr, a noted concert pianist. When Burr was a year old, his parents went to China where for five years they lived in Shanghai, Peking and Hong Kong. That would have been adequate exotic geography for most people. But, since then, Burr has also traveled around the world five times.

He made his first professional appearance as an actor at the age of 12, when he replaced a child actor who had become ill while playing with a stock company in Vancouver, B.C. In the ensuing years, he worked as a traveling salesman, engaged in radio and little theatre work in San Francisco, and he even found time to teach school, following his completion of six years at Stanford and the University of California.

In 1937 he went to Hollywood to fulfill his first picture commitment, but he never made the picture because he became seriously ill shortly after his arrival in the film capital. However, after playing on the Broadway and London stage, he returned to Hollywood in 1944 and took a screen test that resulted in a long term contract at RKO, and his eventual recognition by noted producer Jack Broder for a top role in "Bride of the Gorilla."

Burr considers himself very fortunate to have been cast in the important role of Barney Chavez in "Bride of the Gorilla," for he numbers among his co-stars such outstanding screen personalities as the lovely blonde Barbara Payton, Lon Chaney and Tom Conway.

Success In Movies Not All A 'Break'

There are many still unknown actors and actresses who are destined to remain unknown, if they think that success can come to them with one wildly lucky "break."

That is the conclusion reached by pretty Barbara Payton, who plays her latest starring role in the thrilling Jack Broder production, "Bride of the Gorilla," now showing at the .... Theatre, and which co-stars Lon Chaney, Raymond Burr and Tom Conway.

By way of explanation, Miss Payton points out that she did not just get into motion pictures by accident, or simply waiting for that "one break." When she came to Hollywood, she knew that she wanted to be a film actress. And so, fitting action to the thought, she prepared herself for a screen career by taking both charm and modeling courses as well as studying dramatics intensively.

That her determined ambition has paid off is evidenced by the impressive screen credits she has already acquired in the space of a few short years. She has played opposite such noted stars as James Cagney, Gregory Peck and Lloyd Bridges. And she is constantly growing in demand at all major studios. Her role in "Bride of the Gorilla" climaxes her career to date. For she has been given top line billing by Producer Jack Broder.

Released by Realart Pictures, "Bride of the Gorilla" has already been acclaimed by preview audiences as "a topdrawer chiller-thriller," in the best traditions of Hollywood film-making.

Passion

1 Col. Scene Mat No. 1A

Beauteous blonde Barbara Payton and rugged Raymond Burr portray a pair of passionately ill-starred lovers in the new and exciting Jack Broder Production, "Bride of the Gorilla," which starts here .... at the .... Theatre, through Realart Pictures release. Lon Chaney and suave Tom Conway are also co-starred in the film.

Coming Soon

The widely heralded suspense-thriller, "Bride of the Gorilla," is coming soon to its screen, it has been announced by the .... Theatre. The story of a mysterious plant drug in a remote jungle land and its strange effects on human beings, the film is a Jack Broder Production for Realart Pictures release and co-stars Barbara Payton, Raymond Burr, Lon Chaney and Tom Conway.

PUBLICITY

'Bride of the Gorilla' Stars Barbara Payton In Top Role

It was not too long ago that blonde and lovely Barbara Payton was running a modeling school in Hollywood, appearing in pictures whenever she could snare assignments. Then she was spotted by William Cagney. He gave her the break of her career by casting her as James Cagney's leading lady in "Kiss Tomorrow Goodbye."

Beauteous

1 Col. Scene Mat No. 1B

Lovely blonde screen star Barbara Payton has the top role in the exciting and thrilling Jack Broder adventure film production, "Bride of the Gorilla," which opens .... at the .... Theatre, through Realart Pictures release.

She followed that with a top role opposite Gregory Peck in "Only the Valiant." And now she has completed her most recent starring role in Jack Broder's thriller production, "Bride of the Gorilla," which opens .... at the .... Theatre, through Realart Pictures release, with a co-starring trio of noted actors including Lon Chaney, Raymond Burr and Tom Conway.

this pert, blonde actress, who was born in the little town of Cloquet, Minnesota, on November 16, 1927, enthusiastically admits that she has one of her best starring roles to date in "Bride of the Gorilla." In her part as a professional dancer who goes to live on a jungle plantation, Barbara declared recently that she is given an opportunity to fully reveal her acting and dancing talents.

When she isn't emoting before the cameras, Barbara finds her favorite recreation in sports. These are tennis, swimming and water skiing at Lake Arrowhead in the summer. Her favorite food is chicken, whether she cooks it herself, which she does very well, or eats it out. She does not care much for pajamas. And since she loves to sleep, she says she has discovered real sleeping comfort in shortie nightgowns.

In top featured roles in "Bride of the Gorilla" are such well-known players as Paul Cavanagh, Giselle Werbisek and Carol Varga.

'Bride of the Gorilla'

For his latest film production, "Bride of the Gorilla," noted producer Jack Broder has brought together a quartet of top-ranking film stars. Cast in the picture's top role are blonde and lovely Barbara Payton, Lon Chaney, Raymond Burr and suave and handsome Tom Conway.

Slated to open .... at the .... Theatre, "Bride of the Gorilla" has been enthusiastically acclaimed by preview audiences as a "great suspense thriller" in the finest traditions of Hollywood. Realart Pictures is releasing the picture.

CREDITS

JACK BRODER PRODUCTIONS
presents
"BRIDE OF THE GORILLA"
starring
Barbara Payton Lon Chaney
Raymond Burr Tom Conway
Written and Directed by
Curt Siodmak

Associate Producer	Edward Leven
Assistant to Producer	Herman Cohen
Assistant Director	Richard Dixon
Art Director	Frank Sylos
Set Director	Edward Boyle
Men's Wardrobe	Elmer Ellsworth
Women's Wardrobe	Betty Zachin
Hairdresser	Ann Kirk
Makeup	Gus Norin
Sound	Bud Meyers
Special Effects	Lee Zavits
Director of Photography	Charles Van Enger, A.S.C.
Editorial Supervision	Francis D. Lyon, A.C.E
Music By	Raoul Kraushaar

A Jack Broder Production
Released by Realart Pictures Inc.

CAST

Dina	BARBARA PAYTON
Taro	LON CHANEY
Barney Chavez	RAYMOND BURR
Doctor Viet	TOM CONWAY
Klaas Van Gelder	PAUL CAVANAGH
Al Long	GISELLE WERBISEK
Larina	CAROL VARGA
Van Heussen	PAUL MAXEY
Policeman	WOODY STRODE
Native Man	MARTIN GARRALAGA
Mrs. Van Heussen	MOYNA MacGILL
Van Heussen's Daughter	FELIPPA ROCK

SYNOPSIS

(Not for Publication)

KLAAS VAN GELDER (Paul Cavanagh), a middle-aged and pious, but very jealous, rubber plantation owner, has married Dina (Barbara Payton), a young and beautiful professional dancer in her middle twenties. He takes her to his domain in the wild jungle wastes of Spanish America to be mistress of his household, consisting of his old native servant woman, Al Long (Giselle Werbisek); a young native girl, Larina (Carol Varga), who acts as Dina's maid; and Barney Chavez (Raymond Burr), manager of the plantation.

Dina knows that Klaas has married her for her love, youth and charm. In return, she has received a sense of security she did not know in her professional work. Nevertheless, the overwhelming sense of loneliness in the midst of the dark and mysterious jungle drives her to seek the attentions and admirations of Barney Chavez, whose personal magnetism has cast a spell over her.

The Governmental Doctor Viet (Tom Conway) becomes an unusually constant visitor to this sparsely settled region. Since he is also a younger man than Klaas, his visits to the plantation are easily ascribed to the presence of the attractive mistress of the Van Gelder household.

One night, during dinner, Klaas brings up a complaint of one of the workers against Barney's attentions to Larina, (whom we later learn is really Klaas' half-caste daughter). A heated argument ensues and Klaas dismisses Barney on the spot. Klaas and Barney become embroiled in a bitter fist fight, which results in Klaas' death from the bite of a venemous snake during a knockdown.

Taro, (Lon Chaney), the native police commissioner, is convinced that Barney alone is guilty. But he is overruled by the doctor's official autopsy which proves "death by snake bite." This verdict is substantiated by Al Long, who witnessed the whole affair. However, she has decided on a plan to mete out jungle justice to the murderer of her dead employer. She uses a rare native plant, "pe de guine," known for its powers to put a curse on evid-doers.

In time, Dina and Barney are married by Taro. The ceremony is barely over when the curse of the plant begins to work. Barney notices one of his hands turning to the claw of a gorilla. He rushes to his room and bolts himself in. As he unsuspectingly is fed more of the terrible plant potion in his innocent-looking drinks, Barney is nightly driven by uncontrollable desires to take to the jungle with the gorilla's instincts of prowling and killing.

Each morning, Dina finds him as his normal self, but exhausted and tormented from his nightly tirades. The native rubber workers become alarmed when cattle are found mauled and torn. They report descriptions of a horrible two-legged marauder, and they set traps for his capture. In following Barney one night, Dina's fears are heightened by finding him caught in one of the traps.

Dina really loves Barney and she persuades him that they should sell the plantation and leave for the nearest large city. A deal is made for a neighboring plantation owner to buy them out. But, before the deal is consummated, Barney is seized with an uncontrollable anxiety, and he takes off into the jungle. Two days later, when Dina finds him, he confesses that the jungle has a hold on him and he won't leave.

Dina refuses to go without him and that night accompanies him into the jungle. As the curse overcomes him, he begs her to go back. Soon both have gone far into the jungle. Barney's transformation overpowers him, and he seeks out Dina and tries to strangle her. The Doctor and Taro, who have followed them into the jungle, shoot him dead, and he crashes to the ground.

Running Time: 65 minutes

2 Col. Scene Mat No. 2B

A spine-tingling highlight in the thrill-packed adventure melodrama, "Bride of the Gorilla," is pictured here when the towering and ferocious gorilla picks up lovely blonde Barbara Payton and rushes headlong with her into the sinister jungle. The film, a Jack Broder Production for Realart Pictures release, starts an engagement here .... at the .... Theatre. Lon Chaney, Raymond Burr and Tom Conway co-star with Miss Payton.

BOXOFFICE BUSINESS BOOSTERS

Lobbies and Fronts

"Bride of the Gorilla" is an exploitation natural. Sell it with a maximum community-wide saturation promotion campaign for outstanding boxoffice grosses. Here's a batch of showmanship ideas, stunts and gimmicks that you can use to promote "Bride of the Gorilla" and pre-sell your patrons and the whole community:

* * *

An important feature of your lobby and theatre front should be photo blowups of the outstanding action stills from your theatre set.

* * *

Build a miniature jungle in your lobby, using stuffed animals promoted from local museum or tax'dermy shop. Dramatize it with wild animal noises played up from hidden phonograph. Local sporting goods store will be glad to co-operate with display of rifles and shells to give added effect of action realism.

* * *

For an eye-catching backdrop in lobby, get a large map of South America — or have one blown up — with an arrow pointing to the wild interior of the country as the locale of "Bride of the Gorilla."

* * *

Another theatre front stunt can be a "native" beating a tom-tom and making your bally pitch. Variation on this could be hidden phonograph playing weird jungle music, interspersed with a woman's frantic screams.

Local Tieups Pay Off

A tie in natural is with a local sporting goods store. Set up window displays using exchange set of stills from picture and surround them with guns, hunting garb and other material that lends itself to window display. Tie in hunting items with the gorilla hunt in "Bride of the Gorilla."

* * *

Local photography store can be counted on for help in animal picture content. Prizes can be guest tickets or merchandise promoted from co-operating dealer.

* * *

Certain of the stills from the picture lend themselves admirably to merchandise tie-ups for window displays. Here are a few and where you can use them: Still BG-49 (Barbara Payton) lends itself to tie in with local dress shops. Still BG-52 (Carol Varga) can be used in women's sporting goods shops for a bathing suit tie in or informal dress wear. Still BG-56 (Raymond Burr) can be used in conjunction with men's wear shops featuring men's suits and haberdashery. The same could be applied to Still BG-57 (Tom Conway).

Street Bally Plugs Playdate

A huge gorilla figures importantly in "Bride of the Gorilla." Capitalize on that by locating a gorilla outfit big enough to fit a man and have him parade around town with a sign on his back reading: "Follow me to 'Bride of the Gorilla'!"

* * *

An usherette, or usher — or both — can be dressed in jungle attire, carrying signs reading: "We Are Seeking 'Bride of the Gorilla'."

* * *

Another stunt that will pay boxoffice dividends is an open sound truck carrying a cage of live or stuffed animals. Sounds should stress thrills and excitement in the picture. Copy for signs can be catchlines from ads in this press book.

RADIO

15 SECONDS:

Gripping — Terrifying — Thrilling! Feel all the excitement the screen can hold when the spine-tingling adventure picture, "Bride of the Gorilla" opens .... at the .... Theatre.

15 SECONDS:

What was it like to be the bride of a snarling, ferocious beast? See the terrifying answer for yourself when the exciting adventure film, "Bride of the Gorilla," opens .... at the .... Theatre.

Boxoffice Generator!

Sell "Bride of the Gorilla" with a costume party for kids that will generate plenty of talk, arouse interest in your attraction and give your Kiddie Matinee Day an extra send-off. Announce via lobby poster that all kids are to come to the matinee dressed in jungle costumes. Award merchandise prizes or guest tickets for the outstanding costumes in the following categories: prettiest, most unusual and funniest. This stunt might also provide local newspaper with pictures justifying feature coverage.

Trailer

All the thrills and excitement of "Bride of the Gorilla" have been highlighted in the hard-hitting, seat-selling trailer. It's terrific boxoffice ammunition that can build those "Bride of the Gorilla" grosses up to the high mark. Make your playdate payoff with this sensational boxoffice insurance. Book it now from the nearest National Screen Service exchange and play it early and often.

POSTERS

SIX SHEET

THREE SHEET

ONE SHEET

ACCESSORIES

Style A   TWO 22 x 28's   Style B

INSERT (14 x 36)

ALSO SET OF EIGHT
11 x 14's WITH TITLE CARD

Order your 30 x 40's;
40 x 60's and 24 x 82 banners
from your local National Screen Exchange.

Order trailer, slide, all accessories, ad and scene mats from your local National Screen Service Exchange

www.ingramcontent.com/pod-product-compliance
Lightning Source LLC
Chambersburg PA
CBHW050411110426
42812CB00006BA/1862